# The social significance of dining out

MANCHESTER
1824

Manchester University Press

# The social significance of dining out

## A study of continuity and change

Alan Warde, Jessica Paddock
and Jennifer Whillans

Manchester University Press

Published by Manchester University Press
Oxford Road, Manchester M13 9PL
www.manchesteruniversitypress.co.uk

*British Library Cataloguing-in-Publication Data is available*

ISBN 978 1 5261 3475 2 hardback
ISBN 978 1 5261 6377 6 paperback

First published by Manchester University Press in hardback 2020

This edition published 2022

Typeset by Sunrise Setting Ltd, Brixham

# Contents

## Part V: Continuity and change

# Figures

# Tables

# Notes on authors

**Alan Warde** is Emeritus Professor of Sociology in the School of Social Sciences and Professorial Fellow of the Sustainable Consumption Institute at the University of Manchester. He is well known for his writing on topics of consumption, cultural capital, food and eating. He has written many books on similar and related topics. Works on similar topics to this book include: *Consumption, Food and Taste: Culinary Antinomies and Commodity Culture* (Sage, 1997); (with Martens) *Eating Out: Social Differentiation, Consumption and Pleasure* (Cambridge University Press, 2000); (with Kjaernes and Harvey) *Trust in Food: An Institutional and Comparative Analysis* (Palgrave, 2007); (with Bennett et al.) *Culture, Class, Distinction* (Routledge, 2009); *The Practice of Eating* (Polity, 2016); and *Consumption: A Sociological Analysis* (Palgrave, 2017).

**Jessica Paddock** is a Senior Lecturer in Sociology at the University of Bristol. Her research employs sociological approaches to explore the interaction of everyday life practices, natural resource use, food consumption and social differentiation in the context of environmental change. Her work involves interdisciplinary collaborations across the social and natural sciences, which are published in journals including *Sociology, Journal of Peasant Studies, Journal of Rural Studies, Poetics, Appetite, Sustainability* and *Ecosystem Services*. Jessica has a PhD in Sociology from the Cardiff University School of Social Sciences.

**Jennifer Whillans** is a Lecturer in Sociology and Quantitative Research Methods at the University of Bristol. Her primary academic focus is time use research; specifically, she is interested in the timing of activities across the day and week and examines the temporal organisation of people and practices using both qualitative and advanced quantitative methods. Alongside her work on *Eating Out*, she recently completed a research project, funded by the British Academy under their

Postdoctoral Fellowship scheme, entitled '(De)synchronisation of People and Practices in Working Households: The Relationship between the Temporal Organisation of Employment and Eating in the UK'. She has published articles in *Poetics, Appetite, Public Health*, European Journal of Ageing, *Time and Society* and *Leisure Studies*. Jennifer has a PhD in Sociology from the University of Manchester.

# Acknowledgements

We gratefully acknowledge funding from the Sustainable Consumption Institute (SCI) at the University of Manchester to carry out the research on which this book is based. Other colleagues at the SCI worked with us on the same data and participated in discussions about various aspects of the material; thanks to Helen Holmes, Jo Mylan, Dale Southerton, Dan Welch and Luke Yates. We thank Dan Welch especially for allowing us to draw on material about the UK Foodservices sector from an unpublished working paper of his, 'Political Economy and Sustainability in the UK Food Service Sector'. We benefited enormously throughout from the stimulating and collegial atmosphere in the SCI and the support offered to us by its management teams and its administrative staff.

We are also grateful to participants in a final workshop which presented key results from the project in April 2018. As a result, we enjoyed help-ful discussion of aspects of the project and received detailed comments on part of the manuscript from Bente Halkier and Lydia Martens. Lydia, who was the co-author of the book based on the initial project (Warde and Martens, 2000), has also been involved as an advisor to the project throughout. We say a special thanks to her.

We have also learned much from discussions about our material at the conferences of the British Sociological Association and the European Sociological Association and at seminars in a dozen or more universities in Europe and the UK.

Very sincere thanks to Jukka Gronow who graciously agreed to read the whole manuscript and who offered valuable comments and insightful suggestions for its improvement.

Alan Warde, Jessica Paddock and Jennifer Whillans
Manchester and Bristol
July 2019

# Part I
# Introduction

# 1

# Dining out

Eating away from home used to be considered exceptional. Normality meant eating at home, with other family and household members. Scholarly and popular literature about the social aspects of eating begins from meals at home and their supposed capacity to enhance family relationships (Murcott, 1983; Douglas, 1984; DeVault, 1991; Mennell, 1992; Valentine, 1999; Sobal, 2000; Bugge and Almås, 2006; Fischler, 2011; Phull et al., 2015; Yates and Warde, 2018). Probably the majority of meals in the last 100 years have been consumed within the household. However, much eating takes place away from home. Dining out, or eating a main meal away from home, is now a symbolically significant popular activity which provides a complementary source of food and companionship. This book examines dining out both as customers in commercial venues and as guests of friends and non-resident kin.

The Food Standards Agency (FSA, 2014) reported that one meal in six was eaten away from home in Britain in 2014, an estimate covering all types of eating events away from home, including breakfasts, light lunches during working hours, and other small occasions, as well as the consumption of main meals. Various studies indicate that considerable amounts of money and time are devoted to eating out (Warde, 2004; Cheng et al., 2007; Warde et al., 2007; Lhuissier, 2014). There are many options, including a meal at work, fish and chips on the street corner, a picnic, a school dinner, a snack in a roadside diner or sandwiches taken to work, as well as a substantial meal in a restaurant (Finkelstein, 1989; Warde and Martens, 1995; Jacobs and Scholliers, 2003; Finkelstein, 2013). The alternative sites conjure up images of different events and occasions, some fleeting, others special. Burnett (2004: 320), in the pre-eminent historical account of England, contends that, despite popular impressions to the contrary, the number of events may not be much different now from what it was in the late nineteenth century. Then, having employment at a distance from home was the main contributory cause; people who most frequently purchased cooked food away from home in the nineteenth century were the labouring poor, such as farm labourers and manual workers in the city (Murcott, 2018: 59–60). However, as Burnett (2004: 320) acknowledges, the form of eating out changed significantly in the second half of the twentieth century. Previously being primarily a necessary substitute for an inability to obtain a meal in a family home, dining out became, for the majority of the population, a positive preference as a recreational activity offering pleasure as well as refreshment. Eating out is a popular and heterogeneous activity.

Research on food concentrates more on its production and sale than on its final consumption. Within the domain of consumption more attention is devoted to hunger, poverty and nutritional deficiency than to the symbolic and aesthetic aspects of eating. Nevertheless, scholars in food studies, building on work in anthropology, sociology and mass communications, have increasingly documented the symbolic significance of eating (Albala et al., 2017). Such endeavours include investigation of various aspects of eating away from home. Situations of commercial provision where the buyer has maximum discretion attract the most attention, among which, street food, the burger bar, cafes and restaurants provide the most inspiration because they appear most emphatically to express personal and individual taste. Yet many alternative sources of provision exist. A very large industrial and institutional sector of the catering trade delivers meals in hospitals, schools, prisons and factories. Domestic hospitality is a source of meals for guests who live under a different roof (Julier, 2013a). Charities are also, sadly, providing an increasing number of meals, and their constituent ingredients for home consumption, for the needy and the destitute, as another form of communal provision (Garthwaite, 2016; Lambie-Mumford, 2017). Nevertheless, the retail commercial sector is the most eye-catching feature of provision of food away from home in the early twenty-first century as much for its cultural and symbolic significance as for the sustenance it provides.

Restaurants, and other equivalents such as cafes, pubs and hotel dining rooms which offer table service, attract most attention. They typically deliver substantial meals and define ritual procedures, where culinary content and social contexts are of considerable symbolic significance. Upmarket places which serve elaborate dinners are subject to research on their personnel, increasingly the chef, their social setting and their gastronomic features (Mennell, 1985; Ferguson, 2004; Warde, 2009; Lane, 2014; Pearlman, 2013; Leschziner, 2015; Lane, 2018). The picnic, the hotel breakfast, the dinner party, the barbecue and the street bench are studied much less. Places serving foreign or 'ethnic' cuisine have attracted perhaps even more attention because of what they say about changing tastes and migrant populations (Driver, 1983; Heldke, 2003; Buettner, 2008; Panayi, 2008; Alkon and Agyeman, 2011; Ray, 2016; Oleschuk, 2017; Warde et al., 2019).

Despite now being very common, dining out in a restaurant or cafe is still regarded with some suspicion. People view it positively when they themselves are engaged in the activity but may have reservations about its role in the feeding of others! What is imagined as wrong with eating out which renders it morally ambivalent? First, the kitchen door marks a separation between the backstage conditions (Whyte, 1949; Goffman, 1959; Gabriel, 1988; Fine, 1996) and frontstage display, perhaps considered disingenuous by diners worried they may be getting more than they bargained for (Crang, 1994; Murcott, 2018: 56–59). Many restaurants have been redesigned with open kitchens, possibly to demystify the backstage social world, and to heighten the sense that restaurant is theatre. A second objection might be its fundamental challenge to the ideal of the family meal, the widely held view that dinner is best eaten at home with other members of the elementary family. A moral and practical issue, which has rumbled on inconclusively since the mid-nineteenth century, it could be thought to be especially threatened by the incursion of commercial provision, replacing domestic food preparation and meals eaten together by members of the family household (Murcott, 1997; Jackson, 2009). Inevitably each meal taken away from home eliminates an opportunity to cook. Some think that cooking is good for its own sake, but many more have a morally loaded premonition that it is a matter of resorting to a convenient alternative which defaults on responsibility and is an encouragement to laziness, for it is often contended that home-made food is of better quality than any alternative. This view is bolstered by contentions that eating out has adverse effects on health. Certainly it is less easy to calculate the nutritional value of a meal prepared in a commercial kitchen than one assembled at home. Eating out is also thought to encourage people to suspend any principles of constraint over what might be consumed on a special occasion. This arouses a related suspicion that dining out is extravagant and that people enjoy themselves too much. A Protestant revulsion against hedonistic excess is not uncommon, and since dining out has long been associated with drinking alcohol, the recrimination intensifies. Undeserved pleasure, expense, and the relinquishing of responsibility and control are maybe even more reprehensible than merely avoiding hard work. There is also some general public suspicion about the intrusion of the market into everyday life. People are very used to buying items and services which they would previously have obtained in other ways but they may nevertheless feel some disquiet about it. Against most of these reservations it might be objected that eating out is relatively infrequent even in the richest of western societies such that the anticipated negative consequences are exaggerated. Nevertheless, if the trend were towards ever more events away from home then the primary role of the domestic meal might eventually be fatally compromised. Perhaps ambivalence should not be surprising given a much wider tension in the contemporary treatment of food, its being both pleasurable and a source of great anxiety. Arguably, the anxieties have excessively detained scholars, and even more so policy-makers, to the neglect of the appreciation of the satisfactions and pleasures of eating out.

The activity of eating out inspires many reasons for sociological interest. How people judge themselves and others in their everyday behaviour is a guide to shared norms, and social standing is well revealed in the study of morally ambivalent practices. The apparent disjuncture between much media representation of the activity and how it is experienced by consumers is an endless source of fascination. The mutual effects of the different forms of provision and the substitution between forms potentially reconfigure the ways in which societies eat. The pattern of domestic meals, which Grignon (1993) argued is primarily determined by the obligations of employment and the organisation of the household, is subject to the compounding effects of the greater use of alternative means of provision. Eating in restaurants means exposure in public spaces, involving personal performance and social interaction, during which observation may lead to judgement.

Increased spending on eating in commercial settings reopens questions about commodification as a master process in the development of capitalist societies. The restaurant is interesting because it could be represented as the apogee of consumer choice, a paradigm of the process of individualisation which social theorists propose is a consequence of changes in western societies after the 1960s (Bauman, 1988; Featherstone, 1991; Giddens, 1991; Beck and Beck-Gernsheim, 2001). It is no longer necessary to eat the same food as other people at the table, each restaurant offers many items and there are many types of restaurant. Whims and desires can be satisfied, and opportunities arise to eat unfamiliar foods as the growing availability of dishes and customs associated with foreign cuisines becomes a strongly marked option (Ascher, 2005). The parallel development of a global 'consumer culture' is an ongoing matter of controversy, associated with propping up the ideology of consumer sovereignty and consumer choice. Said to be Britain's most popular leisure pursuit after watching television, the significance of dining out for life and lifestyles is considerable. As an object of enthusiasm for some, and as a common leisure pursuit, much can be gleaned about cultural practice, cultural capital and cultural priorities. What, for instance, does eating out eliminate from the diary, and indeed what does it accompany? In addition, it is open to examination as an instance of social differentiation, of inequalities between classes, men and women, young and old, the staple concern of sociology.

In sum, eating out is a very common and popular recreation, a significant contributor to diet and eating, an instance of commodification and changing modes of provision, and an activity with considerable cultural and symbolic significance. It also throws light on key debates in cultural sociology in the twenty-first century, providing a means to test and elaborate theories of globalisation, cultural omnivorousness, cultural intermediation and aestheticisation. So why would sociologists not study it?

Scholarly interest has risen in parallel with public interest which is reflected in media coverage and popular commentary. Yet eating out is still not a very popular sociological topic. The extent to which buying meals out in restaurants, hotels and cafes has become increasingly common over the last fifty years in Europe and North America has been documented (Kjaernes, 2001; Jacobs and Scholliers, 2003; Levenstein, 2003; Cheng et al., 2007; Holm et al., 2012; Díaz-Méndez and García-Espejo, 2014; Cabiedes-Miragaya, 2017; Díaz-Méndez and García-Espejo, 2017; Díaz-Méndez and Van den Broek, 2017; Gronow and Holm, 2019). In the process, commercial options have multiplied enormously, driven by forces of globalisation, commodification and aestheticisation (Warde, 2016). Venues have diversified, specialising in provision for different types of occasion and serving a wide range of foods and cuisines, rendering the market increasingly large and varied (Finkelstein, 1989; Wood, 1995; Warde et al., 1999; Warde and Martens, 2000; Scholliers, 2001; Berris and Sutton, 2007; Johnston and Baumann, 2010; Julier, 2013b; Díaz-Méndez and García-Espejo, 2014; Ray, 2016; Paddock et al., 2017). Recent studies across Europe and the US have told us about upmarket restaurants and their celebrity chefs (Rao et al., 2003; Lane, 2011; Lane, 2014; Leschziner, 2015). There is also literature on fast foods (Leidner, 1993; Watson, 1997). We know about what is cooked and sold in restaurants and cafes across the globe, arising from a particular interest in the significance of the spread of commercial enterprises purveying different national, ethnic and regional cuisines and their connection with processes of migration (Mintz, 1997; Jacobs and Scholliers, 2003; Wilk, 2006; Berris and Sutton, 2007; Panayi, 2008; Ray, 2016).

Research focusing specifically on the act of consumption is, by contrast, relatively limited. There is more research on provision than consumption. A minor interest in food connoisseurs has developed recently

(Ascher, 2005; Johnston and Baumann, 2010; Warde et al., 2019) and somewhat dated literature exists on the more basic experiences of eating out in Europe and the US (Finkelstein, 1989; Wood, 1995; Warde and Martens, 2000; Warde, 2016). About domestic hospitality we know even less. Apart from Julier's (2013a) full-length study of North America, little else deals with entertaining (Warde and Martens, 2000; Mellor et al., 2010). Our account aims to advance understanding of the experiences of domestic guests and restaurant customers.

## Dining out in England

This book is a second episode in an analysis of continuity and change in the practice of dining out in England. It results from a re-study of eating events which occur away from home. It was not originally intended that the initial investigation carried out in 1995 and reported in the book *Eating Out: Social Differentiation, Consumption and Pleasure* (Warde and Martens, 2000) would be repeated. However, when an opportunity arose to carry out a follow-up project it was grasped because it offered exciting possibilities to examine processes of change in a disciplined sociological fashion. The first study, based on qualitative household interviews and a survey in three English cities, was pioneering insofar as there was no systematic research on eating out from the point of view of consumption and consumers. Instruments were designed which allowed the exploration of an increasingly common but obscure set of activities with a view to understanding what people were doing, and thought they were doing, when they ate food away from home. The focus was explicitly on main meals eaten either on commercial premises or as a guest of friends or non-resident kin. Of the many different types of events where food is eaten outside of the home, we focused on the most elaborate and symbolically significant. When questioning people, two terms, 'main meal' and 'eating out', were used to direct attention to substantial, costly, extended and planned events. In retrospect it might have been more appropriate to refer to the focal activity as 'dining out'. However, that probably would not have had sufficient resonance in the general population; Britons tend to say 'shall we *eat out* tomorrow?' not 'shall we *dine out?*'. The results of the study gave no grounds for thinking that the use of the term eating out, in combination with requests to tell us only about 'main meals', caused any confusion or was in any way misleading. Nevertheless, the etic version 'dining out' would probably have characterised the object of analysis best because it carries intimations of 'dinner', the largest meal of the day, and an 'outing', an excursion not part of the humdrum and mundane domestic routine. In the re-study, we deployed the term 'main meal' explicitly, trying to achieve comparison of like with like, mindful nonetheless that the commercial sector in the intervening twenty years had expanded provision of minor meals in more informal settings.

A sociological re-study is not like a repeated laboratory experiment in which the goal is to eliminate contextual effects. Inevitably in modern societies the context of the action will to some degree change over two decades, making it unfeasible to control contextual conditions. Nevertheless, using the same research instruments and asking the same questions significantly aids the systematic measurement of change. In 1995 we were interested in dining out (main meals eaten away from home) for a number of empirical and theoretical reasons. It was partly that nothing much was known beyond anecdote about the understandings, concerns, objectives, behaviours, purposes and frustrations which are associated with eating away from home. A primary point of departure was the long-running debate about the fate of the family meal. Equally important was the social state of the meal itself, the central sociological concept in the sociological armoury, which has been the subject of much more attention in, for example, French sociology (Herpin, 1988; Poulain, 2002a; Fischler, 2011), but also across the Nordic countries (Gronow and Holm, 2019). Commodification, which entails organisations operating through markets with the purpose of supplying goods and services for sale and with a view to profit, is a defining feature of the modern capitalist economy. Its consequences for social relationships, daily life, connections between family members and friends, as well as employers and workers are profound. Stereotypically, market relations are impersonal, transitory, rationally calculated and carry no obligations beyond the single transaction. The possibility of the logic of calculated exchange invading the most important and symbolic meal occasions may be intrinsically worrying. With that in mind we compared the restaurant meal with that taken as a guest in other people's houses, a form of communal provision based usually upon mutual and durable interpersonal obligation.

Eating meals on commercial premises had clearly become more common during the decades before 1995. Expenditure data are totally unambiguous in recording an increasing proportion of the household budget on food being devoted to eating outside the home and not from the household store cupboard. Warren (1958) provides probably the best estimate of eating out in the period immediately after the Second World War. As part of a market research inquiry, a survey of 4,557 people in England and Scotland in 1955–56 uncovered some basic evidence about the frequency of eating out and variation by class, gender, day of the week and season. Three classes were differentiated – an upper class of professional and managerial occupations (10% of households), a middle class of lower managerial and white- collar households (20%) and a lower class (70%). The results show that eating out occurred more often at the midday meal than in the evening and mostly at the workplace; twice as many midday meals were in a canteen than 'at a cafe/restaurant/hotel'. Approximately 10 per cent of all lunches occurred on commercial premises, and about 3 per cent of evening meals. Men were about twice as likely as women to eat both midday and 'principal evening meals' in such commercial venues, and both men and women living in upper or middle-class households visited commercial venues about twice as often as those in the lower class. Upper and middle-class men ate an evening meal on commercial premises about twice as often as those in the lower class during the summer, but the difference was less in winter. Dining out in the 1950s was thus relatively uncommon and marked by social privilege. These social differences diminished in the succeeding decades as access to meals on commercial premises became more equal, a process which Burnett (2004) perhaps misleadingly called 'democratisation'. Not that it was imagined that all vestiges of class or gender differences had disappeared. Gender continued to be of great importance because of the entrenched role of women in the provision of household meals. Matters of taste remain related to social class, cultural capital and social domination. Dining out persists as an opportunity for the display of distinction and social status. This is possible not only through the purchase of expensive and stylish food, but also through public displays of refinement of manners. Exposure in a public space, both to other diners and staff, for extended periods of time, facilitates the judgement of performances and the attribution of social esteem.

Almost all these considerations remain as sociologically relevant in 2015 as they were in 1995. The underlying social processes behind patterns of social differentiation in the activity persist. Commodification, global diffusion of foreign cuisines, class and gender differences, choice and distinction remain key questions. Additional considerations have emerged. One is the continuing and perhaps intensified pressure towards commodification, coeval with the further erosion of welfare services provided by the state. The ideology and the policy applications of neoliberalism promote and legitimise provision for corporate profit. Only the very rich have gained in income and wealth in real terms during the last decade, in conditions of imposed wage stagnation and growing inequality. Nevertheless, the ideology of consumer sovereignty still sustains a belief that market provision is the most efficient, satisfying and responsive way to obtain goods and services such as a good meal (Ehgartner, 2019). In such a political context, the role of domestic hospitality seems even more important in assessing the sway of commodification.

The process of globalisation is now better understood and there are many signs of reaction against its consequences. Appadurai (1990, 1996) identified globalisation as types of 'flow' accelerating in the contemporary world, among which the circulation of goods, ideas and people are important with regard to eating (Warde, 2012). Access to exotic foodstuffs and the diffusion of foreign cuisine continue to grow (Lane, 2019). High levels of migration make the larger and older population of the UK more diverse. By contrast, reassertion of the virtues of local, seasonal and regional foods, and nationalist reactions against free trade and freedom of movement, have put a brake on globalisation in ways which impact upon food supply and frame tastes. This global–local dialectic flourishes ever more as culinary taste is more extensively mediated. Restaurants are frequently represented in the mass and social media. The details of restaurants and their services are widely circulated. Publicity and promotion have been extended by the Internet. Restaurants have websites; their menus and decor can be inspected by anyone with a suitable electronic device, and they invite reviews by their customers rather than journalists. Customers take photographs of the dishes served to them and publish them to friends and a wider public. This cultural climate, in which discussion of the qualities of food and dining flourishes, begets 'foodyism'. Promises of excitement about change and innovation, perpetually signalled through the media channels, give additional reason for examining dining out in 2015. The challenge for sociology is to establish the nature and degree of change witnessed in a period of twenty years and to judge whether there has really been a significant transformation in the practice of dining out.

## What difference might twenty years make?

Understandings of change are often impressionistic, based on anecdote and extrapolation from personal experience. The paucity of studies of dining out means that available information sources such as government surveys about expenditure, media archives and texts about recipes, menus and restaurant rankings have yet to be fully exploited. Yet trends and innovations in practice are much discussed. Partiality for thinking about change leads to an emphasis on movement, speed and progress, with vehicles such as fashion, novelty and mobility prominent in many accounts. This, however, overlooks the fact that many mechanisms operate persistently over long periods and their effects remain much the same.

Eating is a rather routine and habitual practice and some things change less frequently and less quickly than others (Warde, 2016). Issues about the analysis of social change run throughout the book.

One focus of the analysis is how dining out fits with other eating routines and habits. Dining out is in some respects a voluntary activity. People are rarely forced to participate. They can eat all their meals at home. They can eat in the street, in the office or in a car. Even when they need to eat and cannot get home, they can obtain foodstuffs in different ways. They do not have to purchase meals but can eat snacks and sandwiches instead. Most people engage in a mixture of these activities, and how and why individuals develop specific arrangements to accommodate the range of possibilities is a source of interpersonal and inter-group difference. The composite practice of eating is an emergent effect of how people in different positions solve the problem of feeding. Their arrangements are subject to change in myriad ways because there are many elements that can be organised and reorganised to reconcile the frequency and purposes of meals away from home with domestic arrangements and obligations.

A second major question of interest is how groups represent to themselves and others the symbolic significance of dining out. As has already been alluded to, class and gender affect practice. People's behaviour is a form of expression of social position and identity. Income, ethnicity, age, household structure, generation and place of residence are other sources of differences in behaviour. Dispositions arising from upbringing and education also affect behaviour, sometimes appearing in the guise of commitments to particular styles of life. Food is a source of enthusiasm, antipathy and difference, each of which influences arrangements. We are especially interested in how people express social commitments and connections, and signal identity through their ways of dining out. This taps into core questions of sociology about inequality, structured differences and social hierarchy. Variations between social groupings in the conduct of a practice give symbolic and cultural expression to wider societal relations.

A third research question concerns the nature of the experience of dining out – what it means to people, what gives them cause for concern and what proves a source of delight. Experiences are inevitably mixed. The moral ambivalence surrounding dining out is possible because people do recognise many potential benefits of dining out. Dining out provides flexible and unimpeded access to cooked food, relieves women of some burdens of obligatory domestic labour, transports people to sites of commensality and conviviality, expands culinary horizons and awakens new tastes, increases public interest in cooking and eating, and perhaps elevates British cuisine. To what extent these benefits are attained and whether they are primarily cultivated through dining out is a main thread of this study. If scholarly approaches to consumption have often generated an unfortunate degree of disapproval or condescension towards popular pleasures, an antidote is to listen carefully to ordinary folk talking on the basis of their experience. We attend to detailed accounts obtained from qualitative interviews to plumb the meanings of dining away from home.

Although the research focuses on reports about eating out, a thorough and comprehensive analysis of change requires an examination of the intersection of eating with many other practices. Changes in the composition of the British population, the redesign of cities, flexible working hours, etc. are all potentially relevant. The major sources of change in eating out may actually arise in rather different fields. Interpretation of the broader economic and cultural context of dining out is essential to explain changing tastes and practices.

## How the book unfolds

The book has five parts. The next chapter, which concludes Part I, gives additional details of how the study was conducted, the techniques of data collection and the analytic procedures employed. It also sketches briefly some features of the market provision of eating services in the UK to give context to the ensuing account of consumption. Part II shows how dining out has become more familiar to more people over the twenty years since 1995. It examines who visits which types of restaurant and how frequently (Chapter 3). Chapter 4 considers what these visits mean to people, for what reasons they dine out and how their orientations towards the activity differ. Part III contains four chapters dealing with the three main avenues for obtaining dinner – at home, as the guest of a friend or non-resident family member, or in a commercial setting such as a restaurant or cafe. The nature of experiences on these three different sites is indicated by the use of evidence from both surveys and interviews about practical arrangements, the company kept and the foods eaten. All three avenues are subject to processes of informalisation. Chapter 8 reprises the three modes with a view to explaining how they are integrated in practice. Part IV concerns diversification, exploring orientations towards variety, especially of tastes, examining social differentiation and the pursuit of cultural distinction through the selection of cuisine style. The social and cultural value of an aesthetic approach to dining out, and the unequal distribution of that value along lines primarily of class and ethnicity is assessed. The final Part provides a summary and draws conclusions about continuity and change in dining out between 1995 and 2015. The first of two chapters describes the contours of the shared practice of dining out in England in 2015, while the second considers the direction and extent of change over twenty years in the context of longer-term trends and institutional change.

# 2

## Method and context

### Introduction

This chapter is a prelude to the analysis. It provides the necessary information required to contextualise the results reported in later chapters. It describes some technical details of the study (supplemented in the Appendix), reflecting briefly on the nature of re-studies and some of the challenges in interpreting the results of a sociological revisit. The final section provides brief information about the changes in provision most relevant to the subsequent analysis.

### Research design

#### The first study, 1995

Fieldwork for the initial project, 'Eating Out and Eating In: Households and Food Choice',[1] was conducted in 1995 and reported in Warde and Martens (2000). At the time, research had rarely been concerned with anything other than the nutritional and commercial aspects of eating out, so little was known about eating out as entertainment or as a means to display taste, status and distinction. The study was one of the very first extended empirical social scientific investigations on the nature and experiences of eating out.

The research design entailed two phases of data collection. In the first, Lydia Martens conducted interviews with thirty-three people in thirty

[1]   Funded by grant L209252044, Economic and Social Research Council, Phase II of 'The Nation's Diet: The Social Science of Food Choice' Programme, 1994–96.

households, living in diverse circumstances in Preston and the surrounding area, during the autumn of 1994. The sampling was modelled on DeVault (1991) and interviews were with 'principal food providers', that is, 'anyone, man or woman, who performed a substantial proportion of the feeding work in the household' (Warde and Martens, 2000: 228). Reflecting the prevailing gender division in domestic work, twenty-eight women and five men were interviewed.[2] Concentration on Preston, a city in Lancashire in north-west England, was opportunistic, but there was no reason to think it highly unusual. Interviewees were recruited through organisations including a leisure centre, a community association, a tennis club, an environmental group, a primary school, a trade union branch, and a national DIY chain store.

Semi-structured interviews were conducted first because, in the absence of prior social scientific inquiry, it would otherwise have been difficult to construct informative questions for a survey instrument. Questions about eating out included the interviewees' understanding of the term, the frequency and reasons for using various places and detailed information about a few recent eating out events. Preliminary analysis was undertaken in order to design a questionnaire for the second phase. Subsequently, the interviews were analysed in considerable detail, focusing on shared understandings which defined eating events, differential orientations towards eating out, as well as aspects of eating at home, including descriptions of household routines and the distribution of food preparation tasks.

In the second phase of data collection, 1,001 people aged 18 to 65 were surveyed in three cities in England: London, Bristol and Preston. These cities were chosen for their contrasting socio-demographic composition and cultural ambience. Preston represented a northern freestanding city without any particularly eccentric characteristics. London was selected in anticipation that its unique features, including its diverse market and greater volume of provision, would prompt distinctive consumption behaviour. Central and suburban areas were chosen to illustrate potential differences between areas of the metropolis. Bristol was selected as an example of a southern non-metropolitan city with some claim to be culturally heterogeneous. Since no three cities could be representative of all others in England, these sites were deemed satisfactory. The survey was undertaken in April 1995 and was administered to a quota sample which matched respondents to the overall population of diverse local sub-areas of the cities by age, sex, ethnicity, class and

---

[2]    Three men were interviewed on their own, and two were present in a joint interview with their partner.

employment status. Despite not being a nationally representative sample, there was no reason to consider the survey biased in any particular way as a basis for an initial portrait of the practice in an English context.

Survey questions sought to ascertain each respondent's frequency of eating out, types of outlet visited, attitudes to eating out, extensive detail about the nature of the most recent meal eaten away from home, and rudimentary information about domestic routines. Socio-demographic data were also elicited in order to explore variation by class, income, age, gender, education, place of residence, and so forth.[3] Analysis of this cross-sectional survey data provided a snapshot of the activity of eating out in 1995.

### The second study[4]

In the first phase of data collection for the re-study, in April 2015, 1,101 respondents were surveyed in London, Preston and Bristol. The original rationale for selecting these three cities still resonated (that they offered contrasts of socio-demographic composition and cultural ambience) despite changes in population and provision within these cities since 1995. The survey asked almost identical questions as previously, pertaining to five thematic areas: (1) eating at home, social activities, division of labour; (2) eating out and takeaway food; (3) the last main meal eaten (at a public establishment, or at somebody else's home); (4) domestic entertaining; and (5) miscellaneous matters of attitudes and behaviour. Socio-demographic characteristics, such as age, household structure, income, class trajectory, social connections and cultural capital, were also collected. A few modifications were made to reflect market, technological and sociocultural developments, such as the broadening of styles of cuisine available and the advent of the Internet and social media communication platforms. Very similar information was obtained at each time point, although from different individuals.

In 2015, the survey was administered to a quota sample of 1,101 respondents to reflect the demographic profile of the cities studied. Census Output Areas (OAs), typically comprising around 150 households, were selected at random from across the relevant Local Authorities in proportion to size. Output Areas were stratified by the proportion of residents in social grade AB, using estimated social grade from the Census.

---

3   The Technical Appendix describing the first study fully can be obtained from the ESRC Data Archive, University of Essex, as can the raw survey results.
4   The Technical Report for the 2015 study can be obtained from the authors: alan.warde@manchester.ac.uk.

Interviewers were given quotas based on age and working status, interlocked with gender, to reflect the demographic profile of the OAs selected. While respondents to the 1995 survey were aged 18–65 years, an additional quota of 100 respondents above the age of 65 were surveyed in 2015 to better capture the ageing population (Leach et al., 2013). When conducting analysis of change between survey years these additional cases were removed, but they were included when exploring 2015 data independently. This secured internal validity of comparison while also fortifying the sample for the purposes of understanding the practice in 2015. The social characteristics of the samples of respondents are summarised in the Appendix Table A2.1 (p. 256) and compared with the population of England in Table A2.2 (p. 257).

The survey recorded many features of the eating habits of respondents including those surrounding both eating out and domestic arrangements. We examined many different dependent variables. Among key questions, respondents were asked to estimate the frequency of eating out in restaurants, pubs, cafes or similar establishments over the last twelve months and the range of cuisine styles experienced when eating out in the last year.[5] Scales were constructed to estimate the volume and pattern of attendance at restaurants of different types and styles. Respondents were also asked to describe in detail the last occasion on which they ate a 'main meal' away from home. The terms 'main meal' and 'eating out' leave room for ambiguity, but the interview data suggest that neither was confusing and that answers to the survey questions were based on common understandings.

To examine change we often prefer relatively simple statistical comparisons, partly because of the limitations of the data. However, bivariate and multivariate techniques were used occasionally to address specific explanatory problems, especially with respect to 2015. The independent variables used most frequently were sex, age, whether there were any children under 16 years of age in the household, educational level, class trajectory, ethnic identification, household income and city of residence. Education is a binary variable based on having a university degree or not. Class trajectory, a measure of social mobility, was constructed on

---

[5]   The wording of the questions were: 'Overall how often have you eaten out in a restaurant, pub, cafe, or similar establishment during the last twelve months, excluding times when you were away on holiday (in the UK or abroad)?' and 'Thinking now about restaurants specialising in specific food styles, during the last twelve months, in which of the restaurant types and places listed on this card have you eaten on the premises?'. Note that this question refers to the cuisine style associated with the restaurant and not necessarily the style of the dishes served.

the basis of answers to a question about the occupation of the primary earner in the household when the respondent was aged 16 and the respondent's current occupational class according to the National Statistics Socio-economic Classification (NS-SEC) schema. We considered as meaningful only mobility transitions which crossed the boundary between the service class (i.e. professional and managerial occupations)[6] and the rest (i.e. all intermediate and working-class occupations). Combining the occupational class of respondents and their parents yields a five-category variable: stable service class, upwardly mobile into the service class, the downwardly mobile from it, an 'other mobile' group experiencing sideways mobility between intermediate and working classes, and the stable working class (see further, Li et al., 2015). Most of the analysis uses occupational class trajectory, but additional questions included in 2015 permitted the construction of a measure of social class based on possession of economic, cultural and social capital. This measure of capitals, assets and resources (CARs) (Savage et al., 2005) is used sparingly in chapters 10 and 11. Household income is equivalised to take account of household size and composition, and calculated as tertiles.[7] Due to the sample size, ethnic identification is a binary variable, white British or Other, although greater detail available in 2015 permits some additional descriptive analysis.

In addition, principal component analysis (PCA) was employed to determine whether cuisine styles clustered together to form patterns of taste, and to create factors from a bank of twenty-five questions about attitudes and behaviours, to isolate orientations towards dining out.

### Survey harmonisation

To enhance comparison, we combined the two surveys in repeated cross-sectional data sets which permitted analysis of each survey year separately and patterns of change over time. Although the survey administered in 2015 asked almost identical questions, a number of differences between the two surveys required some adjustments. A few questions found in the 1995 survey were not repeated in 2015 and a few new questions were introduced. In almost all instances, the question wording

---

[6]   We adopt the terminology of Goldthorpe et al. (1980) whose concept of the service class provides a concise and convenient label for all in higher and lower professional and managerial occupations.

[7]   Total household income is divided by the number of household members, converted into equivalised adults, made equivalent by following the modified-OECD equivalence scale.

remained the same across surveys, but in 2015 the response alternatives were amended. Response categories differed mostly in order to accommodate additional items. We also introduced some new socio-demographic questions to accommodate recent developments in the sociology of class and ethnicity.

For the purposes of analysis, respondents aged over 65 were excluded from the harmonised data set in order that the 2015 sample would match the age range surveyed in 1995 (that is, 16 to 65) thus retaining 973 respondents from 2015 and 1,001 from 1995. The statistical analysis used Stata 13.

### The in-depth interviews

At the time of the first study, relatively little was known from an academic point of view about the practice of eating out, although some excellent monographs had described owning and working in restaurants in the US (Leidner, 1993; Fine, 1996) and the UK (Gabriel, 1988). The thirty qualitative interviews conducted in 1995, only with Prestonians, provided for an elementary mixed-methods research design and also a means to explore understandings to frame the survey questions. Twenty years later, the primary purpose of conducting in-depth interviews was different.

In the 2015 revisit, the survey was conducted first, in April 2015, and in-depth interviews followed in January 2016. Thirty-one in-depth follow-up interviews were conducted, ten in each city, with an accidental extra interview in Bristol. Of the survey respondents, 66 per cent agreed to be re-interviewed. Rather than speaking to the 'principal food providers' as in 1995, responses to survey questions about behaviour guided the selection of interviewees. For example, because we wanted to learn about how eating in and out related to each other, and because we were especially interested in domestic hospitality, we avoided contacting respondents who claimed never to eat out, or had little to no interest in food or cooking. We selected people who had some enthusiasm for food and cooking differentiated by age, ethnicity, gender and class trajectory.

Before the in-depth interview we knew a considerable amount about each interviewee – socio-demographic characteristics, class trajectory, tastes and much more. The survey had elicited information which might not have emerged otherwise and certainly not systematically in every narrative account. We matched up qualitative with quantitative responses, albeit with the proviso that these accounts were collected some months apart.

We invited interviewees to speak about the routines that shaped both typical and atypical days. We asked about the frequency of the various eating events mentioned, about their dining companions, as well as their tastes. We ended by inviting interviewees to speak about their experiences of both entertaining others with meals in their own homes and being a guest in the homes of others.

The qualitative interviews were transcribed verbatim and coded using a CAQDAS programme, NVivo 11. Thematic codes were derived both deductively and inductively. Indexed into 'parent and child' nodes, codes were used to retrieve narratives by category when further analysing the data, both in connection with survey evidence and when writing case vignettes. For the latter, we paid attention to the ways in which utterances and stories contributed to a portrait of eating and feeding both inside and outside the home for each respondent. Extracts from these vignettes appear throughout the book, some at length and some as brief illustrations. The characteristics of the interviewees are listed in Appendix Table A2.3 (pp. 258–259). Personal details (age and location) are cited on the first occasion a name appears in the text but thereafter referred to only when pertinent to a specific argument.

### Mixing methods

According to Yin (2006: 41), the challenge in using multiple data sources and methods is 'to maintain the integrity of the single study, compared to inadvertently permitting the study to decompose into two or more parallel studies'. We encountered this challenge not only when fitting together survey and interview data, but also when deciding how to synthesise data from 1995 and 2015. The interpretation of the evidence moves back and forth between the quantitative and the qualitative data in an attempt to represent both the social structural features of the practice and the meanings they have for participants. The latter sometimes involves extended description of individual interviewees and their concerns. More often it involves illustrative quotations from transcripts to give a flavour of the orientations and experiences of different sections of the population.

## Interpreting change

### The logic of the revisit

Our methodological approach can be characterised in Burawoy's (2003) terms as a 'focused revisit'. Its purpose is not simply to reanalyse or update the previous study. For Burawoy (2003: 646) the focused revisit seeks to 'disentangle the movements of the external world from the researcher's own shifting involvement with that same world, all the while recognising that the two are not independent'. The revisit should avoid slavish adherence to a notion of strictly 'replicable' research after the manner of laboratory sciences. Change may be attributed to the effects of external forces and to revised perspectives of the social scientific observer but separating and decomposing these is difficult. Burawoy contends that reflexivity is required to achieve a credible balanced account. Applying the principles of a focused revisit to our mixed-method study permits re-engagement with the topics highlighted by the first visit but brings to the analysis fresh theory and literature to deal with the conceptual priorities of today. This creates a dialogue between the 1995 and 2015 studies, noting interconnections, developments and departures.

Burawoy insists that not only does the empirical world alter but the preoccupations of social science also change. The 'practice turn' (Schatzki, 2001) marked a new phase in sociological research on consumption and on eating (Warde, 2016). A focus upon expressions of individual identity pursued by the 'cultural turn' in the late twentieth century made way for accounts giving less prominence to the agency of social actors. Instead, it was proposed that performance of a practice, such as eating, relies more upon automated and practical senses of reasonable action than calculation or deliberation. The unthinking ways in which social actors repeat performances and adjust to specific situations lead practice-theoretic accounts to suggest that people are the carriers of practices, rather than conscious deliberative actors. Eating is thus understood to be a highly complex, weakly regulated and routinised activity, performed by social actors, and creating, in turn, the structures upon which performances are reproduced (Warde, 2016). Such a turn to practice brings a fresh perspective and greater theoretical sophistication to a long tradition of research that has framed food as a lens through which to view other domains of social life including gender relations (DeVault, 1991; Martens, 1997; Mellor et al., 2010; Meah and Jackson, 2013; Hollows, 2016), sociability (Jacobs and Scholliers, 2003; Julier, 2013b; Díaz-Méndez and García-Espejo, 2017), social differentiation and taste (Mennell, 1985; Warde, 1997; Johnston and Baumann, 2010; Cappellini et al., 2016; Paddock, 2016; Ray, 2016), deprivation and social exclusion (Lambie-Mumford, 2017; Wills and O'Connell, 2018).

Empirically, identifying change independently of perceptions of change is fraught with difficulty. Sociology has become intensely aware that empirical observation cannot be divorced from procedures of measurement (Mallard, 1998). Systematic documentation of change is, even in the most propitious circumstances, problematic. Optimal techniques such as the panel study, or even repeat studies at annual intervals are beyond the financial means of agencies other than governments and consortia of corporations. These expensive projects have mostly been devoted to foundational questions around economic prosperity and social problems. To be able to field a repeat survey after twenty years on a focused topic is thus a social scientific luxury but is far from a perfect tool for capturing change.

Some limitations in the data for examining change should be noted. The first is that the qualitative interviews cannot be systematically compared. Quotations from interviewees are all from the second study. The second is that the surveys are based on quota rather than random samples within each city. The third is that neither study is statistically representative of England as a whole, describing strictly only three cities where research was conducted. The fourth is that taking two time points can never capture sufficiently the difference between linear trends, specific interruptions and constant fluctuation. The data cannot substantiate claims about the effects of the 2008 economic crisis, for example. Finally, explanation necessarily also draws upon knowledge of cultural trends from secondary literature. These reservations are less problematic in respect of the characterisation of the practice in 2015, and their implications have been taken into account throughout our analysis.

## Changing provision

The primary focus of our research is the practice of dining out as a form of popular consumption. Yet consumption cannot be fully understood without reference to the processes of provision because the provider and the eater are inescapably interdependent. Consumption would be different were the system of provision, infrastructures and industrial practices transformed. Hence some brief background about changing commercial provision is necessary.

People compile their eating practices from meals prepared at home, received as guests of friends and family, and provided by commercial suppliers. The last of these has absorbed a growing proportion of food expenditure since the mid-twentieth century. The proportion of household food expenditure on eating away from home increased from 10 per cent in 1960 to 21 per cent in 1990, reached 27 per cent in 1995, increased to 34 per cent in 2004–5, and fell back to 32 per cent in 2015 (Household Family Expenditure Survey; Family Spending). The proportion of food expenditure spent on eating out per person per week fell from 33 per cent to 31 per cent between 2004–5 and 2015. Table 2.1 shows the changing distribution of spending between 1995 and 2015.

The Food Standards Agency (2014) reported that about one meal in six in the UK is eaten away from home. That figure, however, includes breakfasts and sandwiches bought for lunch, and not just main meals.

**Table 2.1** Households in UK, expenditure per week, in total, on food and on food not from the household stock, 1995 and 2015

|  | 1995 | (%) | 2015 | (%) |
|---|---|---|---|---|
| All expenditure | £283.58 |  | £531.30 |  |
| Food expenditure | £50.43 |  | £86.30 |  |
| Percentage of all expenditure | 17.8 |  | 16.2 |  |
| *Food not from household stock (percentage of total food expenditure)* |  |  |  |  |
| Restaurant and cafe meals | £6.74 | (13.4) | £16.60 | (19.3) |
| Takeaway meals at home | £2.06 | (4.1) | £4.40 | (5.1) |
| Other takeaway food and snack food | £3.07 | (6.1) | £4.40 | (5.1) |
| State school meals and meals at work | £1.77 | (3.5) | £2.00 | (2.3) |
| Total away from home | £13.64 |  | £27.40 |  |
| Eaten out as percentage of food expenditure | 27.1 |  | 31.9 |  |
| Eaten out as percentage of total expenditure | 4.8 |  | 5.2 |  |

A little earlier Deloitte (2011) had estimated that the distribution of 'eating and drinking trading occasions' was 17 per cent breakfast, 26 per cent evening meal, 31 per cent lunch and 26 per cent 'drink/quick bite any other time of day' (2011: 5). Of both lunch and dinner events, half were takeaway and half 'sit-in'.

Increasing level of demand has provided many more commercial opportunities, and the number of businesses providing prepared food, their turnover and the numbers of people employed has risen fairly steadily. The total UK foodservice sector in 2015 comprised 164,549 enterprises, employed 5.5 per cent of the total UK workforce (1.78 million workers) (ONS, 2017) and had annual revenues of £68.3bn in 2016 (Mintel, 2017). Industry statistics distinguish between retail and contract catering sectors. Operational organisations in the former are typically divided into restaurants, quick service restaurants (QSR), pubs and hotels. Operations within contract catering include leisure, staff catering, health care, education and transport services, some being for 'profit' and others provided at 'cost' (Edwards, 2013). Our study deals almost exclusively with the retail sector which Mintel (2015) estimated as having revenues of £34.5bn. The rate of growth of the sector fluctuates, being briefly negative during recessions, but overall it has grown remorselessly for several decades. It contains a small number of large companies and many small independent operators. The latter have a precarious existence; of 18,155 restaurants and mobile food service enterprises opened in 2011 only a third were still operating five years later (ONS, 2017). The market share of the large companies is increasing steadily; independents accounted for 58 per cent of revenue in the Consumer Foodservice sector in 2016, which was 6 per cent less than in 2011.

Market research reports are the main regular source of information about the commercial sector. This material is difficult to piece together, partly because it is restrictively costly for academic users and partly because of its focus. Reports are mostly formulaic and too superficial for the extraction of long-term changes and trends. As short-term forecasting exercises, they try to identify how recent movements in markets and consumer behaviour trends might require practical adjustments to company strategies. Their very high prices and the small number of subscribers – mainly large competitor organisations within the sector – mean that they are diffuse and generic. Nevertheless, they give some indication of the state of the market for the services of restaurants, cafes and takeaway outlets, and they pinpoint some recent innovations and tendencies. For example, highlights from the annual Mintel *Eating Out Review for 2015*, the year of our fieldwork, include continuing modest growth in the market, improvement in 'food in informal and convenience-driven settings', discounting, growth of 'all-day dining', greater use of 'fast-food outlets, cafes or coffee shops', judicious combination of home delivery and restaurant meals, and taking advantage of price promotions in casual settings. Mintel's sample of consumers use takeaway or home delivery a little more often than they eat a meal in a restaurant, indicating a concern with value for money. They estimate that 30 per cent of the population eat a meal in a restaurant once a week.

Occasionally a firm is commissioned to write a focused report for a single company, which has greater depth and is potentially of greater academic interest. One such is an Allegra (2009) report, commissioned by McDonalds, called 'Eating Out in the UK, 2009: A Comprehensive Analysis of the Informal Eating Out Market'. It included a section called 'Market history and evolution' portraying the 1990s as a decade of 'The emergence of "fast casual" dining'; gastropubs and mid-market chains are at the centre of the story as venues which offer both table service and speed. It characterised the 2000s by cafe culture, a growing concern with healthy food, and informal outlets selling higher quality food. Huxley et al. (2011:17) report that 'Pub food had become very popular during the growth period of the late 90s and early 2000s'. Like other sources, they indicate that activity in the sector dipped after the 2008 economic crisis but began to grow again after 2011; 'allowing for the effects of inflation, spending on eating out fell almost 9%' between 2006 and 2010 when pubs closed but 'quick serve restaurants (fast food and casual dining) increased by over 5%'. Mintel (2014) noted an increase in eating out, but a reduction in spending per head across the sector, as 'meal deals', 'buy-one-get-one-free' offers, and 'early bird' set menus provided opportunities for many on restricted budgets.

Information about other modes of provision is less well documented. Institutional catering is rarely examined from the consumer's point of view. Our study adds little except to note that 29 per cent of respondents in 1995 had eaten in a workplace canteen during the previous year, a proportion which declined to 17 per cent in 2015 (73% of those for whom such a facility was available). The extent and organisation of the communal sector, where guests are entertained by friends or non-resident kin, is even less well understood; there is little commercial profit to be made from its investigation. Our study may therefore be particularly valuable because it deals in some detail with domestic hospitality. Most people are sometimes hosts and sometimes guests, and the proportion of the population involved remains very much as it was in 2015.

# Part II

# Familiarisation

# 3

## Patterns of dining out

### Introduction: the pleasures of dining out

When introducing the results of the first study we sometimes quipped that despite Britain's reputation as a gastronomic desert, respondents to the survey almost universally loved every aspect of their experiences of dining out. This, admittedly rather feeble, joke went down well in Europe, especially France. The supporting evidence was, nevertheless, compelling and initially surprising. We asked people in great detail about the last occasion when they had eaten a main meal away from home, whether in a commercial outlet or at the home of a friend or a family member (non-resident kin). A summary evaluation of several dimensions of that event – the food, the company, the atmosphere, the service and the conversation – was obtained by asking respondents to declare whether they liked or disliked these aspects 'a lot' or 'a little'. Table 3.1 lists the dimensions and the responses in both 1995 and 2015, distinguishing between meals on commercial premises and those delivered through the communal mode of provision. It shows that in 1995 enjoyment was exceptionally high,[1] which was one of the grounds for concluding that eating out was special, always appreciated, something to be looked forward to, with defects readily excused because of other positive features of the event.

Only minor changes occurred over the twenty years, the clearest being a decline in satisfaction with some aspects of the restaurant experience. Liking 'a lot' reduced for every aspect of the last restaurant meal, most sharply the food, atmosphere and service. The decline was, however, mostly compensated by the proportion of people declaring that

---

[1] So few respondents recorded dislikes that (not only for ease of reading) they can be disregarded.

**Table 3.1** Enjoyment of last occasion at commercial establishment and someone else's home, 1995–2015 (percentage)

| | Commercial | | Someone's home | |
|---|---|---|---|---|
| | Change since 1995 | 2015 | Change since 1995 | 2015 |
| *Food* | | | | |
| Liked a lot | −8 | 72 | −1 | 87 |
| Liked a little | 8 | 21 | 0 | 10 |
| Neither liked nor disliked | 1 | 4 | 1 | 3 |
| *Company* | | | | |
| Liked a lot | −5 | 86 | −1 | 94 |
| Liked a little | 3 | 9 | 1 | 6 |
| Neither liked nor disliked | 2 | 5 | 0 | 1 |
| *Decor* | | | | |
| Liked a lot | −9 | 48 | 2 | 93 |
| Liked a little | 5 | 29 | −2 | 4 |
| Neither liked nor disliked | 5 | 20 | 0 | 2 |
| *Service* | | | | |
| Liked a lot | −8 | 57 | −6 | 78 |
| Liked a little | 6 | 28 | 0 | 9 |
| Neither liked nor disliked | 4 | 10 | 5 | 12 |
| *Conversation* | | | | |
| Liked a lot | −3 | 79 | 1 | 89 |
| Liked a little | 1 | 15 | −1 | 8 |
| Neither liked nor disliked | 2 | 6 | 0 | 3 |
| *Value* | | | | |
| Liked a lot | −14 | 56 | | |
| Liked a little | 10 | 28 | | |
| Neither liked nor disliked | 5 | 11 | | |
| *Overall* | | | | |
| Liked a lot | −5 | 77 | 2 | 94 |
| Liked a little | 4 | 18 | −2 | 5 |
| Neither liked nor disliked | 2 | 5 | 0 | 0 |

*Note:* Respondents between ages 16–65. Shaded cell indicates a decline over time

they liked these features 'a little'. Respondents' summary judgements of their last meal 'overall' reveal 77 per cent having liked it a lot and 18 per cent a little. A satisfaction rate of 95 per cent is not to be sniffed at in any market context. Remarkably, enjoyment of the last meal in someone else's home, which had in 1995 been marginally greater than in restaurants, further increased; 94 per cent reported that overall they had liked the event a lot. Thus, despite some slightly greater reservations in 2015, eating out remains a source of great enjoyment. Paradise retained.

Given the level of satisfaction expressed in 1995 it was surprising that not more of our respondents wanted to eat out more frequently. In response to the question 'I would like to eat out more often than I do now', 60 per cent agreed and 27 per cent disagreed. By 2015, however, only 45 per cent agreed that they would like to eat out more (and only 17% strongly) while 34 per cent disagreed. Reasons for disagreement are not hard to imagine,[2] but the simplest hypothesis for explaining the change is that by 2015 some people were eating out more often than before and had become satiated. So, in 1995 when eating out was still special and relatively unfamiliar to many, a thirst for more existed. By 2015, when restaurants were more commonplace, despite still delivering great satisfaction, they ceased to be candidates for further investment of financial resources or scarce leisure time. Such a conjecture would best be explored by establishing to what extent, if indeed at all, the rate of eating out had increased. However, deriving a reliable estimate of how often respondents eat out proves remarkably and instructively difficult.

### How often do respondents eat out?

The surveys elicit retrospective annual estimates of the frequency of eating out in restaurants, at the home of a friend, or in the house of non-resident kin.[3] The results for the two years can be viewed in Table 3.2. This suggests almost no change. In both years about a fifth of people (21%) reported eating in a restaurant or cafe weekly or more often, with a small and diminishing proportion recording 'never'. For eating out on commercial premises both the mean and the median recorded was monthly, equating to the average respondent eating out in a restaurant a little more often than once every three weeks. Eating at the home of non-resident family

---

[2]  People might currently be so happy as to feel too much of a good thing would be imprudent.

[3]  In 1995 and 2015 all respondents were asked 'Overall, how often have you eaten out in a restaurant, pub, cafe or similar establishment during the last twelve months, excluding times when you were away on holiday (in the UK or abroad)?' For the other modes of provision, the questions were: 'Overall how often have you eaten a main meal at the home of a *friend* during the last twelve months?' and 'And how often have you eaten a main meal at the home of a *relative* during the last twelve months?'

**Table 3.2** Frequency of eating out, main meal, 1995–2015, retrospective annual estimate (percentage)

|                | Commercial premises | | Relative's house | | Friend's house | |
|----------------|------|------|------|------|------|------|
|                | 1995 | 2015 | 1995 | 2015 | 1995 | 2015 |
| Weekly or more | 21   | 21   | 10   | 9    | 6    | 6    |
| Fortnightly    | 18   | 19   | 10   | 8    | 7    | 8    |
| Monthly        | 25   | 26   | 20   | 21   | 19   | 21   |
| Less often     | 29   | 29   | 41   | 43   | 35   | 42   |
| Never          | 6    | 5    | 19   | 19   | 34   | 22   |
| N              | 976  | 972  | 965  | 970  | 949  | 973  |

*Note:* Respondents between ages 16–65. Those recording a 'don't know' response have been excluded. In 1995 between 3 and 5% of respondents recorded 'don't know' but scarcely any did in 2015

members remained constant; approaching 40 per cent make a visit at least once a month. The most significant change in the twenty-year period was that fewer people never ate at the home of a friend; in 1995 34 per cent had not, a figure which had fallen to 22 per cent by 2015, and there was a 2 per cent increase in monthly visiting.

Although, by this measure, not much has changed, we might pause to reflect, as it is commonly presumed that eating out on commercial premises has increased recently. Given also that a majority in 1995 had declared that they would like to eat out more often, is there a technical problem? Questions in the surveys about the last occasion on which the respondent ate a main meal out might suggest so, since answers about exactly when the last meal occurred and what was its purpose offer a somewhat different picture of frequency.

Table 3.3 shows a 5 per cent increase in taking a meal within the last seven days, indicating that a section of the population is eating out more often. A last meal out occurred within the last seven days for 45 per cent of respondents and within the last fortnight for at least 59 per cent. A fair estimate might be that the average respondent who ever eats out, irrespective of whether in a restaurant or at someone's home, does so every ten days. On this evidence, people are, on average, eating out more frequently. The rate of increase is greatest for eating with friends but also significant for eating in restaurants. A much greater proportion of last occasions were reported to be on commercial premises in 2015, suggesting that, on aggregate, this would be the primary source of greater frequency of meals out overall.

**Table 3.3** When was last main meal eaten away from home taken? 1995 and 2015 (percentage by column). All locations

|  | 1995 | | 2015 | |
|---|---|---|---|---|
|  | N | % | N | % |
| Within the last 7 days | 396 | 40 | 441 | 45 |
| Within a fortnight | 96 | 10 | 133 | 14 |
| Within a month | 157 | 16 | 143 | 15 |
| More than a month ago | 287 | 29 | 222 | 23 |
| Never | 65 | 6 | 34 | 3 |
|  | 1,001 | 100 | 973 | 100 |

*Note:* Respondents between ages 16–65

As we will show in detail in Chapter 4, processes of familiarisation and casualisation have affected the restaurant sector over the last twenty years. More people are taking impromptu meals, shorter, with fewer courses, and more often alone. This is captured in a significant shift in the number of meals in restaurants that respondents designated as 'Quick and convenient'. The proportion of such meals rose by 7 per cent and comprised 22 per cent of all meals in 2015 and 25 per cent of meals in restaurants. Such meals are especially likely to have occurred within the last seven days. Casualisation, contingent upon a simultaneous shift in provision and consumption occurring during the last twenty years, might account for a substantial proportion of the shift in the reporting of a restaurant meal as the most recent. Since most people's definition of 'eating out' involves consuming a substantial meal, with others, ideally of more than one course, etc., then 'Quick/Convenient' episodes might seem marginal. Symbolically less significant, they are easier to forget and hence do not register in retrospective reconstructions of the last year's experiences.

Overall, dining out has increased, although to a more modest degree than popularly imagined. The impression common among the public arises from a real increase in the consumption of minor, rather than main, meals. As market research shows, sales of breakfasts, brunches, light lunches and coffee with snacks have flourished. The marketing device of 'the meal deal' which in this context often combines a drink and a sandwich, may have unsettled understandings of the term meal. Growth in the frequency of main meals is slower. Inspection of what was eaten on the last occasion shows the reporting of a handful of minor meals such as: 'ham and tomato sandwich', 'toasted teacake', 'panini with cheese and tomato'. Interviewees, however, reflecting on the place of lunch and snacks in a definition of eating out, almost always set these occasions to one side in favour of more major events involving a hot meal, usually the largest eaten in the day, taking place overwhelmingly in the evening. This suggests the reporting of minor meals is not likely to be skewing our data towards an unreasonable interpretation of frequency. While eating out has increased modestly, it is unlikely that what is reported disproportionately comprises 'minor' events. Rather, we suspect overall under-reporting due to recall. Interviewees tend to recall additional events as the interview progresses.[4]

If the most symbolically significant meals are no more common than before, annual estimates may be reasonable indicators of actual frequency of main meals taken by respondents. However, obtaining an accurate estimate may be fetishistic in a realm of activity where precise measurement is elusive. Reassuringly, given the incapacity to obtain a precise estimate of frequency of eating out, the social determinants of greater and lesser frequency are not sensitive to the exact numbers derived from the two alternative modes of estimation.[5] We thus feel most comfortable in using the retrospective annual estimates, which are

[4]   Our study is restricted to main meals. We explicitly asked respondents to the survey in both years to focus on 'main meals' when reporting on the last occasion eating at the homes of family or friends. However, only by implication was this applied to the most recent meal in a commercial outlet. We asked about the last time a respondent had 'eaten out' in a restaurant, pub, cafe or similar establishment'. This would allow people to report something other than a 'main meal' in either year. It might however be more likely that something less substantial than a main meal might be reported in 2015. In 1995 respondents automatically associated 'eating out in restaurants and pubs' with main meals, but changing provision, changing practice and changing advertising might loosen this connection in many people's minds. Very probably the major increases in commercial provision involve the supply of smaller supplementary eating occasions. On balance, people are not often reporting minor events.

[5]   Exploratory investigation extrapolating from the timing of the last occasion to an estimate of the total annual number of occasions for each respondent, when subjected to regression analysis, showed underlying patterns of social differentiation almost identical to that derived from the retrospective measure. This alleviates anxiety associated with the imprecise estimates.

the respondents' own, as the dependent variable when examining who eats out often and who infrequently.

## Determinants of frequency of eating out

### Who eats out most?

Table 3.4 reports associations between some social characteristics of respondents and the frequency with which they ate out at commercial premises, as guests of friends, and as guests of kin in 1995 and 2015. This illustrates how people with different socio-demographic character-istics access meals out unequally. It also demonstrates that the social credentials required for access to the different modes of delivery are not the same, although some characteristics affect all.

As can be seen, many social and socio-demographic characteristics impinge upon the frequency of eating away from home. They are mostly similar across the years. For instance, those with a degree, the stable ser-vice class and those with the highest incomes engage more frequently in all activities. In all apart from one instance, younger people eat out more frequently and the stable working class and the least well off participate infrequently. Women are more frequent guests of non-resident kin than men. Having children in the household reduces visits to restaurants and to friends but increases eating with family and acting as host(ess). There are no changes in the direction of associations between the years, and indeed changes are not common. Patterns mostly persist over the twen-ty-year period with the main exceptions being that a general greater fre-quency that characterised the upwardly mobile in 1995 did not carry over to 2015, and the association with city of residence fluctuated. So, while changes may hint at future trends, these were mostly minor.

This patchwork of associations is fascinating in its own right and indicates the probabilities with which a specific social characteristic affects frequency of eating out. However, it is not easy to determine the relative importance of such characteristics, not least because for any individual they inevitably occur in combination. For example, women are better educated than men but they are less likely to have service class employment. The purpose of regression analysis is to estimate how one variable alters when all others are held constant, helping with inference about which are the most important causes. However, for technical rea-sons, regression analysis demands that a small number of independent variables are entered into the models. Thus, most of our regression models use a small number of core variables, ones which sociological

**Table 3.4** Association between frequency of eating out in commercial and communal settings and socio-demographic characteristics, 1995 and 2015

| | Restaurant | | Relatives | | Friends | | Hosting | |
|---|---|---|---|---|---|---|---|---|
| | 1995 | 2015 | 1995 | 2015 | 1995 | 2015 | 1995 | 2015 |
| **Sex** | | | | | | | | |
| Male | 0.10 | | −0.08 | −0.09 | | | −0.11 | −0.12 |
| **Age** | | | | | | | | |
| Age | −0.23 | −0.17 | −0.16 | −0.18 | −0.25 | −0.18 | | −0.07 |
| **Ethnicity** | | | | | | | | |
| White British | | 0.08 | | | −0.08 | | | |
| **Cohabitation** | | | | | | | | |
| Lives as a couple | −0.11 | | | | −0.16 | −0.07 | 0.08 | |
| **Child(ren) in household** | | | | | | | | |
| Children in household (under 16s) | −0.11 | −0.15 | 0.05 | 0.06 | −0.01 | −0.09 | 0.03 | 0.01 |
| **Degree educated** | | | | | | | | |
| Has degree | 0.20 | 0.17 | 0.07 | 0.08 | 0.28 | 0.23 | 0.15 | 0.15 |
| **Class mobility** | | | | | | | | |
| Stable service class | 0.11 | 0.20 | 0.11 | 0.08 | 0.18 | 0.21 | 0.10 | 0.13 |
| Upwardly mobile into service class | 0.09 | | 0.07 | | 0.14 | | 0.10 | 0.03 |
| Downwardly mobile from service class | | | | | | | | |
| Other (sideways mobile) | | −0.08 | | | | −0.07 | | |
| Stable working class | −0.08 | −0.16 | | −0.13 | −0.15 | −0.16 | −0.08 | −0.17 |
| Unknown | | −0.11 | −0.13 | | −0.09 | | | |
| **Equivalised household income (tertiles)** | | | | | | | | |
| Highest | 0.23 | 0.16 | 0.10 | | 0.16 | 0.10 | 0.09 | 0.08 |
| Middle | | | | | | | 0.09 | 0.07 |
| Lowest | −0.17 | −0.19 | | −0.07 | −0.09 | −0.15 | −0.08 | −0.13 |
| Unknown | | | | −0.08 | −0.08 | | −0.08 | |
| **City** | | | | | | | | |
| London | 0.09 | | | −0.07 | 0.15 | 0.08 | | |
| Bristol | −0.11 | | | | | 0.10 | | 0.07 |
| Preston | | −0.08 | | | −0.12 | −0.18 | −0.07 | |

Note: Only spearman correlation coefficients significant at the 5% level or lower are shown. Light grey indicates negative association, dark grey indicates positive association and no colour indicates no statistically significant association. Excludes observations with missing data on frequency of eating at restaurant, relatives, friends, or frequency of hosting: 1995 n = 906, 2015 n = 964

tradition expects will differentiate observed behaviour and help sustain meaningful explanation of behaviour.

### Evidence from regression analysis

The pattern is further specified in Table 3.5 which reports the results of linear regression analyses of the 8-item response variables to the question of how often a respondent eats out on commercial premises, at the home of a friend, and at the home of non-resident kin.

Look first at eating on commercial premises. The explained variance is modest ($R^2 = 0.14$). The factors associated with greater frequency are lower age, identifying as white British, not having children under 16 years of age in the household, having a degree, being currently a member of the service class, and not being in the poorest third of the households surveyed. Notably the variable measuring year of the response is not statistically significant, implying no great overall change in underlying patterns of association over the twenty years since 1995. Gender and city of residence were also insignificant. Examining the samples for 1995 and 2015 separately (not shown here) indicates a minor tendency for change. Education becomes less important (there was no statistically significant association with having a degree in 2015); there was some greater residualisation of the stable working class (people in all other social trajectories were more frequent restaurant-goers); and the tendency, shown in 1995, for Bristolians to eat out less frequently disappeared. The overall impression is that eating out in restaurants is associated with particular social positions – higher social class, higher incomes and being a member of the dominant ethnic majority.

Some of the same social characteristics sustain greater frequency of eating at the home of friends. Again, the amount of variance explained is small ($R^2 = 0.20$) but there are clear patterns. Having a degree, not having dependent children, living in London or Bristol, and being currently in the service class, register as powerful influences on receiving invitations from friends. In addition, with a lesser degree of significance, being sideways mobile increases this behaviour. Thus, many of the same factors affecting restaurant attendance recur, implying that people in more privileged positions accumulate opportunities for eating out. Gender, age and year of survey are insignificant.[6]

---

[6]   A closer look at the models for each year separately indicates that youthfulness ceased to be a significant factor, education reduced to some degree, as did membership of the service class, while the role of city of residence moved very sharply to the detriment of Preston.

**Table 3.5** Regression models: frequency of eating out in commercial and communal settings, 1995–2015 (pooled sample)

| | Restaurant | | Friends | | Relatives | |
|---|---|---|---|---|---|---|
| | (1) | (2) | (1) | (2) | (1) | (2) |
| *Year of Survey* | | | | | | |
| 2015 | −0.076 | −0.213** | 0.090 | −0.118 | −0.225* | −0.288** |
| *Sex* | | | | | | |
| Male | 0.007 | 0.047 | −0.142 | −0.089 | −0.314*** | −0.247** |
| *Age* | | | | | | |
| Age | −0.062** | −0.058*** | −0.027 | −0.026 | −0.073** | −0.073** |
| Age$^2$ | 0.000 | 0.000* | 0.000 | 0.000 | 0.001* | 0.001* |
| *Ethnicity* | | | | | | |
| White British | 0.296** | 0.034 | −0.153 | −0.157 | 0.161 | 0.139 |
| *Child(ren) in household* | | | | | | |
| Children in household (under 16s) | −0.406*** | −0.203** | −0.238** | −0.192* | 0.176 | 0.151 |
| *Education* | | | | | | |
| Degree or higher | 0.347*** | 0.244** | 0.577*** | 0.447*** | 0.167 | 0.133 |
| *Social mobility* | | | | | | |
| Stable service class | 0.693*** | 0.454** | 0.840*** | 0.695*** | 0.383* | 0.339 |
| Upwardly mobile into service class | 0.496*** | 0.261 | 0.577*** | 0.459** | 0.328* | 0.299 |
| Downwardly mobile from service class | 0.326 | 0.174 | 0.339 | 0.241 | 0.371 | 0.350 |
| Other (sideways mobile) | 0.207 | 0.145 | 0.336* | 0.271* | 0.097 | 0.068 |
| Stable working class | 0.000 | 0.000 | 0.000 | 0.000 | 0.000 | 0.000 |
| Unknown | 0.167 | 0.177 | 0.261 | 0.211 | −0.135 | −0.120 |
| *Equivalised household income (tertiles)* | | | | | | |
| Highest | 0.874*** | 0.405*** | 0.062 | −0.065 | 0.135 | 0.053 |
| Middle | 0.545*** | 0.204* | 0.181 | 0.094 | 0.115 | 0.049 |
| Lowest | 0.000 | 0.000 | 0.000 | 0.000 | 0.000 | 0.000 |
| Unknown | 0.167 | 0.177 | 0.261 | 0.211 | −0.135 | −0.120 |

**Table 3.5** Continued

|  | Restaurant | | Friends | | Relatives | |
|---|---|---|---|---|---|---|
|  | (1) | (2) | (1) | (2) | (1) | (2) |
| *City* | | | | | | |
| London | 0.019 | −0.029 | 0.384*** | 0.297** | −0.225* | −0.229* |
| Bristol | −0.134 | −0.161 | 0.407*** | 0.336*** | −0.033 | −0.070 |
| Preston | 0.000 | 0.000 | 0.000 | 0.000 | 0.000 | 0.000 |
| *Attitudes* | | | | | | |
| 1 Exploration | | 0.295*** | | 0.242*** | | 0.136*** |
| 2 Relief | | −0.060* | | −0.053 | | 0.024 |
| 3 Home-centredness | | −0.350*** | | 0.003 | | −0.008 |
| 4 Caution | | −0.063* | | −0.128*** | | −0.036 |
| 5 Indulgence | | 0.037 | | −0.082* | | −0.011 |
| 6 Decorum | | −0.025 | | −0.034 | | −0.004 |
| 7 Efficiency | | 0.224*** | | 0.025 | | −0.009 |
| 8 Sociability | | −0.050 | | −0.020 | | 0.090* |
| *Frequency of eating out* | | | | | | |
| In a restaurant | | | 0.251*** | 0.182*** | 0.126*** | 0.094** |
| Constant | 4.847*** | 5.193*** | 1.824*** | 2.332*** | 4.018*** | 4.209*** |
| Obs | 1948 | 1948 | 1901 | 1901 | 1914 | 1914 |
| $R^2$ | 0.144 | 0.306 | 0.209 | 0.240 | 0.080 | 0.094 |
| Adjusted $R^2$ | 0.137 | 0.297 | 0.202 | 0.230 | 0.072 | 0.082 |

Note: *$p < 0.05$, **$p < 0.01$, ***$p < 0.001$

As regards visiting kin, models are extremely weak and barely worthy of consideration. This is a reassuring finding, as it would seem harsh if privileged families also enjoyed greater contact between parents and children. Over the twenty-year period, being female, being in the age range 26–45 and having a stable service class trajectory prove relevant.[7]

These three models overall suggest that social characteristics and social position are not especially strong predictors of frequency of eating

[7] In 1995 only being a woman and living in London (which had a negative effect) were significant factors. This suggests a mild trend, as younger women with service class experience are the most frequent guests of family. Again, people stable in working-class positions are the least well provided for by 2015.

out, although there is a weak propensity for those more privileged by class, income and ethnicity to enjoy more frequent occasions for eating out. There is little evidence of a significant change in the years between 1995 and 2015.

### Personal orientations and frequency of eating in restaurants

The limited variance explained by socio-demographic differences in the frequency of attendance at restaurants can be partly attributed to the fact that a good deal of eating out is more necessity than inclination or personal expression. The need to eat away from home is often a matter of contingent circumstance, when travelling or if delayed by a chance encounter. Some social positions *require* engagement, regardless of personal inclinations towards the practice. The marginal tendency for the privileged to eat out more frequently in commercial settings reflects expectations and norms associating material prosperity with more extensive engagement in this particular market. However, the effect is weak and the range of discretion commensurately large.

Strictly speaking, eating out in a restaurant can almost always be avoided. Provisioning from home, takeaway food and postponement of an eating event are almost always available as alternatives. With foresight and planning, one can take provisions to cover most eventualities. A packed lunch, a picnic, packets of nuts and biscuits – from snacks to a fairly complex set combination of items – there are strategies for avoiding having to buy prepared food when in transit. Exceptions may include foreign holidays, extended periods in hotel accommodation and business trips. However, forethought is often absent, whether regrettable or not. Away from home, many eventualities and many opportunities arise, such that the urge to eat will be met by retail purchases when there is little option except to buy food for immediate consumption. This may involve takeaway food, hot or cold, purchased from myriad outlets – supermarkets, newsagents, chemists, delicatessens, garages, cafes or specialised takeaway outlets. At the other end of the spectrum some meals are planned months ahead. Then, for sure, people could easily do otherwise, as there is no immediate threat of hunger. Such instances clearly are voluntary in the sense that they are within someone's discretion. However, the obligations surrounding commensality mean that with whom we eat, and where, is often not simply a matter of personal choice.

So, people are rarely forced into restaurants. There is usually a place for discretion, which is likely to be a function of attachment to the activity or practice of eating out. Personal variations can be expected. It is therefore interesting to find that introducing measures of orientation towards eating out substantially increase the explained variance in eating in restaurants, although not for the communal mode (Table 3.5, model (2)).

We used factor scores from a principal component analysis of twenty-five attitude questions in the surveys to explore whether they might account for variation in the frequency of eating out. The statistical operation is described in detail in Chapter 4, where changes in attitudes towards eating out are examined. For present purposes, however, including measures of orientation when modelling frequency of attendance at restaurants increases explained variance by between 14 and 16 per cent. Comparison with 1995 suggests that orientations to eating out may have become stronger drivers of behaviour. The very limited effect of orientations on the frequency of eating with friends or family is also worthy of note. This may partly be because, implicitly, the battery of questions probing orientations are directed towards the activity of eating out in restaurants rather than in other people's homes, hence failing to much increase the explanatory power of models of eating with friends and family. However, the effect on eating with friends is greater than for eating with family, suggesting that the circumstances surrounding and the experience of eating with friends is closer to that of the restaurant.[8] This is corroborated by evidence of the relationship between the frequency of eating in restaurants and the frequency of being a domestic guest; eating monthly or more often at the home of friends increases significantly the frequency of eating out in restaurants (see further, Chapter 6).

### Frequency summarised

Eating out frequently is a practice of the more privileged sections of the population, and that inequality may be increasing. Class, education and income are of increasing significance in determining frequency. Nevertheless, how often a person goes out is probably not a key element in games of distinction. Orientations towards eating out appear to be almost equally as important as social characteristics as sources of variation. Expressed attitudes are both a distillation of previous experience and an indication of future behaviour.[9] We might expect those who are home-centric and cautious about food to eat out relatively less frequently in the foreseeable

---

[8]  Exploration and efficiency increase frequency in restaurants while home-centredness acts as a brake. Being a guest of friends is made more likely by an orientation of exploration and less likely for the cautious.

[9]  That some people say they are content to stay at home while others like to get out of the house may be both a rationalisation of previous experience and a declaration of intent for the future.

future, to the extent that their work and leisure routines offer flexibility. As regards distinction, however, it is where people go, rather than how often they go, which is most likely to express discriminating taste, their social identity, and sense of social status.

## Variety of types of restaurant in 2015

Where people go has greater symbolic capacity for signalling status than how often. Respondents were asked which of fourteen types of restaurant they had visited in the last year. Figure 3.1 (top panel) shows

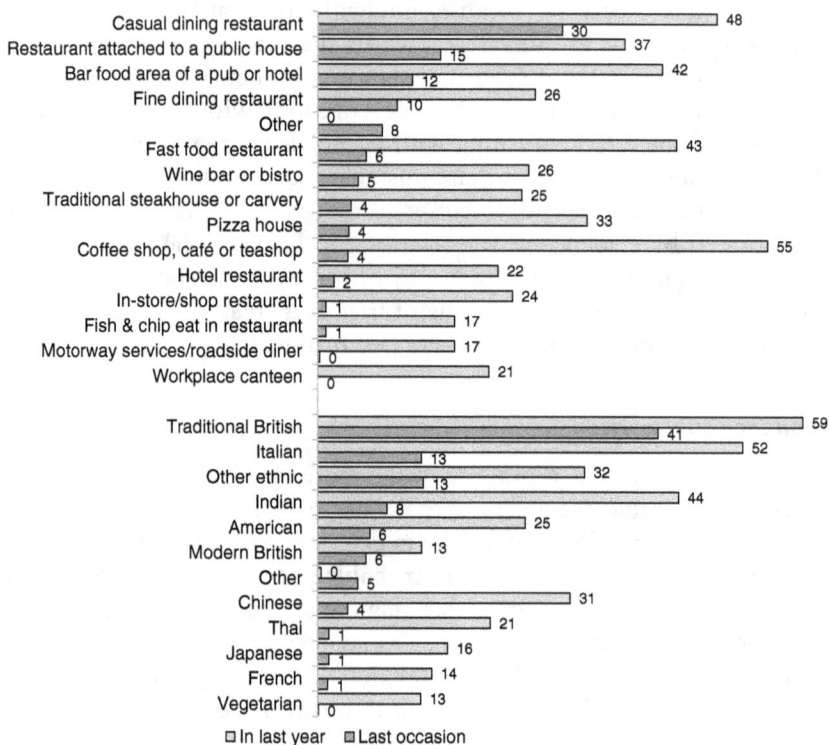

**Figure 3.1** Restaurant type (top) and restaurant cuisine style (bottom) visited within the last year, and on the last occasion, 2015 (percentage)

*Note:* Categories of restaurant type and restaurant cuisine style are ordered by their popularity as a destination on the last occasion

*Observations:* In the last year (N = 1100: One respondent did not answer this set of questions); On the last occasion (N = 817: 822 people ate in a commercial establishment on the last occasion but five respondents did not answer questions on type and/or cuisine style of the restaurant)

exposure of respondents to the different types listed in the survey, both the proportion of the respondents who had visited the various types in the previous year and also the site where, on the last occasion, the respondent had eaten a main meal.

Over half the population had been to a cafe during the last year. Between 40 and 50 per cent had visited a casual dining restaurant, a fast-food restaurant, or the bar food area of a pub or hotel. A third had eaten in a restaurant attached to a public house or a pizza house. A slightly smaller proportion, a quarter or more, had eaten in a fine dining restaurant, a wine bar/bistro, or a traditional steak house or carvery. However, extrapolating from the type of venue attended on the last occasion gives a better indication of which are most often attended. The casual dining restaurant and the pub were the main locations for the majority of meals eaten away from home in 2015 and their impact on the understanding of food or cuisine in Britain must be commensurately significant. The next most popular venues are the fine dining restaurant (10% of last occasions), fast-food restaurants (6%), wine bar or bistro (5%), with steak house and pizza house next (4%).

In light of the cultural omnivore thesis, and its prediction that particular groups in the population will seek greater variety than others, we constructed a variable summing the degree of exposure of each respondent to fourteen types of venue and subjected it to linear regression analysis.[10] We employed the same independent variables as before, but added a measure of frequency of eating out, because people who eat out more have greater opportunity for exposure to different sorts of experience. This variable proved highly significant, but tests (not reported here) showed that while including it reduced a little the strength of effects of socio-demographic variables it did not alter their relative importance or change the direction of their impact (Table 3.6, column 1).

The regression equation, explaining 41 per cent of the variance, shows that the most important factors influencing breadth of experience of different types of restaurant are ethnicity, class trajectory and income. Identifying as white British is highly significant, probably a function of many menus catering to traditional British tastes, availability of alcohol, and because being a member of the white British majority population minimises anticipation that places might be unwelcoming. Having had either personal or childhood experience of life in a service class

10   The mean score on the scale (which could run from 0–14) was 4.125, and the median 4.

**Table 3.6** Regression models: range of type and style of restaurant, 2015. All ages

| | Volume of types of restaurants (0–14) | Volume of styles of restaurants (0–11) |
|---|---|---|
| *Sex* | | |
| Male | 0.025 | 0.036 |
| *Age* | | |
| Age | 0.038 | 0.062* |
| Age$^2$ | −0.001 | −0.001** |
| *Ethnicity* | | |
| White British | 0.948*** | 0.445** |
| *Child(ren) in household* | | |
| Children in household (under 16s) | 0.184 | −0.307 |
| *Education* | | |
| Degree or higher | 0.458* | 0.799*** |
| *Class mobility* | | |
| Stable service class | 1.612*** | 1.627*** |
| Upwardly mobile into service class | 1.160*** | 1.025*** |
| Downwardly mobile from service class | 1.231*** | 1.105*** |
| Other (sideways mobile) | 0.884** | 0.734** |
| Stable working class | 0.000 | 0.000 |
| Unknown | 0.037 | 0.356 |
| *Equivalised household income (tertiles)* | | |
| Highest | 1.083*** | 0.526* |
| Middle | 0.766** | 0.272 |
| Lowest | 0.000 | 0.000 |
| Unknown | 0.037 | 0.356 |
| *City* | | |
| London | −0.091 | 0.708*** |
| Bristol | −0.241 | 0.446** |
| Preston | 0.000 | 0.000 |
| *Frequency of eating out* | | |
| In a restaurant | 0.973*** | 0.784*** |
| Constant | −2.309** | −3.038*** |
| N | 1100 | 1100 |
| R$^2$ | 0.419 | 0.445 |
| Adjusted R$^2$ | 0.410 | 0.436 |

Note: $*p < 0.05$, $**p < 0.01$, $***p < 0.000$

household increases the range of venues visited in the last year.[11] This
presumably also is related to feeling comfortable in and entitled to a
presence in a wide range of places.[12] Household income is also highly
significant, the more wealthy the household the broader the experience.
In addition, having a university degree is significant at the lowest level of
confidence, perhaps indicating that the pursuit of variety, but not frequency, is associated with the possession of cultural capital.[13]

Using genres of establishment as a measure of variety is, however,
rather crude, for types of venue come in many qualities. There are smart
pubs and rough pubs; some fish and chip restaurants have national reputations and have entries in the upmarket independent *Good Food
Guide*, others are much less elevated. Close analysis nevertheless reveals
that different types of restaurant have significantly different customers.
The chances of finding the same people in fine dining, fast food and the
bar in the pub are not high. For example, fast-food venues are disproportionately attended by men, from households with children, living in
Preston, and who do not have a university degree, while fine dining
establishments attract people with service class connections, high or
medium household incomes, and who hold degree level qualifications.[14]
Despite the genre labels being imprecise, the models are powerful and
hint at distinction.

### Exposure to variety, 2015 (styles of restaurant)

Figure 3.1 (lower panel) indicates the pattern of use of restaurants serving different styles of cuisine. The survey named eleven styles when
asking about behaviour in the previous year. When asking about the
previous visit, the option of 'other' was available, and on 5 per cent of

---

[11]  Significance declines monotonically from those who are second-generation
      service class, to the upwardly mobile and to the downwardly mobile.
[12]  Those most likely to agree with the statement 'I feel comfortable in any type
      of restaurant' have high or medium household incomes, eat out more fre-
      quently, are stable in the service class, and do *not* have a degree. Why grad-
      uates should feel less comfortable than others is not clear.
[13]  Unsurprisingly there are similarities between the models predicting fre-
      quency of eating out and range of exposure to different types of venue.
      Income, ethnicity and class trajectory are common to both models, but edu-
      cational qualifications enters the second model, while age and city of resi-
      dence drop out.
[14]  Regression models show that wine bars and fine dining restaurants have
      clientele of higher socio-economic status.

occasions the respondent nominated some version of a mixture of styles. This reflects the popularity of fusion foods and the accessibility of food halls which allow permutations of dishes from several culinary traditions at the same eating event.

We take up the subtleties of the combinations and permutations of different styles and their symbolic significance in chapters 9 and 10 but this section concerns only the total volume of respondents' experience of variety in cuisine styles. Some respondents have narrow and limited experience, others are much more expansive. Range can be considered as some measure of openness and tolerance, of wealth and privilege, and of curiosity and culinary enthusiasm.

Almost 60 per cent of the population had eaten traditional British cuisine in a restaurant setting (10% had eaten no other) and over half had eaten Italian. Indian is the next most widely experienced (44%), while 32 per cent reported at least one 'other' type of ethnic cuisine not specifically nominated by the survey questionnaire, likely to include Mexican, Spanish, Greek or Middle Eastern. About a third of the population had eaten a Chinese meal. Some of the styles pre-identified in the survey were visited infrequently: Vegetarian, Modern British, French, Japanese and Thai had been visited by a fifth or fewer respondents.

The report of the *last* occasion best indicates relative popularity, as cuisines that are experienced more often are more likely to feature as their last experience. 'Traditional British' predominates. Over 40 per cent of respondents classified their last restaurant meal as traditional British. The next most popular (each 13% of last occasions) were Italian and 'other ethnic', the latter witness to the increasingly wide range of styles of cuisine appealing to Britons in 2015.[15] The last meal was Indian cuisine for 8 per cent of respondents, and both American-style and modern British for 6 per cent. Another way to sum up these results is that 47 per cent of meals were in British style, and 46 per cent were designated as exotic cuisines,[16] implying a more or less even attachment to British and 'foreign' cuisines.[17]

---

[15] This point is further underlined by the fact that a majority of respondents volunteering explicit clarification of the 'other' option, nominated a mix of cuisines or fusion style to characterise their last meal.
[16] Neither 'American-style' nor vegetarian are included in this calculation.
[17] Were we, instead, to take 'exotic' to mean non-European, between 15 and 32 per cent – depending upon the geographical provenance of 'other' ethnic and 'mix of different cuisines' – might be deemed exotic. Then British meals outweigh the exotic by approximately two to one.

Considered overall, a significant proportion of the sample were conversant with a wide range of different culinary styles, a feature which must impact upon the overall tastes and diets of contemporary Britons. As a point of comparison, 48 per cent of respondents reported in 1995 that they had not eaten in an ethnic restaurant of any kind in the last twelve months, but by 2015 that proportion had fallen to 22 per cent. In 1995, the propensity to visit restaurants defined by their selling of ethnic cuisine was a strong indicator of social position; people with high levels of cultural and economic capital were much more likely during the previous year to have visited several different types of ethnic restaurant than those with less education and working-class occupations (Warde and Martens, 2000: 81ff). It was argued that having a broad familiarity with ethnic cuisines was evidence of culinary curiosity and adventurousness and, hence, probably also a mark of distinction. However, to the extent that visits to foreign or ethnic restaurants have become more common, their capacity to act as a marker of social distinction might be reduced, since the rarity of items consumed often confers honour. To investigate, we summed up the number of different styles of cuisine that each respondent had reported in the previous twelve months.[18]

Table 3.6 (column 2) reports the linear regression analysis of this measure of overall exposure to culinary variety. With frequency of eating out included as a control,[19] the model explains 44 per cent of the variance, showing that most independent variables are significant, many of them at the highest confidence interval, including, again, identifying as white British, belonging to the service class and having the highest level of income. Education is very significant, suggesting that breadth of culinary taste is an expression of cultural capital. Living in Preston reduces adventurousness. Middle age bands (frequencies, not shown, indicate those aged 26–45 years) display the broadest range of culinary tastes. There is no effect for gender.

Overall an association between social privilege and adventurous taste pertains. Ethnicity, class and income are all significant contributors to explanation of breadth of experience, confirming the joint operation of class and other types of social division upon a symbolically significant activity.

[18]  The maximum was 11 (out of a possible 12), the minimum was 0, the mean was 3, the median 3, and the mode 1.
[19]  The exclusion of frequency of eating out from the model renders linear age statistically insignificant.

## Comparing 1995

For technical reasons exact comparison between 1995 and 2015 on the measures of variety just considered is impossible. The survey instrument in 1995 did not distinguish so clearly between type of venue and cuisine style. Instead a longer list, mixing types and styles, had been presented, in the manner of the market research categories current at that time. The resulting pool of information included much less information about culinary variety. Nevertheless, although less than perfect, an approximate comparison is feasible by adjusting the 2015 data to match the 'hybridity' and 'curiosity' indexes calculated for 1995 (Warde et al., 1999).

An approximation to the older measure offers seventeen options, including most of the same types of venue and four specified ethnic restaurants (e.g. 'Chinese restaurant').[20] Regression analysis was applied to this 'hybrid scale' for each year independently and using the harmonised data set. Neither measure reveals statistically significant differences in breadth of experience between the years. Each of the three models using the core set of independent variables and a measure of frequency of eating out (which is, unsurprisingly, always very significant) explains 40 per cent or more of the variance in each model. Social characteristics strongly influence the experience of variety. Being white British, having a degree, and being in the two highest income bands are very significant. Class trajectory is also very significant in both years. Having some service class experience was a significant determinant in 1995, but in 2015 the line of division lies between the stable working class and the rest. This seems evidence of this section of the population becoming more separated. Another mild emergent tendency is for men to have greater breadth of experience, despite sex being a statistically insignificant factor in the harmonised model, as is age, having dependent children at home, and city of residence. Variety, then, remains primarily the effect of education, income, class and ethnic identity – or, it might be said, a function of cultural and economic capital.

---

[20]  The 'hybrid scale' is a simple arithmetic scale, ranging from 0 to 17, comprising seven cuisine styles (Indian, Chinese/Thai, Italian, American, other ethnic, vegetarian, and 'other') and ten types of establishment patronised (pizza house, fast-food restaurant, fish and chip restaurant, wine bar or bistro, motorway services or roadside diner, in-store/shop restaurant, cafe or coffee shop, traditional steakhouse or carvery, bar food area of a pub, or a restaurant attached to a pub). A second scale was created, the 'curiosity scale', which ranges from 0 to 4 and comprises four 'ethnic' style cuisines (Indian, Chinese/Thai, Italian, other ethnic). Both of these scales are constructed using cuisine styles and restaurant types that were surveyed in both years.

## Conclusion

Eating out is both necessary and discretionary. There has been a modest increase in the rate of eating out as the tempo has stepped up. The retrospective estimate of frequency of eating out over the previous twelve months is almost certainly an underestimate of the true rate, but the discrepancy with the evidence about the last occasion was more or less the same in 2015 as in 1995. Frequency and variety are still subject to social inequalities. Broad patterns have not changed much in the years between 1995 and 2015. However, there are some symbolically significant differences. Familiarisation with the practice makes dining out less special, so while it is still highly pleasurable, satisfaction with commercially provided meals has declined.

The fact that responses to statements about attitudes and preferred behaviour contribute so heavily to a statistical explanation of frequency of eating out in restaurants, but little (though never zero) to eating out with friends or family, or to experience of variety of types or styles of restaurant, raises philosophical and methodological questions about the nature of attitude statements and their measurement (discussed in Chapter 4). The specific result regarding frequency of eating out in restaurants suggests that frequency is associated with social position, but that there is a supplementary effect which might be attributed to how any person is engaged with the practice of eating out. Including attitudes does not eliminate the hypothesis that frequency of eating out is primarily a response to necessity. (Some questions tap preferences, others constraints.) This is partly because orientations are the product of prior experience; those who must eat out a lot come to manage events more comfortably and more competently, irrespective of their social position. But there might still be a presumption that, in the matter of orientations, a degree of discretion remains for those with most interest in the activity to pursue it more assiduously and seize more available opportunities for eating away from home. These issues are pursued further in Chapter 4.

# 4

## The meaning of eating out

### Introduction

A foundational question for our first study was what people would understand when we asked them questions in a survey about eating out. Six themes were isolated which, in combination, constituted the prevailing definition among the people interviewed in Preston in 1994 (Warde and Martens, 2000: 46f). The three most prominent features of the definition were that it happened in delimited types of socio-spatial location outside the home, involved commercial provision, and the work was done by somebody else. Three secondary themes, elicited more during qualifying discussion, were that it implied a social occasion, was deemed a special occasion, and involved a meal rather than a snack. Interviewees debated, for instance, whether being a guest at someone's house counted, and whether some commercial events were not sufficiently special by virtue of the company present, the reason for the event, or its food content. All in all, there were some ambiguities about what occasions should be included, but a broad degree of common ground.

As we were interested rather more in the symbolic and recreational aspects of the practice than in the refuelling role played by eating away from home, we directed survey questions towards eating main meals in socially organised situations on commercial premises or at someone else's home. We did not repeat the listing exercise in 2015 but did ask explicitly at the beginning of the household interviews what people understood by the two terms 'eating out' and 'main meal'. The answers cannot be directly compared to those of 1995 because in the later year interviewees had already completed the survey and interviews occurred in all three cities not just in Preston. A systematic approach to change over time is possible by comparing answers to attitude questions on the survey (see below) but first consider how interviewees in 2015 defined eating out.

## What does it now mean to eat out?

As in 1995, when interviewees were asked what they understood by the term 'eating out', some were taken aback at a social scientist asking such a stupid question. However, most were prepared to volunteer an answer. Some responses were terse and matter-of-fact. Douglas (35, London)[1] gives the most succinct response to being asked what the term 'eating out' means to him: 'Dinner. Hot meal at a sit-down restaurant.' For him, there was very little ambiguity. This is the core of popular understanding. Other features were added by others. For Siobhan (35, London), eating out is defined by the service: 'Going out to a restaurant I think is all that I would term as eating out really. So somewhere you're being served.' However, Angela (40, Preston) counts anything not eaten at home as a meal out:

> Well any meal not eaten at home is eating out really. So yes, that could be anywhere. Restaurant, fast-food place, anything not eaten at home I would say.

Tyler (20, Preston) is more discriminating:

> Probably a restaurant, eating out. It doesn't really matter, as long as you're sitting down. I wouldn't count a fast-food chain as eating out, that would be more of a snack, like you'd get a Subway or a McDonald's. I wouldn't turn round to my missus and say I'd take her out for a meal and then take her to Subway.

Eating out conjures up images of main meals, hence interviewees are unsure how to categorise snacks, lunches in sandwich bars or coffee shops as well as the takeaway. They think aloud as to what they count as 'eating out', but often settle on a description akin to their descriptions of main meals at home, i.e. dinner. For example, Camilla (40, Bristol) says:

> I suppose eating out would be going out for the main meal. Not just going out and picking up lunch somewhere, but actually sitting somewhere away from home where you pay for the food and have a main meal.

Perhaps the most perceptive observation came from Eleni (35, London), originally from Greece, who suggests that eating out includes for her a greater variety of occasions than her British friends and colleagues acknowledge:

> There are different types of eating out. One is planned eating out because you're at work and then you go to have something to snack or to eat or to …

[1]   We list the respondent's age – rounded to the nearest five – and city of residence when first mentioned in the main body of the text. Thereafter, the reader can refer to Appendix Table A2.3 to learn more about the respondents' demographic characteristics.

but eating out in an English sense I think … isn't it also that you have plans with your … to go to a restaurant, a nice restaurant and have a nice meal as well. So there are two types of it. One … you're already on the street. You're hungry so you stop somewhere to have something to eat. Eating out can be … I think in English terms isn't it more like going to a restaurant?

Uncertainty exists whether meals at the home a friend or non-resident family member count. Thus Magdalina (30, Bristol) says, 'Well, I would say it's either at the restaurant or either at my friends, well I don't know if that counts as eating out but it's not in my house so.' Others discount meals with family: Penny (35, London) says, 'For me, eating out is either where I'm not eating in the flat or with my family.' The first reaction of Nadine (30, Bristol), is similar, 'Not eating in your home. Or a close family member.' Meals eaten at the home of family are considered as routine events that are not out of the ordinary. Nadine makes this explicit in saying,

> I suppose it depends doesn't it, but if you're eating at parents' or best friends' where you eat regularly I suppose. So I'd say eating out is something that you do out of routine, but where we both eat at my grandparents and my parents weekly so that's not eating out because that's a routine.

The uncertainty about whether eating in other people's homes is really eating out underlines the point that market provision is core to common understanding, and Nadine, by potentially discounting places visited routinely, shows strong vestiges of the idea that eating out should still be special.

From these deliberations comes a sense of how the term is typically employed. Its dominant meaning continues to be much the same as in 1995. It refers primarily to events occurring outside the home at a commercial site, usually indoors around a table, involving a financial transaction, and not requiring labour on the part of the customer. So while no one baulked at being asked about main meals eaten at the homes of friends and non-resident kin as part of a study of eating out, this was not a primary element of the everyday understanding of the term.

More debatable, and perhaps revealing some shifts, are the supplementary qualifying features of the definition of eating out. It continues to be assumed that eating out will be a social occasion, even though people do eat out alone sometimes and a little more often than in 1995. However, the degree to which it should be treated as a special event is more open to question, a matter which is tied up with the content of the food consumed. Interviewees still see some events as very special and out of the ordinary occasions, where there is opportunity for indulgence and conviviality when celebrating an anniversary or a rite of passage or sometimes purely for its own sake. However, these kinds of event are a decreasing proportion, which is reflected partly in what is eaten and understandings of the types of food appropriate to a particular event. Some foods and dishes are marked as incompatible with the eating event being designated 'eating out'. Fast-food restaurants are on the cusp, although 6 per cent of respondents reported their last meal as being in a fast-food restaurant.

Suitable food is something akin to dinner at home, the instance par excellence of a main meal (which term the survey used). These are hot meals, comprising vegetables, often meat and carbohydrates. Almost universally, interviewees view a main meal as one eaten with companions, usually with other members of the family or household, once the daily work tasks (for those with engagements outside of the home in employment or education) have been completed. Cheryl (65, Bristol), who lives with her husband, explains:

> To me a main meal has always been the one that we have as a family, which is the evening usually, when my husband's home and the children. The children are here, we're here coming in from work and that would be the main meal of the day.

Some people incline to denying that snacks or tapas count. For example, Pete (55, London) says

> I had Mexican fajitas. Now when I see that in one restaurant that was pretty good, but when it comes up I think it's not what I would call a meal, it's more a snack. More than a snack but not quite a meal, you know.

Others make a distinction between the form and content of main meals at home and main meals when eating out, the latter being more elaborate.

## Special and ordinary meals

In 1995 there were more celebratory meals, classified by respondents as 'special occasions' and eating out itself was referred to as an exceptional, and thus a 'special', event. Greater familiarity with the activity reduces the sense of specialness, and the grounds for that can be detected in the interviewees' accounts which depict ordinary events of two types.

Comparing features of the last meal out as reported in the surveys indicates some significant casualisation and simplification of dining out in restaurants. Table 4.1 shows that the number of people at the table declined; more people reported eating out alone and fewer people reported eating with very large groups. Respondents tend not to dress up especially for the occasion as much as they did twenty years ago.

**Table 4.1** Characteristics of the last meal occasion in a restaurant, 1999, 2015 and change over time (percentage)

|  | 1995 | 2015 | Change |
|---|---|---|---|
| *Company* |  |  |  |
| Ate alone | 3 | 6 | 3 |
| 20 people or more | 5 | 3 | –2 |
| *Dressed up* |  |  |  |
| Yes | 39 | 26 | –13 |
| *Day of the week* |  |  |  |
| Weekend (Fri–Sun) | 65 | 58 | –7 |
| *Decided in advance* |  |  |  |
| Walking past | 27 | 27 | 0 |
| One hour | 11 | 17 | 6 |
| On the day | 16 | 19 | 3 |
| Several weeks or more *before* | 14 | 7 | –7 |
| *Duration* |  |  |  |
| 1 hour or less | 20 | 35 | 15 |
| 1–2 hours | 45 | 48 | 3 |
| 2 or more hours | 35 | 18 | –17 |
| *Courses* |  |  |  |
| Starter | 52 | 39 | –13 |
| Dessert | 41 | 30 | –11 |
| One course | 35 | 43 | 8 |
| Two courses | 32 | 35 | 3 |
| Three courses or more | 33 | 22 | –11 |
| *Returning customer* |  |  |  |
| Been before | 62 | 67 | 5 |
| Go again ('Very likely') | 55 | 64 | 9 |

*Note:* Using data from respondents between ages 16–65

Events are planned less far in the future; many more decide to eat out one hour before or on the day of the meal and fewer make arrangements several weeks or more in advance. People now spend less time eating their meal when in a restaurant; meals taking less than one hour increased from 20 per cent in 1995 to 35 per cent in 2015. Meals are also simplified, with one course more frequent and three-course meals much less common; fewer people had dessert while even fewer had starters. Finally, respondents were more likely to return to a restaurant previously visited (67% compared with 62%) and also more likely to report that they would go back there again. It is thus no coincidence that in the survey more events were designated as convenient/quick and fewer as special occasions.

## Special meals

Interviewees talked of special occasions which they associated with celebratory life events such as birthdays or anniversaries,[2] but also with 'treating' oneself to a more elaborate dining out experience than usual, such as in what Arlie (70, London) described as a 'posh restaurant'. Such meals are often booked weeks or even months in advance and, for some, provide the opportunity to dress up more than one would usually. On these occasions, typically more than one course is ordered and rules of everyday eating are temporarily suspended. Menus are sometimes previewed online and a decision about what to eat made in advance (Penny). Such occasions are described in ways that suggest anticipation of both the meal itself and the atmosphere of the restaurant. For Simon (40, Preston), the special occasion would be a birthday or an anniversary, and would involve going out with his wife for what he describes as a fine dining experience:

> I suppose it's the experience of, you know, the level of service. I suppose it's the atmosphere. It's not being pressured. It feels like you're being I suppose waited on without being kind of hurried [...] I suppose it's got to be the [...] quality of the food and the drinks, [...] food that I know I can't turn out at home, you know, because for me if it's home-cooking, then to me that's not fine dining.

Interviewees commonly refuse to accept disappointment with any aspect of a special event. The atmosphere and service are of equal if not greater importance than the quality of the food, for it is an occasion out of the ordinary.

Increasingly over the last twenty years people have eaten out at commercial premises more routinely and more informally. While in 1995 exactly the same proportion of last meals were reported as being 'just social occasions', those allocated to the category of 'quick/convenient' has increased. Nevertheless, while the meaning of those terms probably has not changed, the substance of such events may have. Interviews reveal distinct types of ordinary meals. While there is a clear shared understanding that special meals should be 'memorable events', most meals described by interviewees are less exceptional. These 'ordinary' meals are shaped and inspired by myriad related practices and are

2   Asked to describe such special occasions, mention was made of special birthdays (twenty-first, fiftieth etc.), 'ordinary' birthdays, special anniversary celebrations, 'ordinary' anniversary celebrations, weddings, christenings, engagements, religious festivities, Mother's Day, passing an exam and a farewell meal.

unremarkable; fewer are planned in advance, they are interwoven with everyday responsibilities for 'feeding work' (DeVault, 1991). They are more informal and also more affordable, but nevertheless central to repertoires of eating and sociability. Respondents across all three cities use 'special price menus' and dining out discount and membership cards to discover deals and promotions and bring down costs.[3] Others find pubs an affordable and convenient alternative to the 'nice restaurant':

> We more regularly go to a pub kind of place which has nice food, just for convenience, I think. Really nice restaurants are expensive, so just time and circumstance, we just would more go to a nice pub out of the city. I suppose it's less informal as well. (Angela)

Miranda (50, Bristol) notes the transformation of many establishments that primarily sold drinks, into places for eating informal and simple meals. One could argue that they offer a compromise between the 'nice restaurant' and the public house by combining dining room service with informality and what is understood as relatively inexpensive meals yet served with alcohol.[4]

One unifying feature across all forms of eating out, special or ordinary, is that interviewees enjoy a range of eating events. To eat out is not an obligation. Routinisation does not detract from pleasure derived. Asking Crispin (50, Bristol) to explain what he means by eating out being a 'treat', he explains,

> I don't know. I don't know. I think it's because we don't do it every day and the kids get to choose what they eat and it's sort of... it's seen as a bit of an occasion, so... and there might be nice food even. I don't think... it's not like it's an amazing treat, sort of like we all ... It's just something nice.

Being 'just something nice' rather than 'an amazing treat' sums up the status of the increasingly frequent and less exceptional meals. Two types of *ordinary* meal out can be detected, the impromptu and the regularised.

### Ordinary meals: impromptu and regularised

The *impromptu* meal out is not planned in advance and is a response to the culmination of particular circumstances or events. It is a form of

---

[3]  The survey question about 'how did you decide what to eat' for the last occasion showed that in 1995, 5 per cent of last meals in a commercial establishment were a fixed menu but in 2015, 17 per cent were from fixed price menus.

[4]  UK fast-food venues and cafeterias do not serve beer and wine unlike in many other European countries, such as Spain and Germany.

'ordinary consumption' which takes place as the result of other daily life demands (Gronow and Warde, 2001). For example, hunger might strike suddenly, or the inclination to cook might be lacking, or there may be insufficient ingredients in the cupboard to make a satisfactory meal; in such circumstances access to a nearby restaurant suggests an impromptu meal out. Pete, for example, reports a spontaneous event when he succumbed to the smell of pie and mashed potato while shopping for a new pair of shoes.

Isaac (45, London) reports that he uses digital technologies to locate a venue and make last-minute arrangements with dining companions. Increasingly, communication technology facilitates impromptu events. Mal (25, Bristol) lives alone and claims that meals are for him 'a social thing' which he prefers to take in company. In this way, he will 'call people and be like, "come and have lunch with me"' Also several men described nights out in bars with their male friends, eating burgers or steaks in a pub or from an outlet en route to the next venue. Edward describes this as food to fill you up so that you 'don't fall over'. Echoing the survey results, Tyler notes that a convenience or quick meal with his friends will often involve 'just a main'.

> Sometimes I'll eat out with my mates but that's more of a burger and beers eating out. [...] Yeah, there's no planning. It might just be we're going for a couple of drinks and then go to a Wetherspoon's and get some food there because we fancy it. Or we might just be out and someone might fancy something to eat so we might go across. But that's more of a small portion rather than sitting down and eating a full three-course meal. It's just a main really.

Commercial casual venues provide last-minute opportunities to meet immediate requirements. In addition, the landscape of provision has altered, with changes to the opening hours of kitchens in public houses allowing meals to be consumed away from home throughout the day, creating opportunities for impromptu meals more readily synchronised with other activities and other people.[5]

Last-minute impromptu meals are not necessarily characterised by convenience or junk foods. They are often full, cooked, 'proper' meals, for example roast dinners eaten in pubs or carveries or pasta dishes in local Italian restaurants (Murcott, 1982; Holm, 2001; Marshall and Anderson, 2002). For Simon, stopping for a carvery meal extends the family Sunday

---

[5]   Still, many pubs and some restaurants respect traditional lunchtimes (12.00–14.00) and evening serving times (18.00–21.00).

outing and allows him and his partner to return home ready to prepare for the week ahead. No one has to stay behind to prepare dinner.

Interviewees speak of release from the labour of food preparation as well as other domestic obligations and chores competing for their attention. For example, Tristan eats out more 'if it's a busy week'. Nicola explains that, as she turns her mind to thinking about preparing the evening meal, she will say to herself '"I can't be bothered, so let's go out." It's just easier.' Similarly, Cheryl's husband convinces her it is not worth the effort unless their grown-up children visit as planned.

> By the time you go and buy a piece of beef that's ten pound. By the time you go and get all the veg, then you've got to cook it, then you've got to wash it all up and it's three o'clock in the afternoon before you've done all that. He says 'well, we'll go have a natter, a lunch'. He says it's no more expensive.

Replacing the home-cooked with an impromptu meal in a restaurant reduces effort, cost and waste.

Not all 'ordinary' meals are impromptu. Accounts of eating out are peppered with references to appointments made with family or friends as a way of staying in touch with people outside of the household on a regular basis. What we call *regularised meals* take place at intervals by mutual agreement, a means for those living outside the household to stay in touch with each other, or which have emerged over time as a pattern of sociability. For Gerald (70, Preston) 'there's four of us usually go out together [...] friends of ours, we usually go out with them once a month or something like that, different restaurants'. Such meals take place regularly although not repeated at exact intervals. For Penny, lunchtimes and early evenings are key moments to eat out with friends who work nearby but who live at opposite edges of the city. It is a way to meet friends she would otherwise struggle to see. Such planned social events are key forms of regularised 'ordinary' meals out.

A couple of survey questions reaffirmed a shift towards informalisation and simplification. The proposition that 'I only eat out on special occasions' found greater agreement in 1995 (by 10%), and agreement with the statement 'When I eat out I feel I am on show a little bit' fell from 37 to 25 per cent. More people are more comfortable and familiar with eating out and therefore feel less part of a spectacle. This shift reflects familiarisation with eating out as it becomes increasingly incorporated into people's ordinary daily lives and an increasingly mundane mode of food provisioning rather than being limited to formal, special occasions.

Informality is the basis of a significant cohort effect because familiarity with and knowledge of the practice of eating out among the population has grown in the last twenty years. Being able to call into a restaurant on a whim to satisfy one's fancy in the moment might be considered a pure case of consumer freedom. However, despite occurring on the spur of the moment, most such events are expected, reported as 'tending' to happen. They have happened before and are likely to happen again.

In 1995 many older people had only recent experience of dining out, for until the 1970s it had been uncommon for anyone on a moderate or low income to eat out except on holiday or at midday in the working week (Caplan, 1997; Jacobs and Scholliers, 2003). More people have more experience in 2015 than in 1995. Then the experience of eating out might still be deemed special, for even though it was not much less frequent in 1995 it was not yet taken for granted. Another twenty years of regular and normalised eating out has meant that almost everyone is familiar with the activity. The practice has matured along with a cohort, currently aged less than 45, which has more or less a lifetime of experience of eating meals out on commercial premises. Some of these new features are affirmed by looking at changes in dispositions recorded in the surveys.

## Changing orientations to eating out

### *Measuring orientations*

One means at our disposal for identifying popular understandings and the meaning of eating out is the analysis of responses to twenty-five statements included in the survey at both dates. They indicate what people like and dislike, hope and fear, think and do. The questions asked tap into rationales for eating away from home, culinary preferences, aspirations, habits and routines, and social anxieties about presence in public space. In association with other evidence, the questions throw light on the terrain of meanings, understandings, reasons, motives and reactions to prior experience – although they do not distinguish among these dimensions. Thus, they uncover general orientations that people hold. They also provide basic evidence about changes in the public climate of opinion.

We have due sociological scepticism about attitude questions in surveys. People evolve attitudes and orientations which make sense of their past behaviour and their perceived options. In pragmatist fashion, we view them as feelings about past experience (imagined or real) probably most closely connected to their immediate past behaviour, although longer-held memories and anticipations of future projects are likely also to be relevant. These orientations are one means for justifying past and future action, and they are likely to be tailored to objective constraints on their opportunities. Bourdieu controversially captured this sensibility among the working class in the phrase 'having a taste for necessity'. This condition probably affects behaviour more than attitudes. Nevertheless, orientations are adjusted to the social and material circumstances of typical adherents and it can be presumed that changes in the external environment over twenty years might alter attitudes.

We approach the analysis of these attitude questions in three steps. We first look at broad shifts of opinion by looking at answers to individual questions. Second, we examine how answers cluster together, revealing, more reliably, basic orientations towards the activity of eating out. Third, we look at the social and demographic underpinnings of those orientations – the associations between orientations and different categories of person. Of course, individuals are often not in a position to act in accordance with their orientations. They may hold inconsistent attitudes and desires, and those with whom they dine may have different orientations, requiring negotiation and compromise. Social patterns of behaviour cannot be reduced to the attitudes of individuals with isolated preferences.

### Shifting orientations

Figure 4.1 shows that some attitudes have gained in prevalence, others diminished, but all except two were subject to a statistically significant shift. For example, answers indicate greater openness to new culinary experiences. Many more declared that they became 'excited about going to a new place' (the proportion in strong agreement rose by 18%). The percentage of people agreeing that they often talk to others about eating out rose too. A great deal of culinary education occurs around eating away from home.

Shifts occurred over many other issues. Eating out has become less a matter of relief from the burdens of domestic food preparation. Half agreed strongly with the proposition 'I like to eat out because it means I do not have to prepare the meal at home' in 1995, but only 29 per cent hold the same view in 2015, indicating that some of the burden of domestic meal preparation may have been alleviated. Fewer people are repelled by the trappings of formality in restaurants, and fewer are averse to vegetarian meals. People are also more comfortable eating out alone in a restaurant, more tolerant of the presence of children, and less likely to worry about poor or slow service. Fewer people say that they eat out only on special occasions and fewer declare that they would like to eat out more often.

Most statements divide the population, revealing competing and contrasting attitudes towards the practice. Disagreement is most marked

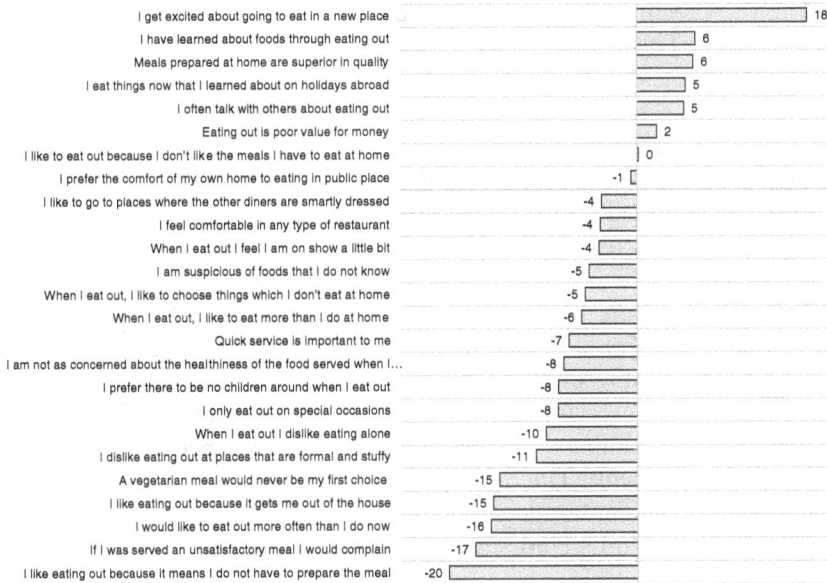

**Figure 4.1** Changing attitudes, 1995–2015 (percentage change in 'Agree strongly')
*Note:* Respondents between ages 16–65

over suspicion of unfamiliar food, concern for health, and preference for vegetarian meals. Nevertheless, no question posed grew more controversial in the twenty-year period.

It is generally held that attitudes clustering together command greater confidence than single questions when interpreting a person's stance towards activities or controversial issues. To show how responses coincide or cluster together, what we call 'orientations', we employ PCA. We conducted several analyses on the data, on samples from 1995 and 2015 separately and also on the harmonised data. The differences in how attitudes clustered were few, implying that basic orientations were stable over the twenty years and hence could be economically represented by reporting from the analysis of the harmonised data.[6]

---

[6] We divided the sample by year of completion and modelled the association with the clusters of attitudes generated from the harmonised data. We also conducted PCA on each year sample separately and undertook the same modelling procedures, on the basis of which we are confident in concluding that little information is lost (and many words saved) by proceeding to analyse the combined sample.

The PCA technique generated an 8-factor solution for the harmonised sample. The results describe differing fundamental orientations towards eating out, indicating aspects that some people appreciate and others reject. Thus, for example, someone who says they learned about foods through eating out is also likely to get excited about going to eat in a new place. Some underlying (latent) understanding is therefore presumed which draws these reflections on past experience together. The patterns reveal some strong and stable orientations towards eating out which suggest competing and contrasting rationales for behaviour.

The eight clusters identified in Table 4.2 identify alternative orientations towards eating out. We find echoes of these orientations in the discourse of the interviewees, contributing to an understanding of the patchwork of meanings, reasons and feelings that people associated with restaurant meals. The first and statistically most powerful component captures openness, adventurousness and a disposition for *exploration*. The orientation includes acknowledgement of learning about food from eating out, of liking to talk about eating out with others, and of excitement about going to eat for the first time in a new place. It announces a willingness to address unfamiliar food with an open mind and a certain enthusiasm for eating out.

The second orientation, *relief*, revolves around the satisfaction to be gained from escaping domestic confinement, avoiding having to prepare food or eat it at home, with a concomitant aspiration to eat out more often.

The third component, *home-centredness*, draws together largely social and resource justifications for preferring to eat at home; it is economical, produces better quality meals and is more comfortable. Hence eating out primarily occurs on special occasions. A fourth syndrome, *caution*, also justifies restricting occasions for eating out, primarily driven by culinary conservatism as reported in suspicion of unfamiliar food, although also there is a hint of embarrassment about eating in public. It conveys a firm embrace of the familiar foods of the domestic table and anxiety about being presented with unfamiliar or unpalatable dishes in a restaurant.

A fifth bundle of concerns, *indulgence*, appreciates opportunities for relaxation of everyday constraints afforded by the restaurant, where health concerns can be suspended, portion sizes increased, and children banished. The associated rejection of vegetarian meals may result from a suspicion that vegetables are insufficiently filling or a mark of frugality but may also be a refusal of the ethical associations of vegetarianism.

**Table 4.2** Principal component analysis, eight orientations: 1995 and 2015 combined

| | | Eigenvalue | Rotated loadings |
|---|---|---|---|
| 1 | **Exploration** | 3.601 | |
| | I have learned about foods through eating out | | 0.522 |
| | I eat things now that I learned about on holidays abroad | | 0.466 |
| | I often talk with others about eating out | | 0.462 |
| | I get excited about going to eat in a new place | | 0.423 |
| 2 | **Relief** | 2.343 | |
| | I like eating out because it means I do not have to prepare the meal myself | | 0.575 |
| | I like eating out because it gets me out of the house | | 0.538 |
| | I would like to eat out more often than I do now | | 0.403 |
| 3 | **Home-centredness** | 1.538 | |
| | Eating out is poor value for money | | 0.551 |
| | Meals prepared at home are superior in quality | | 0.467 |
| | I prefer the comfort of my own home to eating in public place | | 0.432 |
| | I only eat out on special occasions | | 0.407 |
| 4 | **Caution** | 1.395 | |
| | I am suspicious of foods that I do not know | | 0.584 |
| | When I eat out, I like to choose things which I don't eat at home | | −0.430 |
| | Quick service is important to me | | 0.307 |
| | When I eat out I feel I am on show a little bit | | 0.306 |
| 5 | **Indulgence** | 1.211 | |
| | I am not as concerned about the healthiness of the food served | | 0.673 |
| | A vegetarian meal would never be my first choice | | 0.508 |
| | When I eat out, I like to eat more than I do at home | | 0.317 |
| | I prefer there to be no children around when I eat out | | 0.312 |
| 6 | **Decorum** | 1.143 | |
| | I dislike eating out at places that are formal and stuffy | | −0.600 |
| | I like to go to places where the other diners are smartly dressed | | 0.581 |
| | I feel comfortable in any type of restaurant | | 0.471 |

(Continued)

**Table 4.2** Continued

|   |   | Eigenvalue | Rotated loadings |
|---|---|---|---|
| 7 | **Efficiency** | 1.085 | |
| | If I was served an unsatisfactory meal I would complain | | 0.646 |
| | Quick service is important to me | | 0.439 |
| | I prefer there to be no children around when I eat out | | 0.343 |
| 8 | **Sociability** | 1.061 | |
| | I like to eat out because I don't like the meals I have to eat at home | | −0.613 |
| | When I eat out I dislike eating alone | | 0.587 |
| | I prefer there to be no children around when I eat out | | −0.366 |

The sixth factor, *decorum*, commends formality, a sense that at least on some occasions being in a place with white tablecloths among smartly dressed diners is to be welcomed. A seventh set of considerations, *efficiency*, revolves around expectations of service, and suggests a utilitarian and business-like attitude to eating out.

The final factor, *sociability*, pulls together sociable and familial themes, being happy with the meals eaten at home, disliking eating out without company and being pleased to be in the presence of children.

These eight blocs of sentiment each have a degree of meaningful coherence and thematise recognisable aspects of eating out and ways to justify behaviour. They are commonly circulating ways of understanding the meaning of eating out, founded in different ways of appreciating the culinary and the social features of the experience of dining out. They are not necessarily mutually exclusive. One might, for example, appreciate both novelty and relief from the domestic drudgery of food preparation. Other combinations are potentially contradictory. The first factor ('exploration'), which captures culinary openness and adventurousness, is manifestly in opposition to the third and fourth orientations which signify a preference for the domestic table and a liking for familiar foods. Nor does relief from domestic labour sit easily with a view that home is best (factors two and three). Those who favour opportunities for formal dining in public will probably seek venues where other customers prioritise neither indulgence nor efficient service. The nature of such oppositions can be further exposed both by examining the associations between orientation and the social characteristics of the respondents.

### The social foundations of different orientations

Attitudes correspond to some degree with social position, but the relationship is often weak. Using the $R^2$ measure of association to assess the relationship between social characteristics and attitudes, only ten of twenty-five individual questions exceeded 10 per cent. 'I only eat out on special occasions', 'I often talk with others about eating out' and 'I am suspicious of foods I don't know' displayed the strongest associations; not insignificantly, they were questions about routine behaviour rather than judgements of taste. The power of socio-demographic characteristics to 'explain' the distribution of orientations (i.e. the clustered responses) was greater, although still comparatively weak. As measured by survey questions, attitudes are weak social facts.

The meaningfulness and the distinctiveness of the eight orientations is emphasised by considering the association of each with sub-populations. Table A4.1 (pp. 262–264) supplies evidence for the social characteristics and material resources of the people most likely to adopt each orientation.[7] All but one orientation (relief from domestic constraints) was subject to a shift in intensity between 1995 and 2015. The orientations to exploration, decorum and efficiency are all associated with high frequency of eating out, while the sentiments of home-centredness and caution are held by people who eat out comparatively infrequently.

Thereafter each orientation has some distinct social foundations. For instance, the orientation of culinary openness is associated with being a woman and having high and middle incomes. This was true in both 1995 and 2015.[8] Having a degree-level qualification had no effect at all on exploration in 1995, but has a positive effect in 2015. Women and those identifying as white British are most keen to get out of the house. The best predictor of the 'home is best' orientation is having a low income, hence a low frequency of eating out; being female, not being in the ethnic majority and having dependent children are supporting conditions. The three last-mentioned variables were insignificant in 1995, when indeed low income was a more powerful determinant, but became more significant in 2015. Predictors of caution are eating out

---

[7]  The results are based on a linear regression analysis of the factor scores, using the same independent variables as in Chapter 3 but including a dummy variable for the year in which the response was given.

[8]  This is shown in columns 5 and 6 of Table A4.1 (pp. 262–264) which list the statistically associated social variables calculated by considering the samples of each year independently. Where variables listed as significant are not identical in the three columns ('All', '1995' and '2015') there is a presumption that the social basis for an orientation has changed.

infrequently, not having a higher education qualification, being stable working class and living in Preston. In 1995 having children was significant and by 2015 so was ethnic minority status. A propensity for indulgence is strong among white, non-degree-holding and non-metropolitan men. The pursuit of decorum has few social associations. Men, of older age, without a degree but with high incomes are most likely to orient in business-like fashion to restaurant service. The final orientation, sociability, was common among households with children, those living in Bristol rather than London, with middle and high income and minority ethnic status as emergent features.

Examining the evidence from another angle shows how the social characteristics of respondents impact upon orientations. In general, it appears that pragmatic adjustment to material circumstances and personal obligations are the main source of variations in orientation. Those with low incomes are more restricted than the more affluent in their horizons and their behaviour. Those with children appreciate domestic settings. Women with domestic obligations seek respite. However, some of the detail is instructive.

Gender is a primary basis for seeking relief from labour, the sole orientation where no statistically significant difference is detected between the two years. Ethnic status has a broad compass, strong with respect to relief from domestic labour, home-centredness, caution and indulgence. Minorities apparently hold attitudes keeping them out of many types of restaurants while the more confident ethnic majority members hold views pushing them more often into a wide range of public settings. The minority population is less likely to see eating out as relief from unwelcome domesticity. The stable working class is much more likely to be cautious in culinary taste than any other class and is attracted to indulgence a little more than those with service class connections. Income affects most orientations, with home-centredness apparently destiny for the poor. The presence of dependent children increases feelings of caution and sociability. Having a higher education qualification strongly militates against caution, indulgence and efficiency. City of residence has some impact, with Bristol more sociable, London less 'laddish', and Preston more cautious and more expressive of working-class culture. Intriguingly, age has little association with the distribution of orientations.

In broad-brush terms, the same categories of people adopt the orientations identified in both years. The association between factor scores and the social composition of the sub-categories of the population in the sample suggests considerable continuity throughout the twenty-year period.

### How real people thrive

The testimonies of interviewees are fully consistent with, and thus illustrative of, the principal orientations isolated by the statistical analysis. However, they almost always hold more complex views, for it is not the case that anyone is solely inquisitive, or cautious, or indulgent. Any inconsistency or dissonance between orientations will always be muted because any individual who eats out with moderate frequency can experience a range of alternatives, eating Greek one day and traditional British the next. Crispin, when asked what he likes about eating out, replies:

> I don't know really. I'd say for me personally it would be something of...
> a bit sort of... I was going to say exotic, but I don't know, I like Thai and
> Vietnamese food and something that you wouldn't normally cook at home
> so much, but I also like wholesome food. I like pub lunches and things. It's
> not convenience food. Something that's sort of nice and well cooked.

He is not alone in liking a balance between traditional and more exotic foods; one of the joys of eating out in restaurants is that it becomes possible to permutate different culinary experiences on separate occasions (or indeed sometimes during the same meal). The interesting and important differences lie in the degree to which these orientations vary from person to person.

Patterns identify clear differences between individuals but they are not absolute, nor necessarily even strongly marked. Everyone is at least a little cautious, a little pleased to be relieved of work, a little tempted to indulge. Also, by the same token, everyone is at least a little adventurous. We take exploration as an example because it is the strongest attitude syndrome, pulling more like people together more strongly, and because it has increased the most markedly between 1995 and 2015.

Thus, there are meaningful differences in orientation. Answers to attitude questions do discriminate between different ways of approaching and appreciating eating out, and have some association with behaviour. At the same time, there is an underlying similarity in understandings of what eating out might be and what standards are relevant to judging one's own and others' behaviour. Exploration is good, escaping labour is often good, and the value of home is contested.

### Conclusion

Eating out is primarily understood, as it was in 1995, as a substantial meal, paid for in a commercial establishment, eaten with other people, and usually primarily for enjoyment. Basic reasons for wanting to eat out are similar in 2015, but the activity has become more familiar and rather less special. Most meals out now are best considered as ordinary, occurring in an impromptu or regularised manner which renders them normal.

There are many reasons for eating out. Most anticipate a pleasurable experience, although appreciating that there are different dimensions of enjoyment. Food quality and companionship are the primary concerns, but service, comfort and relief from domestic labour all signify. When a full balance sheet is drawn up, many people (55%) would not wish to eat out more often. Some who are sceptical may feel either uncomfortable in some venues or contexts, or simply prefer to stay at home. Siobhan for example, who likes eating out, thinks it would take up too much time for other activities if it occurred more frequently. Some interviewees are very enthusiastic about dining out, and food more generally, and take great pleasure and interest in what might be gained by eating out in restaurants. Others take a much more cautious approach, while still affirming that they try new and different things, being more reserved, less enthusiastic, and more concerned with the sociability afforded or the convenience of an accessible meal requiring no preparation.

Orientations have shifted over the twenty-year period, a consequence of diversification of opportunities. There is greater excitement about food overall, and acknowledgement that eating out can be used to extend and expand culinary horizons. People are more relaxed about eating out. Some constricting aversions are in retreat, for instance the fear of unfamiliar food or dislike of vegetarian meals. However, how the attitudes underlying orientations cluster together and which categories of person subscribe to particular clusters of attitude have altered very little. Attitudes remain anchored to gender, ethnicity, education, class, income and city of residence with all these factors significant sources of variation. The evidence indicates a changing climate of understanding and evaluation but differential orientations remain associated mostly with the same sub-categories in the population. The experience of eating out is socially sedimented in a similar fashion in both years.

# Part III

Informalisation

# 5

## Food at home

### Introduction

The attractiveness of eating out partly depends on how satisfactory arrangements are for eating at home. The stove and hearth represent symbolically the core spatial location for eating. Eating at home remains the norm, and most meals are taken at home. Eating out is thus usually considered as exceptional, a punctuation in the routine of domestic meals. However, given the normalisation of eating out, it may be necessary to reconsider. More breakfasts are taken out. Lunch, at least on workdays, is mostly eaten away from home. Weekends are less predictable, but often include regular eating out events. A radical scenario might be that eating out has become an ineradicably fixed and regular part of the eating regime of many households. It is even possible that domestic meals will become the residual element of eating arrangements, despite being still numerically preponderant, with adverse consequences for the ideal of the family meal. In this regard we might expect differences.

### Domestic meal patterns

The study does not have the same degree of information about domestic meals as for meals out. What casual information we have gleaned suggests that households have routines, but that these differ between households, perhaps depending on household type and generation, and are mostly not adhered to rigidly. The existence of routine is evidenced in the way that people respond in interview to questions about how and what they eat. One striking point is that increasingly people organise their domestic regimes around one main meal, on weekdays eaten in the early evening. Another is that they almost all have in their minds some sense of a regular eating pattern which is implied through reference to what they 'usually' do. Understandings are formulated with household members in mind as companions.

### Who do people eat with?

The surveys asked about companions at breakfast, lunch and dinner on the previous day. The answers indicate that while respondents very often eat with other household members, the proportion is declining (Table 5.1). There was no specification of where those meals were eaten, but since most people eat most of their main meals at home it gives some indication of a decline in the frequency of the ideal family meal as family members eat together less often.

Respondents eat fewer meals with partners and children than in 1995. Only a minority of couples eat breakfast or lunch together, and the proportion has fallen sharply. For example, having breakfast together reduced by 25 per cent. Four in five had their partner present in 2015, a

**Table 5.1** Household members present at various meals 1995–2015 (percentage)

|                      |                                  | 1995 | 2015 | Change |
|----------------------|----------------------------------|------|------|--------|
| **Couple only household** | | | | |
| *Breakfast* | Partner only | 60 | 45 | −14 |
| | Did not eat with household member | 40 | 55 | 14 |
| *Lunch* | Partner only | 44 | 35 | −9 |
| | Did not eat with household member | 56 | 65 | 9 |
| *Dinner* | Partner only | 87 | 80 | −7 |
| | Did not eat with household member | 13 | 20 | 7 |
| **Couple with child(ren)** | | | | |
| *Breakfast* | Partner only | 6 | 10 | 4 |
| | Child(ren) only | 22 | 16 | −6 |
| | Partner and child(ren) | 43 | 33 | −9 |
| | Did not eat with household member | 30 | 41 | 11 |
| *Lunch* | Partner only | 11 | 9 | −2 |
| | Child(ren) only | 17 | 13 | −3 |
| | Partner and child(ren) | 27 | 15 | −12 |
| | Did not eat with household member | 45 | 62 | 17 |
| *Dinner* | Partner only | 8 | 18 | 10 |
| | Child(ren) only | 8 | 11 | 3 |
| | Partner and child(ren) | 76 | 57 | −19 |
| | Did not eat with household member | 8 | 14 | 6 |

*Note:* Respondents between ages 16–65

fall of 7 per cent. Among couples with dependent children, respondents ate without any family member present more frequently at each meal. At dinner, having both the partner and, at minimum, one child present fell by 19 per cent (from 76% in 1995 to 57% in 2015). Nevertheless, in 2015, 86 per cent of respondents with children did eat dinner on the previous day with a family member. The family dinner is far from being eliminated from the schedule of meals.

### Dinner as the main meal

Inquiring about main meals reveals some fundamental features of mundane domestic activities, with no points of strong disagreement. Accounts variously emphasise portion size, the company of household members, the food content, the location, and the time of day. Main meals are generally understood to be the largest of the day, eaten in the early evening, typically hot and including vegetables, and eaten with other members of one's household on a daily basis. It is universally agreed that a main meal should be nutritious. Dinner is central to the organisation of eating and a fulcrum of daily rhythms.

The tenor of the accounts is captured by two contrasting, though ultimately not very different, responses to the question of what is a main meal. Simon says:

> For me, a sort of regular meal is I suppose for all intents and purposes a cooked meal, so it's sitting with the family round the corner [at the kitchen table] and it usually involves just a main course. [...] Usually round about seven o'clock in the evening, through the week anyway. The weekend ... it's usually a bit earlier, so it's about 5.30 p.m.

Eating events have a structure which pivots around the idea of a main meal, eaten in the evening or late afternoon, dependent upon the differing structure of weekends and weekdays. It is eaten with other household members and is characterised as a 'cooked' meal. Any ambiguity as to a meal being cooked 'to all intents and purposes' refers to the use of uncooked accompaniments, such as salads, but also refers to meals not cooked entirely from 'scratch'.

Camilla sums up well the features of cooked main meals:

> Something that is wholesome, healthy, has to have vegetables in it. I think I would usually think of a main meal as something cooked, but I suppose it could also be a salad, although I'd struggle to get the kids to eat it. It's something that we'd sit down and eat together – not today, but usually. [...] It takes place in the afternoon, when we come back from school and work, in the week anyway, late afternoon, early evening.

Camilla emphasises the healthfulness of the food content. Others emphasise portion size. Some include that 'it's important to us to sit around the dining table'. It may be called tea, dinner or supper. It is clear that eating together (for those who do not live alone) is a feature of main meals, as is their timing, taking place in the evening, once the working day is done. Interestingly, Camilla declares what is usual, in order to mark the day of the interview as an exception. Perhaps the story of the family meal now is precisely that there are more exceptions to the rule.

Work, the hobbies of young children, business trips, social gatherings with kin outside the household, and trips to the cinema and theatre interfere with the performance of family meals which conform to the ideal, the template for which is the whole family together, at one table, at the same time, eating a shared substantial meal. Disturbances are not haphazard but arise because of difficulties in synchronising the commitments and routines of household members.

Family members still eat with one another, but not always all together at the same time. Interviewees share understandings concerning the purpose and format of family meals not taken together. The sequencing of other activities, most commonly work commitments and children's hobbies which occur some distance away from home rely upon alternative forms of provision. Meals may be taken at times different from other family members or at the home of a member of the extended family. For example, Pete's grown-up son takes his daughter to evening swimming lessons and they are fed a hot meal by grandad on the way back home. Camilla sometimes eats with her children at their leisure centre's own commercial catering facility. Greater provision of casual dining thus offers opportunities for dining together outside the home (Karsten et al., 2015). Conduct nevertheless displays temporal regularity. Southerton (2013) suggests that routines and habits are set in time by ingrained dispositions and by sequences shaped at institutional level. School and work finish at a given time and meals have to happen in the intervals between daytime responsibilities and evening leisure and learning which are governed by the timetables of leisure centres, cinemas and music teachers. Synchronisation with household members is unsurprisingly complicated as a result.

Timing varies in accordance with the day of the week and the routines and responsibilities of different days of the week. Both Simon and Camilla explicitly distinguish behaviour during the week and at the weekend. Such variation is probably most pronounced among households containing dependent children and where one or more adults are in employment. Like many other interviewees they both use the term 'usually'. The implication is that there is a fairly strong sense of a household routine, a normal way of organising meals. Yet there is a good degree of flexibility, a consciousness that the normal may be disrupted. Other household members, especially family members, are central to the accounts; the terms 'we' and 'us' abound, implying collective events and joint meanings.

## Eating at home

### What do people eat at main meals?

We did not seek in the interviews to discover systematically what people ate at home at their main meals. We did, however, obtain a good deal of information in passing. For instance, asking what is understood by the term main meal and whether people learned new tastes or new foods from eating out in restaurants or while on holiday elicited examples of typical content. Discussions included mention of hundreds of ingredients and dozens of dishes. Most are not dishes with names, as might appear on a restaurant menu. Nor are the foods mentioned as cooked at home predominantly derived from any tradition-defined British cuisine. True, roast dinners, dishes whose main element is roasted meat, are mentioned by all except four interviewees (Noah (35, London), Laxmikant (60, Bristol), Eleni (35, London) and Felicity (30, Preston)) suggesting that it remains the paradigmatic main meal and continues to symbolise a rich and significant, usually weekend, culinary event. However, pasta, rice and pizza (rarely home-made) are mentioned very often as components of the limited range of dishes that households repeat at regular intervals. Weekday meals seem often to be brief encounters over dishes which lack nothing in nutritional quality but take little time to prepare and clean up. Omelettes, beans on toast, jacket potatoes, meals prepared in a slow cooker and pasta dishes are commonly referenced weekday home-cooked meals.

### Home-cooking: a recipe book from Bristol

Miranda showed us her kitchen diary. This, she says, is a notebook that contains a weekly plan of meals she will prepare, and in which she records any fluctuation to that plan. Inspired by a radio programme which stated that each household in the UK typically cooks approximately ten dishes, Miranda made a list of her 'go to' meals:

• Lasagne
• Chilli, rice and salad

- Chicken casserole
- Sausage casserole
- Christine's Chinese chicken
- Chicken and mushroom pie
- Spaghetti bolognese
- Chicken curry Monday
- Fajitas
- Veg pasta bake
- Burgers and salad
- Pizza
- Shepherd's pie
- Sausage, mash and peas
- Quiche, salad and French stick
- Chicken in breadcrumbs
- Veggie burgers and chunky chips
- Ottolenghi roast squash salad
- Madhur Jaffrey marinated chicken in yoghurt and roasted
- Risotto Italian style
- Risotto 'my old flat days' style
- Moussaka

As well as demonstrating the variety of dishes that Miranda prepares, they mirror the evolution of British cuisine style over time. Miranda talks of cooking what she now calls 'risotto "my old flat days" style', a concoction that pre-dates her later knowledge about Italian cuisine.

> Risotto, so I've got risotto Italian style, so that's cooked with wine and stock and you know, then has got things added to it like butternut squash or sage leaves and spinach and whatnot. And then there's the risotto from my old flat days. And that's before we really knew what risotto was. So for us, me and my flatmate we used to roast ... because she was vegetarian so we'd roast a load of vegetables which was just becoming trendy 30 plus years ago, 35 years ago, 40 years ago actually I suppose. We'd roast vegetables ... no, we used to pan fry them, sorry, and that would be courgette, aubergine, tomato, red onion and things like that. And then we used to make the rice in a pan and then we'd mix it all up together and have that.

The main purpose of her kitchen notebook is to plan meals a week ahead of time and to look back on previous weeks in order to avoid repetition (Figure 5.2). This demonstrates how dishes depend on factors such as day of the week (roast only served on Sunday), who is present (a note appears that 'Jaima' will be present for a Thursday serving of 'Chicken flamenco'), and what other activities Miranda has planned for

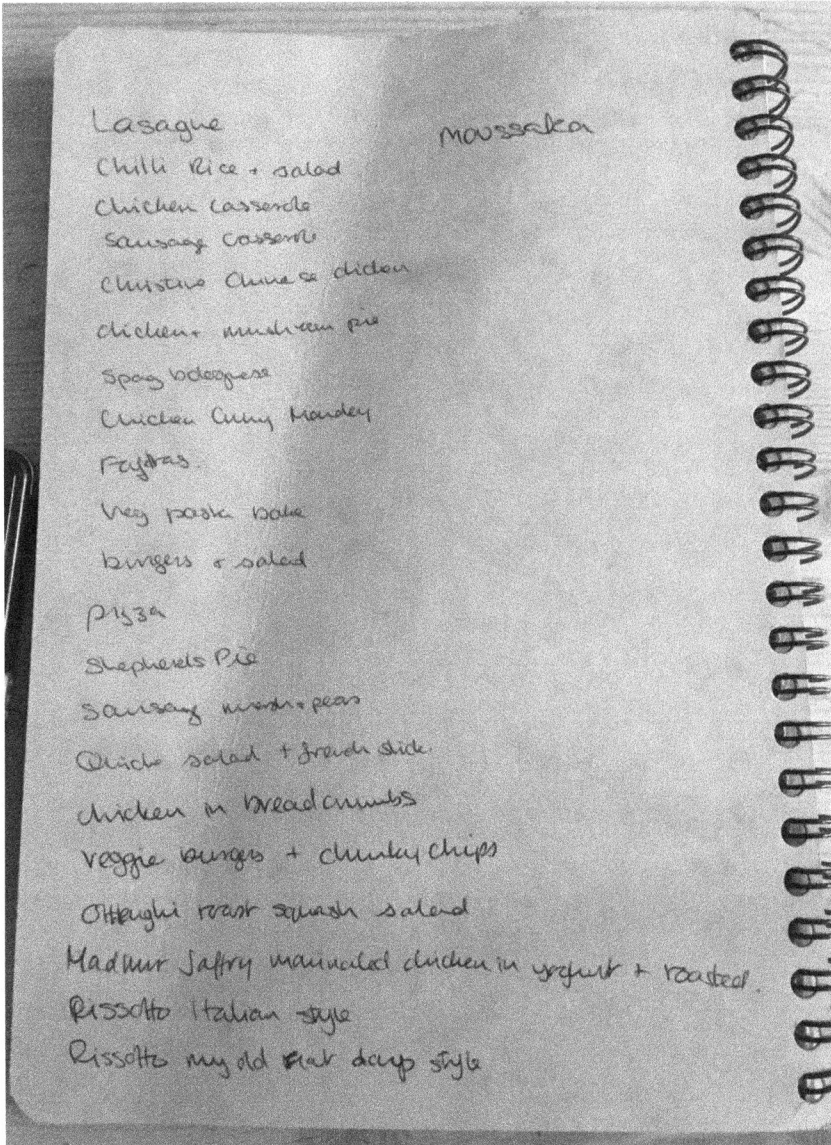

**Figure 5.1** Miranda's list of regular meals: 'go to' meals, written on the cover of her kitchen diary, in which she plans forthcoming meals in order to avoid repetition

herself (a Saturday trip to London). Often, a planned meal is crossed out, evidently to accommodate a change in the available ingredients, the company, or her own plans outside the kitchen, and replaced by another meal.

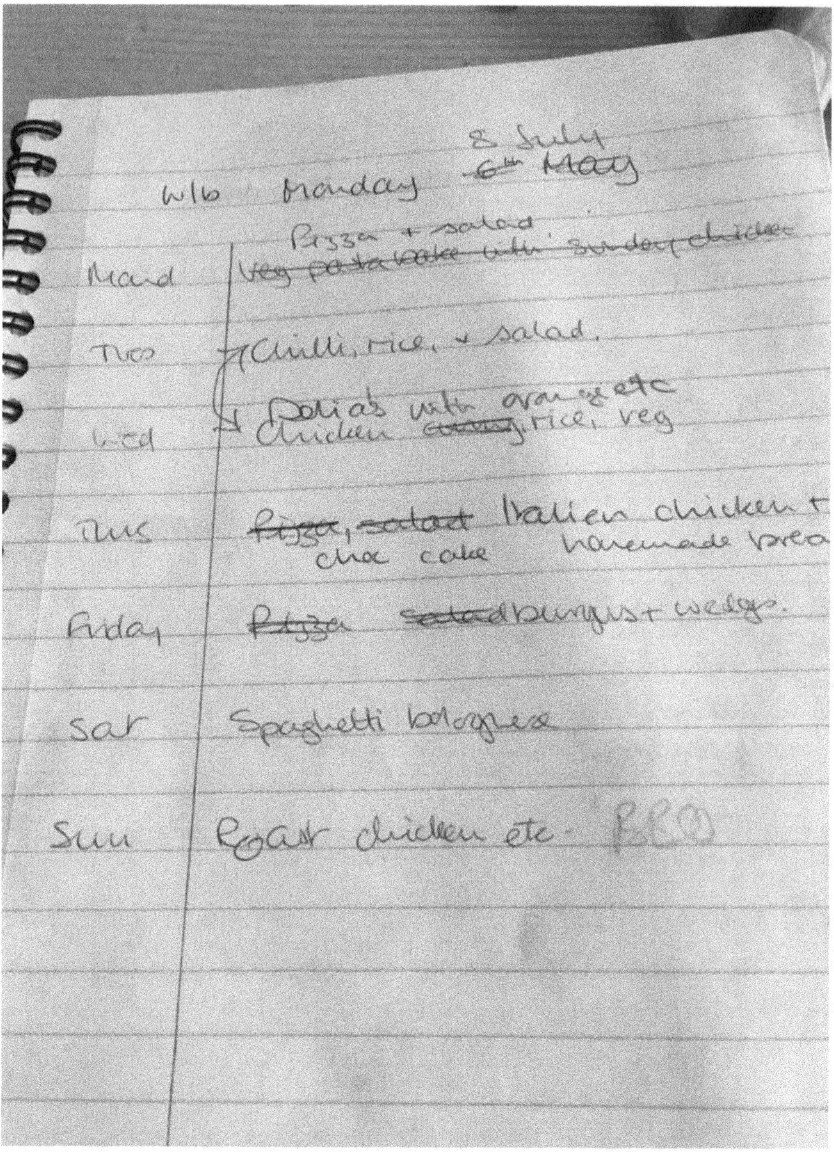

|  |  |
|---|---|
| w/b | Monday ~~6th May~~ 8 July |
| Mond | Pizza + salad <br> ~~Veg pasta bake with~~ Sunday chicken |
| Tues | Chilli, rice, + salad. |
| Wed | Dolias with orange etc <br> Chicken ~~curry~~ rice, veg |
| Thus | ~~Pizza, salad~~ Italien chicken + <br> choc cake    homemade brea |
| Friday | ~~Pizza~~ ~~salad~~ burgus + wedgs. |
| Sat | Spaghetti bolognese |
| Sun | Roast chicken etc. BBQ |

**Figure 5.2** A week in the diary of Miranda's food work

In this excerpt, Miranda replaces the date '6 May' with '8 July' for, as two months have passed, it is reasonable to repeat a week's menu, but with some adjustments evident in the crossing out and marking up. On the first occasions, it is evident that she changes her mind as she works through the week

## Domestic labour

Eating at home involves labour. Preparing a meal is a skilled and often complex task but doing so every day has often been seen as repetitive and boring. Meal preparation came to the forefront of social scientific research when issues of the extent and fairness of the domestic division of labour between men and women was identified by second-wave feminism in the 1960s (Lopata, 1971; Oakley, 1974; DeVault, 1991). Once a ferocious debate, the topic is now part of normal social science, the trends and tendencies in the organisation of housework, the changing tasks and the distribution of effort between partners (Sullivan, 1997), as well as outsourcing of domestic labour being monitored in many countries (Cohen, 1998; Bianchi et al., 2006; Hook, 2006; Hochschild, 2012; Sullivan and Gershuny, 2013).

Food work was traditionally understood as 'women's work' (Murcott, 1983; Charles and Kerr, 1988; DeVault, 1991; Mennell et al., 1992). In many households the female partner did all, or almost all, of the tasks associated with food provision such as planning, shopping, cooking, laying tables and clearing up afterwards. Many women felt that level of responsibility to be burdensome and perhaps oppressive (Thompson, 1991; Lupton, 2000; Sullivan, 2000; Meah and Jackson, 2013). An increasingly popular perception is that men are spending more time in the kitchen, doing the cooking. Those optimistic about equalisation emphasise the broad direction of the change of labour towards gender convergence in domestic divisions of labour, albeit that convergence is 'slow and incomplete' (Kan et al., 2011). Cross-national trends show a decline in the level of women's time in domestic work, as their engagement in paid work has risen, and an increase for men. The implication is a fall in the *relative* contribution of women (Kan et al., 2011). Others emphasise that women still undertake the major share of domestic labour, and that the decrease in domestic labour has not offset the increase in paid work time. Furthermore, the decrease in women's time has been greater than the increase in men's uptake of domestic work (Kan et al., 2011) raising the broader question of the transformation and reduction of housework (Bianchi et al., 2000, 2012). The evidence from our surveys mostly confirms a slow shift towards a more equitable distribution of tasks around food among partners.[1]

---

[1] The survey did not inquire about sexual orientation. The couples interviewed were, contingently, all heterosexual. There is therefore no basis for examining the effects of sexual orientation on divisions of labour. Supplementary interviews (e.g. Warde, 2018) and other sources suggest that gay men are typically more aesthetically interested in dining out in both commercial and communal settings.

**Table 5.2** Who carried out each task last time? 2015 (row percentage)

|  | Female | Male | Shared | Other | Never done |
|---|---|---|---|---|---|
| *Essential food tasks* | | | | | |
| Food shopping | 50 | 25 | 20 | 4 | 0 |
| Deciding what to eat | 68 | 21 | 7 | 5 | 0 |
| Preparing food | 64 | 25 | 6 | 4 | 0 |
| Serving food | 60 | 25 | 8 | 7 | 0 |
| *Subsidiary food tasks* | | | | | |
| Setting table | 38 | 26 | 7 | 17 | 12 |
| Clearing table | 36 | 31 | 13 | 15 | 5 |
| Washing up | 42 | 34 | 11 | 10 | 2 |

Note: Respondents between ages 16–65. Includes only respondents living as a heterosexual couple

### Trends in the division of food work

For all food tasks, women are most likely to have carried out the task on the last occasion, including deciding what to eat (68%), preparing food (64%), serving food (60%), food shopping (50%), setting and clearing the table (38 and 36%), and washing up (42%) (Table 5.2). Essential food tasks, those most immediately concerned with getting the food on the table (i.e. deciding what to eat, preparation and serving food) tend to be the sole responsibility of one adult, usually a woman, with little sharing of tasks or delegating of tasks to children within the household. Men are more often responsible for subsidiary tasks which are much more equitably shared between men and women and more often enlist the help of a child. The exception to this is food shopping, which was the task most likely to be carried out together (one in five last shopping trips were carried out together).

The most notable increases over the twenty-year period are in men's responsibility for essential food tasks, with men in couple households now more likely to decide what to eat (greater by 6%), prepare food (6%), serve food (9%) and, the largest increase, do the food shopping (12%). Men's responsibility for subsidiary food tasks remains unchanged over time. Women were less likely than in 1995 to have done each food task 'last time', with the exception of washing up, where women were marginally more likely to do this than twenty years ago (up 2%) (Figure 5.3).

Women's decreased ownership of tasks has been met with (1) an increase in men taking ownership of tasks, (2) an increase in male

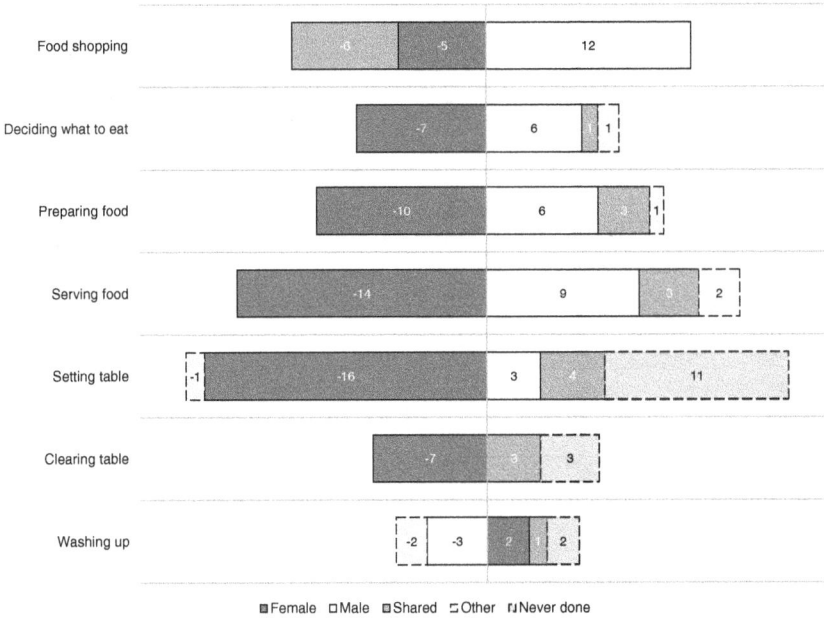

Figure 5.3 Percentage change in who carried out tasks last time, 1995–2015
Note: Respondents between ages 16–65. Includes only respondents living as a heterosexual couple

*involvement* in tasks over time with women's undertaking of tasks becoming a *shared* undertaking of tasks,[2] and (3) a 'disappearance' of certain tasks over time. The proportion of households reporting that tasks are 'never done' has risen (11% fewer set the table and 3% fewer clear the table), emphasising the growing informality of the domestic meal. This is indicative of the simplification of meals at home, fewer meals being eaten at a table and the declining use of a dedicated dining room.

### Perceived fairness in division of food work

Responses to the question 'Overall do you think that you do your fair share, or more, or less, of these tasks?' barely changed between 1995 and 2015 (Figure 5.4). However, disaggregating men's and women's responses shows a redistribution of perceptions of equity, with men

[2]   Not necessarily reducing the workload as there is a difference between taking full responsibility for a task and contribution to a task (see also Meah and Jackson, 2013, on kitchens becoming crowded spaces).

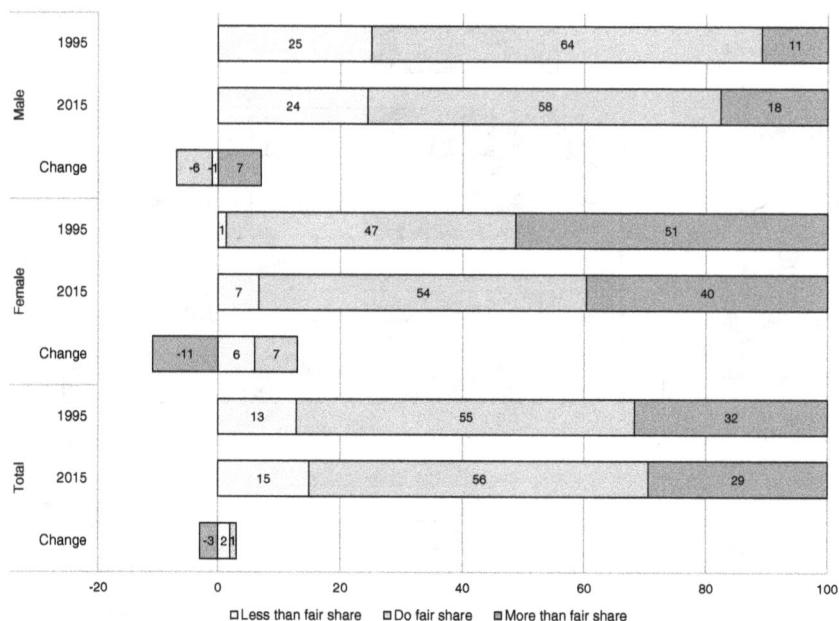

**Figure 5.4** Fair share of food tasks in couple households, 1995–2015 (percentage)
*Note:* Respondents between ages 16–65. Includes only respondents living as a heterosexual couple

more likely to report that they do *more* than their fair share of food work in 2015 (an increase of 7%), and an 11 per cent decline in women reporting doing more than their fair share. This suggests that women view their decreased responsibility as redressing an imbalance in the direction of a 'fairer' division of labour. Nevertheless, in 2015, two women in five still said they did more than their fair share, which is twice the proportion for men.

Like other studies, this suggests that inequality in domestic labour within couples is gradually diminishing. How men and women perceive the labour of meal preparation is revealed in part in their discussions of eating out.

## How people feel about preparing meals

### Women and domestic burdens: coping with irritation

If less time is spent cooking, women have reduced their contribution, and men are doing relatively more now than in 1995, it is valuable to see how interviewees view these matters and how they deal with them.

Several accounts describe arrangements no different from those of fifty years ago. Gerald's experience reflects an old mid-twentieth-century orthodoxy regarding role allocations in the nuclear family when he says, 'She's the boss. Jean [his wife] is a good cook. Excellent. Varied menus.' As Kaufman (2010) showed, many older women, in particular, develop a sense of discontentedness with the obligations of a mundane routine requiring activity from which they derive almost no pleasure. Whether that discontent remains muted or leads to open conflict is not just a matter of how much a woman dislikes cooking but also of the climate of the marital relationship and life-course stage. The arrival and departure of children are often critical turning points in the form and level of commitment that women have to food preparation. So even when accepted as an obligatory burden of marriage, there is much room for resentment and dissatisfaction on the part of women. Reports in interviews reveal a number of different tactics or strategies that women develop to deal with the burden associated with having primary responsibility for daily food preparation. We have no evidence of constant or open conflict about such matters, but women clearly do use different tactics and strategies to alleviate their irritation or annoyance.

Cheryl asked whether her husband shares in the cooking, answers

No [laughter]. Don't even know if he knows where a saucepan is. The only thing he does cook, he will cook an omelette but apart from that, no, never, nothing. No, typical Italian, don't know where the kitchen is.

She is an example of a woman who has grown tired of the work involved in cooking and she perceives the source of the problem to be not only her husband but also her adult children. Asked if anyone helps her with the family roast dinners she replies, 'pigs might fly'. She deals with her predicament by means of disgruntled resignation.

A second form of accommodation involves favourable comparison between one's own burden and that of other women. Nadine consoles herself that 'I'm quite lucky in that [my husband] is not a fussy eater as long as he's got a hot meal in front of him'. She therefore cooks what she wants:

[M]y mum and my dad is very much like me, so we've been brought up in that we get quite bored of food, so I won't eat the same meal sort of once in two weeks. So I need variety and that's what I've grown up with, where if I fed him the same meal all week he wouldn't care.

A third tactic involves the expression of irritation about how current arrangements operate. One example is Crispin who, using a common male explanation of arrangements, claims to be a proficient cook but declares that everyone in his family gets a better meal if his wife prepares it. When she came in at the end of the interview, and Crispin said how he'd been telling the interviewer what a good cook she was, she rolled her eyes and said 'is that what he's been telling you, that's his excuse'. Other examples include Siobhan, who cooks two meals each evening: one for her children, and something more adult for herself and her husband. Her husband is happy with the current arrangement; 'My husband likes it because I do the cooking, he does the dishes.' Although not complaining, she has reason for liking to eat out, 'it's just the treat of somebody making something for you. No dishes, no cleaning up...'

The fourth strategy is to restrict the number of occasions when cooking is required. Gerald's wife, Jean, does not explicitly explain her light lunches in terms of being fed up with cooking, but many women are unwilling to devote the effort required to prepare a full cooked meal for themselves alone. The effect is to make some meals much simpler. This is a standard solution for couples who have just one main meal a day, requiring less major cooking.

That this is not only a function of coupledom is confirmed by women living alone. They often say exactly as does Gerald's wife, that they do not cook proper meals for themselves. Camilla, Lara, Penny and Arlie all mention that they do not cook full meals just for themselves, but instead have something that will get them by. Camilla is a single mother who seems very diligent about preparing what she considers nutritious food for her daughters but when they go for a fortnight's holiday with their father once a year she adopts a very different routine. She suggests that cooking is a real burden for her, one from which she enjoys temporary relief:

> Yeah, it's a real chore to cook. In summer the kids go to their dad's for two weeks and during those two weeks I turn into a teenager, I can't be bothered to tidy up, I can't be bothered to clean, it's like I have no energy to do anything, it's just pathetic. And I don't cook hardly at all for those two weeks. And I always think I'm going to be so healthy and I can eat whatever I want, but it doesn't quite turn out like that. [...] It's just not very satisfying to spend an hour in the kitchen and then sit down and eat a little bit of it for yourself. And then it's like 'okay, that's that then', no one to share it with. I suppose I might invite someone round for dinner and then I would make an effort, but I probably wouldn't, I'd be too lazy. I tend to work more in those two weeks, so get home late and just have a ready meal.

A fifth solution is to make greater use of commercial alternatives to the domestic meal. This is a strong impulse for many women. Many interviewees speak of release from the labour of food preparation as well as other domestic obligations and chores competing for their attention. For example, Nicola explains that as she turns her mind to thinking about preparing the evening meal, she will say to herself '"I can't be bothered, so let's go out." It's just easier.' Similarly, Lara (65, London), who suffers with an ongoing illness, does not always feel well enough to cook and instead takes her family out to a 'carvery' restaurant, making sure 'that the family gets together'. Cheryl's husband convinces her that cooking a Sunday roast is not worth the effort when their grown-up children cancel a planned visit, replacing it with an impromptu meal in a restaurant. The decision is made at the last minute in response to immediate circumstances, thereby reducing effort, cost and waste. In addition, and as an alternative commercial solution, convenience foods brought home from the supermarket, takeaways and fast food all provide options, beyond going to a restaurant, for a radical reduction in the amount of labour and time in the domestic kitchen. (This is dealt with in Chapter 8.)

A final solution is to renegotiate the commensal pact, reallocating tasks within the household division of labour to arrive at a more agreeable set of arrangements. In one case only did this involve total removal of a woman's responsibility for food preparation. Enid (60, Preston) hates cooking. She had shared the task with husband Robert for some years until she was poorly after the birth of their son, when

> he sort of carried on doing the cooking really. We came to the agreement that Richard would do the cooking and I would do the other things, the cleaning and the washing and the ironing etc. So that's our balance, if you will.

She was the only woman to abdicate all involvement, and under a probably rather unfavourable overall trade-off. Other households, especially those in the younger age cohorts, come to arrangements which involve men more in food-related tasks.

### Are men really any help? Older and younger men

Partnered or married men, when asked if they would like to eat out more, often demurred because they were happy with the food provided at home. We have several examples, most conspicuously among those who took the least part in food preparation.

Tyler is happy with food cooked and eaten at home, predominantly by his partner. When she goes out, he does not necessarily eat out, but heats up the food that she has set out for him on the kitchen counter

to defrost during the day. Robert (60, Bristol) plays no role in food provisioning, as his wife plans and executes every evening meal. His food
preparations comprise grazing on leftovers, toasting bread and occasionally boiling an egg, unless his wife is at home, in which case, he says:

> She'll start to make something and she'll sometimes say, 'Do you want
> something?' and I'll say, 'Yes,' but sometimes she just simply announces,
> 'It's ready,' and I was in another world. So it's a very old-fashioned and
> reprehensible way of living but it's a question of expertise. My expertise is
> vestigial, hers is very practical and not particularly advanced, but very
> sensible, always nice.

Were these men to be made responsible for cooking at home they might
be more eager to eat out. For example, neither Crispin nor Isaac (both
in their forties), who cook simple meals at home occasionally, feel any
imperative to feed their children home-cooked food when their partners
are not available. They prefer to take their children out under such circumstances, cooking at home only when there is no alternative.

The most conservative and disengaged men tend to be older. Younger
cohorts of men and women come to different forms of commensal
arrangement influenced perhaps by egalitarian aspirations and feminist
ideas. It is a paradox of the present that many people want to eat family
meals at home but are unprepared to commit the necessary time to their
preparation. How much different are the younger men?

Younger men come up with some of the same excuses for their lack of
involvement as might their fathers. Crispin is one of several saying that
he cooks less because his partner is more skilled and will produce superior meals. In other instances, even where both partners work full time
and when men profess an interest in cooking, the woman cooks most
often on the grounds that she cares more what they eat, or that
she is better at cooking. This last reason is particularly likely to be
offered as an explanation by men. Another explanation of the work
falling to the female partner is that she typically arrives home from work
sooner. Thus Noah (35) says,

> I was between jobs for quite a while and I went through the entire BBC
> web page, cheap, healthy recipes... so I do enjoy cooking. The reason I
> don't cook more probably is a matter of time rather than anything, or
> desire, so yeah, I would say I'm pretty active and I like finding new recipes.
> [...] I mean my... my wife tends to finish work before I do, so she might
> already have cooked by the time I get home.

The coordination of work and school schedules is of course genuinely
problematic. However, no man said that he tended to get home sooner

and *therefore* did the cooking. Yet, some men participate readily, as Angela (40) reports,

> If he's on earlies [a morning shift at work], so he [her husband] will be here for dinner, would quite often start making dinner and, depending on what he's making, sometimes it's easier to just let him finish it himself because he knows where he's up to and things. But other times he might say oh I've just done this, can you do… but usually it's a joint-ish effort. We don't fall out.

This form of sharing is evidence that men do other things besides providing special dishes when entertaining and cooking meat at barbecues. The gendered role of the barbecue is nicely nuanced by Siobhan (35):

> So if it's like a cooked meal, like Sunday lunch or dinner with friends, then I'll do the cooking. If it's a BBQ then my husband does the cooking, which is really just the meat because I still do all the sides and all of that.

Where the cooking is shared, women still make decisions about what is eaten. Thus Tyler, a young man from Preston, does prepare food himself when his partner is at work, but she chooses a piece of meat from the freezer, leaving it to defrost ready for him to cook in the evening. He then adds pasta, rice, or whatever he feels like. The overall impression is that cooking remains the responsibility of the female partner.

Nevertheless, men are involved more than before. Younger men can talk in quite elaborate ways about dishes they enjoy cooking, while older generations see this as the domain of their wives.[3] Very apparent in discussions of entertaining, it spills over into everyday cooking. Simon (40) says 'I tend to cook quite a lot, so you know, I do like to cook curry.' Tristan (35) is also involved in everyday cooking and decision-making:

> Usually our normal routine … because we both work from home, I'll cook a soup at the start of the week and we'll freeze it and we'll have that for lunch a few days. We usually have a cooked lunch. We usually have a cooked breakfast as well really. We try and cook for every meal and then in the evening we'll take it in turns. Or if one of us is very busy the other one will pick up the slack a bit. But usually we go to the supermarket and we decide … this is stupid … we decide in the supermarket, which is not the best, but I guess you can see the food and you get a few ideas or whatever. So that's it really. On the weekend we probably don't eat as well because we're seeing friends or we're going down to see my niece and nephew or whatever, it's a bit more rushed, a bit more on the fly.

---

[3]  The exception is Jeff (65, Preston), an ex-army chef who finds the slowness of his wife's chopping excruciating and tends to take over the cooking.

Luke (25) says 'I really enjoy it and I will cook more as well when I've got like a sense of stability again. I think I cooked a lot when I was living in the flat.' Thus, younger male interviewees claim to be both more interested and more active in the mundane aspects of domestic food provisioning, as the quantitative data imply.

Whether these innovations will survive changes in the life course is unclear. There is some backsliding. Noah (quoted above) does less than before because of his new work commitments. Edward (35, London) explains that his partner has recently replaced him as the main cook in the household:

> She's only just got into it actually, she never used to be into it but she has got into it for some reason, to finally be cooking. Probably when your colleague came round [i.e. at the point of the survey] I was doing all the cooking and now it's the other way round, which I think is pretty unusual maybe to have that switch. [...] I don't think she had any confidence with cooking, whereas I did, just freestyle, just chuck all that together and make it taste nice. But I think she's got into the idea of if you can read a recipe and follow it well you can end up with really nice food because someone who has got a successful cookbook is probably good at it. Whereas for me, I can't follow a recipe.

We cannot be sure that the greater engagement of younger men will not be a function of the early years of a partnership and the problems of managing children. Yet there is some effect. If more men say that they enjoy cooking, as they do, and if, as has been demonstrated in the past, men who like cooking actually cook frequently, more equitable arrangements may gradually transpire.

### Living alone

Our evidence allows us to ask who (or better on which occasions, and under which circumstances) wants to avoid the labour involved in cooking at home. More women than men report eating out so that they don't have to cook themselves (Miranda, Cheryl, Siobhan, Lara, Nicola). Men are less commonly primarily responsible for cooking, so feel differently. To what extent does the wish to avoid labour come from single men and women alike?

At the point of interview, nine interviewees were living alone, two had other people present (Douglas and flatmate, Lara and tenant) and one was in transition (Luke). People living alone seem to divide equally between those who cook systematically and regularly for themselves (e.g. Stephen) and those who explicitly do not bother, or bother less than they feel they might or they have in the past (e.g. Arlie, Penny, and Camilla when her children are away from home).

Dinner is not symbolically any different for those who live alone. Some men (four out of six) cook in a routine manner for themselves; Pete cooks traditional food for himself routinely, Stephen (60, Preston) even more so, Douglas cooks and uses the freezer. A smaller proportion of women do. The two lone mums, Camilla and Karina (40, Preston), put in a lot of effort but are rather reluctant cooks who, when eating alone, select simpler foods (jacket potato, salad and cold meats, pasta dishes, omelettes) and use an array of ready-prepared or partially prepared foods available in portions for one person. There is very little sense that eating alone at home is in any way a hardship. More elaborate foods may then be enjoyed while eating out with friends as part of a social occasion.

## The domestic mode of provision: summary

Domestic arrangements continue to change, slowly. Family meals, although less frequent, because more practically difficult to stage, mean more shared shopping and cooking for busy families. On weekdays, men are perhaps becoming more involved in decision-making and shopping, steps towards their becoming more involved in mundane food preparation. Weekends offer other opportunities. Noah has insufficient time to shop for ingredients during the week but will cook to a recipe at the weekends and make an event out of shopping for the ingredients. Simon speaks of cooking curries and roasts for visiting friends at weekends, whereas during the week his wife will typically arrive home first and take charge of at least starting to cook their main meal. Some younger men are taking more responsibility for everyday food preparation. Neuman et al. (2017) show that, in Sweden, personal and couple relationships may be cemented and effectuated by deciding together, shopping together and cooking together as well as by eating together. Some of the younger couples do seem to be moving in the direction of sharing in these tasks; the households of Felicity, Edward and Simon, all in their thirties, are examples. Perhaps, then, worrying about the loss of commensality is exaggerated, and some of the interpersonal benefits of eating together have been transferred, or extended, to sharing other aspects of food provisioning. Whether younger women can, as a consequence, abdicate primary responsibility remains unlikely, but arrangements for domestic food preparation have become less rigid and the traditional gender role ideology, which was the orthodoxy in the mid-twentieth century, is rarely articulated.

# 6

# Domestic hospitality

## Introduction

Eating in a domestic setting in the company of friends and non-resident kin is a significant form of social occasion in contemporary England. Most people eat out occasionally at the homes of friends or non-resident family members. In 2015, 22 per cent of respondents never ate with friends and only 19 per cent never with kin. People derive exceptionally high levels of enjoyment and satisfaction from such occasions, among the reasons being the particularly high value placed on hospitality in most societies, with the invitation to eat a full meal especially so (Douglas, 1975, 1984; Julier, 2013a, 2013b). This chapter collates the data about hosts and guests.

## Offering domestic hospitality

Most meals in Britain are cooked and eaten together at home by household members. However, meals prepared in the home to be shared with non-household members constitute a significant alternative mode of provision. For this to occur requires some people to act as hosts. Approximately three-quarters of households have other people to a meal at their own home, an insignificant decline of 3 per cent occurring between 1995 and 2015. The same types of people hosted in both years. Regression analysis conducted on harmonised data shows that, at high levels of significance, women, graduates, people with service class connections and those with middle to high incomes host more frequently. However, while levels of significance are high, the variance explained is small.

In 2015, 7 per cent of respondents entertained guests several times a week and a further 13 per cent did so weekly. Among those who ever entertain, the median frequency is approximately once every six weeks.

Thus, a small proportion of the population act as hosts often; one in three of those who host do so at least once a week.

People mostly host friends and family. In 2015, 56 per cent had a family member home to eat in the last year, and 56 per cent entertained a friend. Only one household in ten had entertained a colleague during the previous year. Friends and family are treated differently, although of course many people have both as guests. In aggregate, the circumstances of people who entertain friends and those who provide meals to non-resident family members differ in the same ways in both 1995 and 2015. Those hosting *friends* in 2015 tend to be women, cohabiting, white British, with higher education qualifications and service class connections. Those who entertain *family* members are also partnered women who are not stable working class, are likely to be white British and have a dependent child at home. Hosting is thus a function of social and material attributes of gender, education, class, household income and household structure.

## Forms of domestic hospitality

Domestic hospitality takes many forms. Alice Julier (2013a) conducted a thorough and definitive study of domestic hospitality in the US. She notes that neither she, as the sociological analyst, nor her interviewees were very well able to find distinct names or designations for events, although in practice people mostly distinguish what sort of behaviour is appropriate without knowing what to call the different types of event. She describes a continuum, from the formal dinner party, by way of a modified dinner party, to buffets and barbecues, to the potluck event. Britain displays a similar variation. Adult children visit their parents after work for a quick meal; some extended families converge every weekend around a meal; members of friendship networks meet at intervals at each other's houses for an evening of food and conversation; dating couples eat together at their respective homes; parties are held to celebrate special days such as birthdays, anniversaries, or religious and secular festivals. All of these forms were mentioned by one or more interviewees. The rationale for the occasion significantly affects the format of the event, the people present and the meal content.

Table 6.1 shows a marginal increase in the proportion of last meals taken with friends. The vast majority of meals in both years were described as 'just a social occasion', others nominated as convenient or quick remained at the same low level (8%) and there was a marginal decline in the proportion of special occasions. Significantly fewer meals

**Table 6.1** Comparing eating at someone's home 1995–2015. All events, at a relative's and at a friend's (column percentage)

| | Someone else's house | | | 1995 | | | 2015 | | |
| --- | --- | --- | --- | --- | --- | --- | --- | --- | --- |
| | 1995 | 2015 | Sig | Rel | Frnd | Sig | Rel | Frnd | Sig |
| *Whose home* | | | | | | | | | |
| Relative's | 55 | 52 | | | | | | | |
| Friend's | 45 | 48 | | | | | | | |
| *Number of people* | | | | | | *** | | | |
| 2 people | 10 | 13 | | 5 | 15 | | 9 | 17 | |
| 3–4 people | 35 | 28 | | 28 | 44 | | 23 | 33 | |
| 5–9 people | 46 | 44 | | 58 | 33 | | 49 | 39 | |
| 10 or more people | 8 | 15 | | 9 | 8 | | 19 | 11 | |
| *Reason for meal* | | | | | | ** | | | |
| Special occasion | 19 | 15 | | 25 | 11 | | 19 | 12 | |
| Just a social mealoccasion | 72 | 75 | | 69 | 78 | | 70 | 82 | |
| Convenience/ quick | 8 | 8 | | 6 | 11 | | 10 | 7 | |
| Other | 1 | 1 | | 1 | 1 | | 2 | 0 | |
| *When it took place* | | | | | | | | | |
| Within the last 7 days | 44 | 49 | | 47 | 40 | | 45 | 53 | |
| Within a fortnight | 10 | 15 | | 9 | 11 | | 15 | 15 | |
| Within a month | 16 | 13 | | 14 | 18 | | 12 | 14 | |
| More than a month ago | 31 | 23 | | 29 | 32 | | 29 | 17 | |
| *Day of the week* | | | * | | | *** | | | |
| Monday | 4 | 7 | | 3 | 5 | | 6 | 9 | |
| Tuesday | 4 | 8 | | 4 | 4 | | 9 | 8 | |
| Wednesday | 6 | 8 | | 5 | 8 | | 7 | 9 | |
| Thursday | 7 | 6 | | 6 | 10 | | 8 | 5 | |
| Friday | 12 | 12 | | 6 | 18 | | 10 | 14 | |
| Saturday | 28 | 32 | | 23 | 36 | | 28 | 36 | |
| Sunday | 39 | 26 | | 53 | 20 | | 33 | 19 | |
| *How long the occasion lasted* | | | *** | | | | | | |
| Less than 1 hour | 16 | 39 | | 17 | 15 | | 41 | 37 | |
| 1–2 hours | 24 | 40 | | 23 | 24 | | 39 | 40 | |

**Table 6.1** Continued

| | Someone else's house | | | 1995 | | | 2015 | | |
|---|---|---|---|---|---|---|---|---|---|
| | 1995 | 2015 | Sig | Rel | Frnd | Sig | Rel | Frnd | Sig |
| 2–3 hours | 22 | 14 | | 20 | 26 | | 13 | 15 | |
| 3 hours or more | 37 | 7 | | 40 | 35 | | 7 | 8 | |
| *Number of courses* | | | | | | * | | | |
| 1 course | 23 | 33 | | 19 | 29 | | 35 | 31 | |
| 2 courses | 46 | 38 | | 54 | 37 | | 37 | 40 | |
| 3 courses | 24 | 21 | | 21 | 26 | | 21 | 21 | |
| 4 or more courses | 7 | 7 | | 6 | 8 | | 7 | 8 | |
| *Courses served* | | | | | | | | | |
| Starter | 30 | 31 | | 24 | 36 | * | 29 | 34 | |
| Prior to main | 2 | 15 | *** | 2 | 2 | | 10 | 20 | * |
| Main | 100 | 100 | | 100 | 100 | | 100 | 99 | |
| Dessert | 70 | 52 | *** | 76 | 63 | * | 55 | 49 | |
| Other | 16 | 5 | *** | 13 | 19 | | 6 | 4 | |
| *Eaten similar main course dish before* | | | | | | | | | |
| Outside home | 84 | 88 | | 90 | 75 | *** | 88 | 88 | |
| At own home | 75 | 87 | ** | 77 | 74 | | 85 | 89 | |
| *Drinks consumed* | | | | | | | | | |
| Tap water | 9 | 32 | *** | 11 | 6 | | 30 | 34 | |
| Bottled water | 9 | 14 | * | 7 | 11 | | 16 | 13 | |
| Soft drink | 19 | 31 | ** | 18 | 21 | | 32 | 31 | |
| Wine | 42 | 27 | *** | 36 | 51 | ** | 23 | 30 | |
| Beer/lager | 15 | 19 | | 15 | 14 | | 15 | 23 | |
| Other alcohol | 8 | 7 | | 8 | 9 | | 5 | 10 | |
| Tea or coffee | 50 | 29 | *** | 50 | 29 | | 32 | 27 | |
| *Enjoyed 'a lot'…* | | | | | | | | | |
| Food | 87 | 87 | | 91 | 84 | * | 86 | 88 | |
| Company | 94 | 94 | | 94 | 95 | | 94 | 93 | |
| Service | 84 | 78 | | 90 | 77 | * | 78 | 79 | |
| Conversation | 88 | 89 | | 89 | 88 | | 87 | 91 | |
| Atmosphere | 91 | 93 | | 91 | 92 | | 92 | 94 | |
| Overall | 92 | 94 | | 93 | 92 | | 94 | 95 | |

Note: $\chi^2$ *p < 0.05, **p < 0.01, ***p < 0.001. Respondents between ages 16–65

occurred on a Sunday, marking the gradual erosion of the ritual of family Sunday lunch. A little more than half of the meals eaten at a family member's home were on a Sunday in 1995, but only a fifth by 2015.[1] Intervals between visits had reduced, a change more marked for visits to friends. Middle-sized events diminished in relative frequency and the number where ten or more people were present increased, particularly for family events.

Very striking and significant is the brevity of events, as less time is devoted to these, still highly symbolic, occasions. Two in five meals last less than an hour, the proportion greater by 23 per cent than in 1995. Four in five take less than two hours. Whereas 37 per cent of communal meals had lasted more than three hours in 1995, a mere 7 per cent do in 2015. More meals (a third by 2015) comprise only one course, evidence of the simplification of meals. There was a sharp reduction in the appearance of dessert.[2] Notably, a large and increasing majority of respondents said that they had eaten a similar main course dish before; by 2015, 87 per cent of people had eaten a similar dish in their own home. This suggests wide sharing of know-how and recipes, and implies similarity in the dishes prepared by people belonging to the same social networks. It also hints that most of the dishes served to guests are not very different from ordinary household dinners. Nevertheless, shorter and simpler meals seem no less pleasing; the pleasure derived from these occasions remains remarkably high, 94 per cent of respondents liking 'a lot' their last outing.

Probably the most marked change concerns what is drunk. The highest increase in drinks is in non-alcoholic beverages, with water being served on 46 per cent of occasions in 2015 compared with 18 per cent in 1995. Reasons probably include a greater concern with health (consonant with the decline in the serving of dessert); the extension of a habit, rather uncommon in mid-twentieth-century Britain, of having a jug of water to accompany a meal as well as other kinds of beverages (in 2015 tap water was served on 32% of all occasions); and the increased popularity of bottled mineral water (though still outstripped

---

[1]  As regards kin, there were more visits on weekdays by 2015, although there was not much difference in the days on which people visited their friends. For visiting friends, Saturday was the most popular (28% in 1995 and 36% of such events in 2015), with Sunday and Friday next most common (with about a fifth each in both years).

[2]  At family meals hosts had served dessert on 76 per cent of occasions in 1995, falling to 55 per cent by 2015. Desserts were served a little less often by friends, although this also showed a 14 per cent drop.

by tap water by a proportion of 70:30), appearing on 9 per cent of occasions in 1995 and 14 per cent in 2015. Soft drinks other than water also increased significantly. The consumption of wine declined significantly. At 42 per cent of all occasions in 1995 wine was drunk, falling to 27 per cent in 2015. This occurred at both family and friend events, but more significantly in the latter. As the duration of the meal and the number of courses declines, so does the serving of alcohol. These associations occur in both years but as meals in 2015 have fewer courses, and are of shorter duration, alcohol appears at fewer events. Tea and coffee also fell at both family and friend events.

In the main, the same trends affect meals with both family and friends. A very clear inference from Table 6.1 is that in 1995 there were differences in practice between events involving friends and those with kin. The number of people present, the reason for the occasion, the day of the week, the number of courses served, the likelihood of having a similar main course outside the home, the presence of wine (much more common with friends) and whether the food and service was liked a lot (family settings were preferable) varied between settings. No significant differences are identified in 2015. The structural features of a meal eaten with friends has become almost indistinguishable from one eaten with non-resident kin, being similar in respect of foods, courses, drinks, enjoyment, longevity and sequencing. However, timing differs, the majority of meals with friends being in the evening after 7 p.m., approximately three times the proportion for family events. Families were much more likely to gather together at lunchtime and also favoured early dinners, with a third of all family meals in 2015 beginning between 5 and 6 p.m.

Overall, the evidence suggests gradual informalisation. The proportion of events with between five and nine people, the size of the complement typical of the dinner party, has diminished. A smaller proportion of events celebrate special occasions. Events occur at shorter intervals with more occurring between Monday and Wednesday and many fewer on Sundays. Early dinners have increased and occasions are completed much more quickly, with fewer courses and less wine served. Simplified events further suppress the characteristics of the formal dinner party as feeding friends becomes more like feeding family members.

## What is for dinner?

Comparing the menus of the hosted dinner with domestic family meals and the commercial restaurant is difficult partly because identifying aggregate patterns poses a big coding problem; a great many foodstuffs are served in an exponential number of combinations. Interviewees expose in a more granular way how foods are selected in the light of the meaning or purpose of the event.

### Foods served

Quizzed about their experiences of domestic hospitality, interviewees mentioned many types of food which had been served by them or to them. During the thirty-one interviews, approximately 125 discrete items are mentioned (many occurring more than once). They range from samphire and langoustines to sausage and mash, from tagine to roast, from fish pie to Chinese takeaway, from biltong to tofu, from artichoke pasta to pork pies, from Polish dumplings to fajitas, from beef Wellington to vegan curry. The most frequently mentioned main dishes were curries, roast meats (with lamb especially popular), chicken and salmon. Potatoes were the most often mentioned carbohydrate (nine occurrences), with pasta and rice each appearing four times. Salads and vegetables were mentioned a handful of times each in generic form, supplemented by many discrete items including artichokes, spinach, squash and beetroot. Soup occurred five times. The number of desserts was high, with often more than one being served at the same meal. While the survey indicated many one-course meals and relatively few desserts, the latter seemed memorable when served in domestic settings. Tarts included lemon, salty chocolate, peppermint caramel and tarte tatin, while cakes included strawberry, chocolate and sponge. Also mentioned are apple pie and custard, rice pudding, 'English style puddings' and vanilla slices.

The wide range of foods served is unsurprising, since the urban British population is itself very diverse and has experience of foodstuffs and cuisines from various traditions. The most popular main courses reported in the survey were curries, roast dinners and pasta which comprised 44 per cent of all those recorded. Chicken dishes, grilled or baked fish, barbecued meat, and casseroles accounted for a further 21 per cent of dishes served. Thus, some core items appear very frequently, depicting the predominant staple recipes for domestic cooks in Britain in the twenty-first century: chicken, roast meats, curries and salmon; a mix of carbohydrates in which potatoes dominate; and a range of vegetables, mixed salads and desserts.

### Food for the occasion

One question that arises is how people decide what is suitable for a given occasion. People are constrained by their culinary skills, their imagination, their financial resources, and their own and their guests' tastes. The evidence from the interviews is that almost every host is concerned to mount a performance acceptable to the social circles which they inhabit. For a few, that means concentrating on making the food exceptional, adventurous, out of the ordinary, and perhaps memorable. This consideration sometimes flows over into cooking that might be deemed pretentious or competitive. The majority, however, aim only to serve food similar, but of a higher quality, to that of a normal family meal. As Laxmikant put it, when asked what they would serve to invited guests, 'Something special', by which he meant more flavour is brought to the food and additional dishes are prepared to present a greater variety. What counts as special is, however, not subject to any great consensus. This often means preparing dishes at which the cook is especially proficient, but also involves reflecting on what the guests would prefer. In both scenarios, then, the guests deserve something exceptional.

### Distinctive cooking

People with the greatest interest in food and most invested in cooking propose elaborate and distinctive offerings. Edward, who seeks superior quality and taste, seeks out-of-the-ordinary dishes which require little attention during the event. He describes his preference as:

> something you can throw in the oven. Not that you're compromising on taste, but providing the people coming round with something that they might not have had – instead of having a lasagne or something, which people have been having since they were children – . [...] For example, there's this really nice leg of lamb thing where you can give it this amazing style of spice rub and it's like five hours in the oven and blah blah blah, so hopefully you're giving people things and they're like 'cool, I haven't had this before'. But it's not critical. Obviously the key is to see your friends. Like I said, a lot of my friends are foodies so probably I feel pressure to try and give them something that will maybe impress them or at least not make them think 'that was a bit naff or a bit boring' – spag bol.

For Edward, the food is central, a talking point, something to be noticed. In offering a new experience to the guests, the food is not incidental, not merely a means to keep people fed while they enjoy getting together. Cooking is thus a demonstration of both skill and taste. Lasagne and spaghetti bolognese are not sufficiently distinguished for his friends, whom he describes as 'foodies'. Concern about the quality of the food causes anxiety; Edward feels pressure from a social circle with enthusiasm for gastronomic achievements. The food is not elaborate after the fashion of a fine dining restaurant, but is educated, cognisant of food trends and methods. It is not an expensive meal nor is it showy. The aim is to hit just the right note between comfort and formality while avoiding the accusation of showing off. Edward also notes tensions associated with being a guest. He suggests that his friends are 'more foodie' than he, and that they earn significantly higher salaries. Comparatively impoverished, he seeks out a delicatessen where he can buy a gift that would be appreciated, because a bottle of wine from a high street supermarket would be inappropriate.

Edward was not alone among our interviewees in cooking to impress. Gerald is proud of what his wife serves, although in a different register. He commends her 'fancy starters', identified as prawn cocktail, or 'something with grilled goat's cheese'. He also makes a point: 'We don't have soup'. His wife describes their ideal: 'When we have people over I always do a fancy starter and a sweet of some sort, a nice sweet. And we'll always have cheese and biscuits as well. We do love cheese and biscuits.'

Camilla, who admits to being 'a bit of a foodie', has greater pretension. She has participated in a competition organised with friends annually for the last six years to cook dinner. She says 'we always try to make it home-made gourmet level, food that I wouldn't normally cook. Because that's half of the fun, to stretch yourself a bit and serve matching drinks that go with it and have a really well thought-out menu'. Camilla also hosts parties for her two young children.[3] She alludes to the politics of such events, where, to conform to class and gender roles, the food she serves must be fun but also nutritionally sanctioned. She keeps the chipolata sausages hidden in the fridge for fear of 'offending anyone'. The children's party under the disciplinary eye of other parents may be, therefore, the most anxiety-provoking of occasions.

### Normal cooking

Most people do not joust over culinary perfection. They understand that some sorts of performances are suitable, others not. Their understanding is neither elaborate nor easy to articulate, but common sense gets them by. Typically, they apply a lot of labour in preparing dishes to please their guests. To take an unexceptional example, Angela responds to questions about entertaining by saying: 'My mum comes

[3]   Hosting larger parties is typically described by female participants, and especially women with children. The exception is Jeff (Preston), an ex-army chef, who prepares a buffet of cold meats and snacks for guests at home.

here three times a week. My brother-in-law comes up every other week-end.' She continues,

> [W]hen mum comes she has whatever we're having for tea, because she comes so regularly, it's just what we're having, although, like I say, it might affect what I make.' … 'If mum's coming … the jacket potato or soup or just whatever we're having. I made a stir-fry the other night. Where[as] if my brother-in-law comes, that tends to be Sunday, so it's Sunday roast. If my niece and nephew are coming, well, it depends, I'd probably just do something in the slow cooker probably. So nothing fancy, just home-cooked food.

Interestingly Angela qualifies her comment that her mum just eats what she would be having anyway by admitting that her mother's presence might affect her menu planning. She goes on to distinguish this cooking for the extended family from having friends to visit, where 'a nice din-ner' – 'a fish pie', for example – would be suitable. Respect is shown to guests, even those who are most intimate; and the greater the social distance between host and guests, the greater respect is displayed.

When interviewees were asked about what they served to guests, many responded like Siobhan: 'Depends on who is coming over.' Thus, Simon says that what he serves 'depends on the friends' … '[S]ometimes it will be curry when it is a more kind of social evening' … 'Other times it will be sort of a two-course dinner'. Such relatively simple contrasts comprise the most common way of reflecting on a conventional, and almost universal, understanding that different performances are appro-priate for different occasions. Tyler distinguishes between 'a takeaway and stuff' and 'a sit-down meal', Siobhan between 'lunchtime BBQs' and a 'sit-down dinner', Miranda between 'Sunday lunch' and 'Friday night', and Penny between a 'dinner party' and 'friends to stay'. Few present a long list of alternatives each with their own special characteristics, evi-dence that most people restrict themselves to a few tried-and-tested, rou-tinely occurring, types of event. People make rough distinctions between what is suitable for some guests and what is suitable for others.

When cooking for friends or family many people return to fail-safe favourites and tried-and-tested recipes. They often like to repeat set rec-ipes and formats, with small adjustments made according to preference, dietary requirements, or for the sake of adding variety. As Nicola says:

> If it's a family get-together or whether it's our friends' get-together, I will serve similar. So in fact salmon en croute for the family, I've done it as often as I have for the friends. … if I've got a recipe that's worked for one set of friends or family, I will use it. … But then what I'll tend to do is have [something] different … so I'll do roasted veg one time and then I'll do

normal veg another time. So I tend to change the sort of the bits that goes
around it ... I do have set main courses.

The majority can imagine exceptional feats of cooking but prefer overwhelmingly safe and manageable dishes. Pete once recreated a meal he
had enjoyed in a restaurant for himself and his wife and two other couples, but only once. Nicola raids cookbooks from time to time but has
settled on a salmon dish that she serves to guests each time they visit,
using different side dishes and trimmings for the sake of variation. Robert speaks of how his wife's chestnut roll is a favourite among the neigh-
bours which she is asked to make whenever a gathering calls for
contributions from guests. As we have already seen, some well-known
dishes, such as roast meats, appear very often. Tristan says, when providing for guests: 'We try to make the best vegetarian meal that we've
had that year'. Most people do not experiment when they have hosting
responsibilities.

## Providing food and ensuring comfort

The domestic labour required in giving a dinner party or providing a
buffet for non-resident family members used to fall almost exclusively to
women. As we noted in Chapter 5, there is much speculation about
whether men are doing more. Men were always thought to be more
interested in 'special' cooking and cooking for guests. In 2015 65 per cent
of men claimed to be interested in special cooking, compared with
74 per cent of women, although for some that may mean a barbecue.

### How people feel about hosting

Catering at home can be hard work. Karina is used to both attending
and catering for large family gatherings. South Asian traditions of
large family get-togethers mean that serving food to others, and being
prepared to do so with sometimes little notice, is normal for Karina.
For large family meals she does a huge amount of cooking and goes to
great lengths to make sure that there is something that everyone likes.
She does this without complaint, as her cooking for others is a source of
personal pride and satisfaction. Her network, a large South Asian family, is itself distinctive; social life is heavily organised around visiting the
homes of extended family members. Karina has a regular schedule for
having visitors: 'Nearly every week at weekends, we have a big family
here. Friday I've got some guests at home. Saturday also they will come.

And then Sunday we go to my mum's, so we all gather there.' White British interviewees were in general less heavily engaged, although some people reported very frequent visiting. Angela has her mother to dinner three times a week, as well as having other guests, and Siobhan regularly invites a friend to join their family for Sunday roast dinner. Jeff will entertain friends with a cold buffet and drinks on a Saturday evening, somewhat less often than Angela entertains her mother, but with sufficient regularity to suggest that he is known for these parties. Douglas prepares nachos and dips for similarly drink-led occasions with friends.

Some people clearly get satisfaction from hosting, most obviously Miranda, Simon, Felicity and the food enthusiasts like Noah and Edward. When asked how often she has guests, Miranda says,

Well, Sunday lunch invariably has got somebody coming to Sunday lunch. Well, so on a weekly basis invariably there's somebody here for Sunday lunch. Friday evening if we're in the mood, we'll think let's do a Friday night so and so, something, the cards, let's have a card night or something. And then we'll invite some friends over. So I don't know, very informally once or twice a month, three times a month, something like that.

Nevertheless, sometimes even for them too much hospitality is burdensome. Miranda says of a particular large forthcoming occasion: 'I certainly don't want to be up to my earholes, cooking, and have all those steaming pans etc.' Felicity, just after saying that she liked entertaining, identified

a Hallowe'en party last year which actually was a bit stressful because there were ten people and I did all the cooking and bought everything for them, and I think that was maybe a bit much. At the time I thought it would be fine, but there was a lot of cooking, I didn't really have time to sit and be with them.

If some people grow tired – for Felicity the dinner party is thankfully a distant memory – others get anxious. Tristan says:

I usually mess up when I'm cooking for other people. I'll do exactly the same thing and it will be raw. And they're like 'don't worry about it' but inside you do worry about it, because for us obviously we want to make people think that vegetarian food is okay. It is annoying.

Some people have more or less abandoned entertaining at home and prefer to eat with their friends in a restaurant. For those whose children have left home and who are not poor, eating out is an affordable option for social meals. Lower prices make going out as affordable as eating in, while removal of the hard work means that all can enjoy the evening and the food to the same degree. Nicola goes out a couple of times a week for a light meal with her daughter and/or husband. More elaborate meals, geared towards socialising rather than mere feeding, are more often staged at home. Nicola says that she and her friends can't hear each other so well when out in a restaurant and so now prefer to socialise at each other's homes.

### Orchestrating the occasion

Julier's (2013a) account of how eating together is arranged and managed shows that in almost every case, the exception being competitive cooking for dinner parties among the professional middle class, sociability and conviviality take precedence over the aesthetic quality of the menu. While it is necessary that the food be appropriate to the gathered company, as the type of food served mediates social interactions and facilitates relationships, the cooking is rarely the key to a successful occasion.

Few interviewees currently participate in formal dinner parties. The handful of interviewees exhibiting greatest enthusiasm for cooking and eating recounted events forged in the image of the dinner party where the impression was that eating performances might mirror the procedures of a fine dining restaurant. However, most events are more relaxed, sometimes with the food as background or accompaniment to other forms of entertainment. Simon's vision of the hospitable meal is typical:

> I think sometimes when friends are coming over it, more often than not, is about the kind of social experience with, you know, enjoying an afternoon with family and having dinner, you know, and being able to sit down and just share a dinner because there's something about...I don't know. It just tends to be more relaxed, whereas I think through the week you're eating for the sake of it's dinner time. [...] it's just much more of an event.

Getting the atmosphere right is achieved partly by considering the needs, proclivities and dispositions of particular guests and is also therefore contingent upon established shared understandings. Achieving a relaxed tone is easier within social circles where events are repeated. Levels of informality are negotiated through accumulating experience of joint events that were judged to be suitable. The right atmosphere requires striking an appropriate balance between congeniality, comfort and indulgence. This usually implies informality.

Hosts rarely speak of having extended an invitation to guests. Rather, they list friends and family who 'tend to come over' on particular days of the week, or at particular intervals. The food served goes a long way to setting the tone of informality, as does the preparation required. The less elaborate the meal, the more time one has to be sociable. Another informal move is to serve guests a meal from within the repertoire of family meals. Nor is it a prerequisite to serve guests a home-made meal; Robert sourced a selection of tarts, olives and bread when friends announced they were calling over for lunch. There are also ways of restricting the labour involved in domestic hospitality. Whole meals are purchased from catering companies. Visitors may bring part of the meal or play a role in the preparation of dishes in their host's kitchen.

Julier (2013a) maintains that women are more sensitive to, and take more responsibility for, acts of care for visitors. Making sure that guests are comfortable, ensuring congenial company, and achieving an appropriately convivial atmosphere is very much the domain of hostesses. Women take responsibility for achieving sociability on these, as on most other, occasions. The success of an event, and enjoyment obtained from conversation, company and atmosphere, requires some preparation and orchestration. Several interviewees noted that they don't want to be away from their guests for too long, confirming the impression that socialising is the primary aim of the get-together.

To create the right sort of atmosphere, the older women of the sample (Miranda, Nicola and Gerald's wife Jean), refer to laying a nice table, presenting foods for guests to help themselves in a familial style. For them, while guests may bring a contribution, they are never involved in the cooking. Younger interviewees (Penny, Noah, Douglas) refer to communal cooking as well as commensal eating with guests, perhaps emulating family meals; the guest plays a role in subsidiary food tasks, acting as 'sous chef' by chopping vegetables (Noah) or preparing together simple meals such as a stir-fry (Penny). Cooking together features in the accounts of both young males and females. However, men more generally emphasise the technical and liquid features of events, for instance the mode of cooking (Fred and Stephen roast meat, while Tyler and Isaac barbecue it), or serving foods such as nachos and pizzas as an accompaniment to alcoholic beverages (Douglas, Tyler, Isaac). Older men speak about their role in atmosphere-building.

For all, there is a concern to modulate behaviour to make guests feel comfortable. With or without reflection or great effort, hosts mostly orchestrate enjoyable and highly valued events. Occasionally interviewees implied that their hosts had erred in some way. Laxmikant and his wife, Uma, were shocked when British friends asked them to bring food with them to a party. Nadine, implicitly critical of her friends' skills, expressed a preference for being the hostess to ensure that dishes were freshly prepared rather than purchased in a supermarket. But they were the exceptions. Guests seem duly grateful for whatever they receive, including young men being entirely happy with takeaway items supplying large gatherings of friends.

## Taking turns

One of the most fundamental dilemmas of domestic hospitality concerns the return visit. A basic expectation of reciprocity underpins regularised acts of domestic hospitality. Interviewees talk often about reciprocity. Simon, Jeff, Arlie, Felicity and Stephen explicitly mentioned 'taking turns'. Others (Luke, Miranda, Felicity, Arlie, Elizabeth's husband) used synonyms, or describe practices which routinely involve return visits. Magdalina, for example, says 'They come to us and we go to their place and I would say, yes, probably maybe not even once a month but surely once for two months'. The strength of the ideal of reciprocity is revealed by the survey responses to questions about return visits. Of those whose last main meal had been at the home of friends or family, when asked whether they would expect to entertain their hosts subsequently, 77 per cent said definitely in 2015, 9 per cent said not, and 14 per cent were not sure.

Table 6.2 shows some further differences between dining with friends and with non-resident family members. People eat with kin more frequently; in 2015 over a quarter reported eating at the last home visited at least once a week, twice the proportion for friends. Nevertheless, the bonds of friendship support frequent visits. Disregarding the 11 per cent of first-time visits to a friend's house, 39 per cent (of the remainder) visited at least once a month, and 75 per cent visited the same friends every three months. Many friends, and kin too, make routine repeat visits to eat together.

Table 6.2 indicates changes since 1995. Frequency of visits to the identified hosts has not changed appreciably but the nature of the invitations seems a little different. In 1995, four in five events were at the instigation of the host (81% for both relatives and friends), a figure significantly diminished by 2015. On only 62 per cent of occasions was a family meal the suggestion of a family member, the proportion of all other specified actors having increased. It would seem that on one occasion in five the guests (the respondent or the respondent's partner) had suggested the

**Table 6.2** Reciprocity and sharing in home entertaining with relatives and friends, 1995–2015 (percentage)

| | 1995 | | | 2015 | | |
|---|---|---|---|---|---|---|
| | Relatives | Friends | Sig | Relatives | Friends | Sig |
| *Location of host(ess) home* | | | | | | * |
| In the same street | 2 | 3 | | 4 | 10 | |
| Within 1 mile of your house | 23 | 31 | | 21 | 23 | |
| Over 1 mile but less than 5 | 38 | 34 | | 34 | 42 | |
| Over 5 but less than 10 | 14 | 14 | | 9 | 12 | |
| Over 10 miles from your house | 23 | 18 | | 33 | 13 | |
| *How often eats there* | | | ** | | | *** |
| This is the first time | 2 | 10 | | 0 | 11 | |
| At least once a week | 22 | 10 | | 26 | 13 | |
| At least once a month | 27 | 32 | | 34 | 22 | |
| At least once every 3 months | 28 | 22 | | 22 | 30 | |
| At least once every 6 months | 13 | 18 | | 13 | 12 | |
| Less often | 6 | 8 | | 5 | 13 | |
| *Whose suggestion* | | | *** | | | *** |
| Mine | 7 | 8 | | 13 | 10 | |
| My partner | 4 | 1 | | 9 | 5 | |
| Friend(s) | 2 | 81 | | 7 | 72 | |
| Family | 81 | 1 | | 62 | 5 | |
| Other | 6 | 8 | | 10 | 9 | |
| *Expects to invite host(ess) back* | | | | | | |
| Yes | 73 | 78 | | 77 | 80 | |
| Yes, probably | 12 | 10 | | 5 | 13 | |
| Probably not | 8 | 5 | | 5 | 3 | |
| No | 7 | 7 | | 13 | 5 | |
| *How soon invite host(ess)* | | | * | | | |
| Within a week | 17 | 20 | | 28 | 14 | |
| Within a month | 40 | 31 | | 38 | 49 | |
| Within 3 months | 30 | 28 | | 17 | 25 | |
| Within 6 months | 6 | 17 | | 11 | 9 | |

(Continued)

**Table 6.2** Continued

|  | 1995 | | | 2015 | | |
|---|---|---|---|---|---|---|
|  | Relatives | Friends | Sig | Relatives | Friends | Sig |
| Within a year | 6 | 3 | | 4 | 2 | |
| A year or more later | 1 | 0 | | 1 | 0 | |
| *Takes a gift* | | | | | | |
| Wine | 17 | 35 | *** | 19 | 34 | * |
| Other alcohol | 2 | 6 | | 4 | 10 | |
| Flowers | 7 | 7 | | 7 | 1 | |
| Chocolate | 5 | 8 | | 4 | 10 | |
| Dish | 4 | 6 | | 11 | 13 | |
| Other | 7 | 4 | | 11 | 16 | |
| Nothing | 67 | 42 | *** | 55 | 38 | * |
| *Food preparation* | | | | | | |
| Home-cooked | | | | 91 | 88 | |
| Takeaway | | | | 4 | 10 | |
| Other | | | | 4 | 3 | |

Note: $\chi^2$ *$p$ < 0.05, **$p$ < 0.01, ***$p$ < 0.001. Respondents between ages 16–65

meal. A smaller but still substantial equivalent change is associated with being guests of a friend. Not all visits require an invitation.

Most respondents say that they expect to invite the host back. Only 5 per cent of those referring in 2015 to friends said that they would not return the invitation, a figure which rises to 13 per cent for family. The invitations least likely to be reciprocated come from parents and parents-in-law. Some family return visits occur very soon; more than a quarter will reciprocate within a week. For friends, fewer are within the week, but 63 per cent are within a month and 88 per cent within three months. Repayment to friends is not urgent but return visits apparently cannot be deferred too long.

Another dimension of the balance of credit and debt involves guests bringing gifts for the host. Table 6.2 shows that the gifts guests bestow upon their hosts when visiting have not changed a great deal in the last twenty years; wine, flowers and chocolate are common. However, it has become more common to take a dish to contribute to the meal; 12 per cent of respondents reported this in 2015 compared with 5 per cent in 1995. It is also less common to arrive empty-handed; 9 per cent fewer, although still almost half of the guests, went without a gift in 2015. Part of the rationale for taking a present to the host is explained by different norms or expectations associated with visits to friends rather than

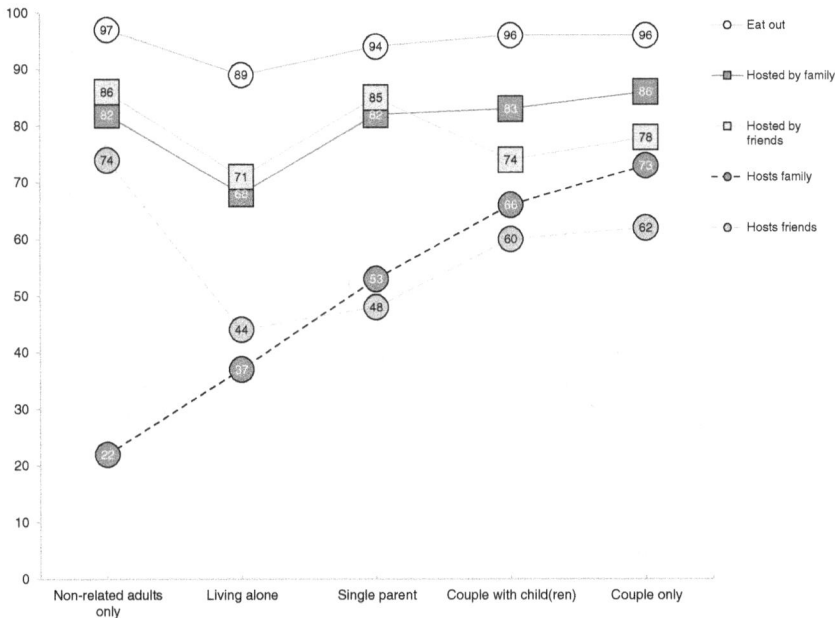

**Figure 6.1** Percentage reporting hosting, being hosted and eating out in the last twelve months, by household type, 2015

family. Guests of friends were much less likely to arrive without a present. In 2015, only a third of them went without a gift, the most popular being wine or some other alcoholic drink.[4] (Alcohol is significantly less prominent a gift at family occasions.) More chocolate is given to friends and more dishes are taken to friends. These small presents presumably symbolise gratitude but might also be seen as temporary payment towards affraying a debt pending, usually a future event where the roles of host and guest will be reversed.

More presents and more invitations issued at shorter intervals suggest a change in the terms of reciprocity, as does the reduction in the proportion of events where the idea about the visit actually came from the host. Informalisation, joint decision-making, and relaxation of roles are elements of a general tendency in the revision of norms governing hospitality.

Yet if reciprocity is the bedrock ideal, it is highly imperfect in practice. Figure 6.1 belies symmetrical reciprocity. Those who live alone or in

---

[4]   Note that the total percentage does not sum to 100 because it was possible to record more than one category of gift.

communal households provide many fewer meals to non-resident kin than they receive. Couples (and couples with children) are very significantly more likely to host family than are single parents, those living alone, or living in shared accommodation. Some people lack the material means to reciprocate and have skill constraints. Tyler lacks money. Elderly or ailing parents are often unable to continue to play their accustomed roles in a family system of exchange, and special arrangements have to be improvised (as was the case with Miranda's mother). Others, most typically men, lack the necessary skills to provide a meal when it is their turn (although they may see themselves as playing a supporting role or have recourse to the buffet or the barbecue).

Hence, some members of extended families tend to be more heavily engaged in providing the contexts for family gatherings. The tally of credit and debt tends to change over the life cycle, as parents with adult children (and perhaps grandchildren) more often give than receive. Couples rely on family more than friends for invitations, while singles visit friends more often.

Thus, reciprocity is intended in the majority of cases, and mostly transpires, but is not a system of perfect exchange. Those less likely to host are men, the less highly educated and the working class. Although hospitality is an example par excellence of a system of reciprocal informal exchange, it is not only more frequently honoured within friendship networks but also concentrated in specific sections of the population.

## Conclusion

Domestic entertaining occurs as frequently in 2015 as in 1995. Women are more likely than men to host events, but otherwise it is richer households, graduates and people with service class connections who are more likely to be involved as both hosts and guests. The main exception is that to be the guest of kinsfolk requires no elevated social attributes.

The formats of domestic hospitality are various, but entertaining is mostly a familiar, informal and sociable affair. The quality and complexity of the food involved are somewhat greater than for the average midweek family dinner, as special care is taken and the hosts are prepared to put effort into the overall experience. Those with the greatest enthusiasm for culinary activity pay a great deal of attention to what they give and what they receive. Their arrangements conform to some version of the template of the dinner party where the central purpose of the occasion is to consume good food and wine. Such events need not be formal and stuffy, but they are likely to occur around a dinner table, to last for at least a couple of hours, to involve several courses, and to have been the object of careful planning. For most others, the food is of lesser importance, although no one suggests that the quality of the food is irrelevant, and the level of informality is higher. Younger people engage in more varied and relaxed events. The differences apparent between meals with friends and meals with kin have diminished significantly. Perhaps formality is reserved now for a minority of restaurant visits. Arrangements are designed to generate a comfortable atmosphere and continue to yield very high rates of satisfaction. Contemporary forms require less labour and less responsibility on the part of the host than does the classic dinner party.

Most occasions are passed off as 'just social occasions'. They are intended as opportunities for relaxed social intercourse, where the primary purpose is to be together with friends or family. Nevertheless, events are orchestrated insofar as guests are carefully selected, activities planned, menus reflected upon, and food quality made to match the social significance of the occasion. Typically, the range of people who might be invited is tightly restricted. Some of the large celebratory events or the big parties of young adults aside, people exchange visits with a small, select, closed bunch of associates, and new participants are added to the guest roster infrequently. People visit the same homes in an agreed sequence. This is a consequence of and consistent with a governing norm of reciprocity which guarantees the repetitive and regularised nature of many of these events.

# 7

## Restaurant performances

### Introduction

Eating out in a restaurant was a very gratifying experience in 1995 and, by and large, it remains so, although on all dimensions satisfaction has diminished, with service, atmosphere and food suffering the sharpest falls (Table 3.1, p. 30). This chapter investigates aspects of the performance of dining out in commercial settings, examining in turn the nature and changes in the purposes of dining out, typical companions, service, dishes and meals. In each instance we describe contemporary practice and where possible make comparison with 1995.

### Changing purposes, changing performances

Figure 4.1 (p. 61) shows that between 1995 and 2015 the proportion of last meals in restaurants described as special occasions has fallen, that the proportion described as 'convenience/quick' has increased, while the proportion which are 'just social occasions' and 'business' remains largely unchanged. Thus, the shift in restaurant meals has been primarily from special occasions to convenience/quick events. Changes in the reasons given for eating out offer a partial explanation of the casualisation and simplification, and also the diminished enjoyment of dining out.

Looking at the characteristics of meals in different categories indicates that they are distinguishably different types of occasion (Table 7.1, compare panels 1–3). The company varies with the reason for the occasion. In 2015 convenience meals are the most likely to be eaten alone (19% of convenience occasions) and rarely in large groups; if not eaten alone, the company at convenience meals is most likely to be family or partner only. Meals described as special occasions tend to be shared with a larger number of people, with 'just social occasions' falling between the two.

**Table 7.1** Characteristics of different meal types in a restaurant, 1995–2015 (column percentage)

| | Quick/Convenient | | | Special occasion | | | Just a social occasion | | | All | | |
|---|---|---|---|---|---|---|---|---|---|---|---|---|
| | 1995 | 2015 | Sig | 1995 | 2015 | Sig | 1995 | 2015 | Sig | 1995 | 2015 | Sig |
| *Number eating* | | | | | | | | | | | | |
| Ate alone | 18 | 19 | | 0 | 0 | | 0 | 2 | | 3 | 6 | |
| 2 | 42 | 44 | | 25 | 16 | | 43 | 37 | | 37 | 35 | |
| 3–4 | 29 | 26 | | 22 | 25 | | 34 | 38 | | 29 | 31 | |
| 5–9 | 11 | 10 | | 29 | 32 | | 18 | 17 | | 20 | 19 | |
| 10 people or more | 1 | 1 | | 24 | 26 | ** | 6 | 6 | * | 11 | 9 | *** |
| *Companions* | | | | | | | | | | | | |
| Partner only | 22 | 22 | | 23 | 10 | | 24 | 16 | | 23 | 16 | |
| Family only | 23 | 31 | | 37 | 47 | | 27 | 32 | | 28 | 35 | |
| Friends only | 26 | 18 | | 13 | 11 | | 29 | 29 | | 23 | 21 | |
| Other combination | 29 | 29 | | 27 | 32 | ** | 20 | 23 | * | 26 | 28 | *** |
| *When took place* | | | | | | | | | | | | |
| Within the last week | 54 | 58 | | 33 | 30 | | 41 | 48 | | 42 | 46 | |
| Within a fortnight | 10 | 12 | | 11 | 13 | | 11 | 15 | | 10 | 14 | |
| Within a month | 15 | 12 | | 16 | 13 | | 19 | 18 | | 17 | 16 | |
| More than a month ago | 21 | 17 | | 40 | 43 | *** | 29 | 19 | * | 31 | 24 | ** |
| *Day of the week* | | | | | | | | | | | | |
| Weekend (Fri–Sun) | 49 | 54 | | 76 | 58 | | 66 | 61 | | 65 | 58 | ** |
| *Decided in advance* | | | * | | | | | | | | | ** |
| Walking past | 58 | 43 | | 8 | 10 | | 27 | 25 | | 27 | 27 | |
| One hour | 11 | 26 | | 5 | 4 | | 14 | 18 | | 11 | 17 | |
| On the day | 18 | 19 | | 8 | 13 | | 19 | 22 | | 16 | 19 | |
| Several weeks or more before | 2 | 2 | | 30 | 17 | *** | 9 | 5 | *** | 14 | 7 | *** |
| *Duration* | | | | | | | | | | | | |
| 1 hour or less | 62 | 63 | | 4 | 12 | *** | 14 | 31 | *** | 20 | 35 | *** |

*(Continued)*

**Table 7.1** Continued

| | Quick/Convenient | | | Special occasion | | | Just a social occasion | | | All | | |
|---|---|---|---|---|---|---|---|---|---|---|---|---|
| | 1995 | 2015 | Sig | 1995 | 2015 | Sig | 1995 | 2015 | Sig | 1995 | 2015 | Sig |
| 1–2 hours | 35 | 30 | | 41 | 52 | | 52 | 54 | | 45 | 48 | |
| 2 or more hours | 3 | 7 | | 55 | 36 | | 34 | 15 | ** | 35 | 18 | *** |
| *Dressed up* | | | | | | | | | | | | |
| Yes | 6 | 7 | | 70 | 62 | | 33 | 21 | ** | 39 | 26 | *** |
| *Courses included* | | | | | | | | | | | | |
| Starter | 21 | 25 | | 63 | 53 | | 57 | 40 | *** | 52 | 39 | *** |
| Dessert | 23 | 19 | | 62 | 42 | *** | 34 | 30 | | 41 | 30 | *** |
| *Number of courses* | | | | | | | | | | | | |
| One course | 62 | 61 | | 20 | 27 | | 34 | 42 | | 35 | 43 | |
| Two courses | 25 | 29 | | 32 | 37 | | 36 | 36 | | 32 | 35 | |
| Three or more courses | 13 | 9 | | 49 | 36 | | 30 | 22 | | 33 | 22 | |
| *Returning customer* | | | | | | | | | | | | |
| Been before | 71 | 76 | | 59 | 62 | | 63 | 66 | | 62 | 67 | |
| Go again ('Very likely') | 60 | 68 | | 57 | 64 | | 54 | 62 | * | 55 | 64 | ** |
| *Satisfaction ('Liked a lot')* | | | | | | | | | | | | |
| Food | 67 | 66 | | 86 | 75 | ** | 83 | 75 | ** | 81 | 72 | ** |
| Company | 75 | 80 | | 96 | 85 | | 94 | 90 | | 91 | 86 | |
| Decor | 40 | 41 | | 62 | 59 | | 60 | 47 | *** | 57 | 48 | ** |
| Service | 49 | 53 | | 75 | 62 | | 67 | 58 | | 65 | 57 | ** |
| Conversation | 66 | 70 | | 88 | 82 | | 85 | 83 | | 82 | 79 | |
| Value for money | 60 | 54 | * | 75 | 60 | * | 70 | 55 | ** | 69 | 56 | *** |
| Overall | 59 | 69 | * | 91 | 85 | | 86 | 78 | * | 81 | 77 | * |
| *Observations* | | | | | | | | | | | | |
| N = | 108 | 185 | | 171 | 158 | | 278 | 357 | | 582 | 723 | |

*Note:* Respondents between ages 16–65; $\chi^2$ *$p < 0.05$, **$p < 0.01$, ***$p < 0.001$; 'All' includes quick/convenient, special occasion, just a social occasion, business, and other reasons for meal

Timing and meal content also vary by type of occasion. For convenient last meals many respondents said they decided when walking past or about an hour before, whereas special occasions tended to be planned several weeks or more in advance. 'Just social occasions' lie in between. Respondents spend less time eating convenience meals; 63 per cent took less than an hour compared with 12 per cent of special occasions and 31 per cent of just social occasions. Nevertheless, almost a third of convenient meals (30%) lasted between one and two hours, demonstrating that convenience does not always equate to shortage of time. The most prolonged meals are special occasions. One explanation for the variation in duration of the meal is the number of courses consumed; convenience meals are most likely to comprise a single course, and special occasion meals least likely. Special occasions are the most likely to contain a starter and the most likely to include a dessert.

Examining satisfaction with the different components of the meal reveals that convenience meals are in all respects inferior. People were much less prepared to say that they liked such a meal 'a lot'. Special occasions, compared with just social occasions, were 'liked a lot' in all aspects except company and conversation, presumably because special occasions bring in a wider group of people not necessarily known intimately by all in the party. Overall, while dining out in restaurants generally meets with strong approval, the convenient type is least appealing. Probably declining overall satisfaction results from many quick and convenient meals being taken in less congenial circumstances, in less smart surroundings and with more casual service or self-service than in 1995 and this reduces the intrinsic pleasure of the occasion (for further discussion of fast food see Chapter 11). Nevertheless, the satisfaction derived from meals described as quick and convenient increased very significantly between 1995 and 2015.

Comparison of meal characteristics *within* each of the categories over time reveals a broader shift. Even the most special of dining occasions reflect a trend towards informalisation (Table 7.1).[1] There was a slight decline in large groups (twenty-plus people) and fewer respondents dressed up for the occasion. Special meals are now less likely to contain a starter (10% decrease) or a dessert (20% fall). Thus, they tend to contain fewer courses than twenty years ago (witness a 13% decrease in meals with three or more courses). Sharp falls are recorded in the proportion of special meals which occur at the weekend (18% fewer); take longer than

[1] Respondents recorded various types of special occasion including ordinary and special (e.g. twenty-first) birthdays; ordinary and special anniversaries; weddings, christening and engagement parties; religious festivals; Mothers' Day; passing examinations and farewell meals.

two hours (19%); were decided several weeks in advance (13%); where the overall event was 'liked a lot' (6%). Satisfaction with all aspects of the special meal has declined: the food (a fall of 11%), the company, decor, service, conversation, value for money, and the overall experience. Special occasions thus exhibit the same trends towards casualisation and simplification as other types of event.

## Companions in restaurants

Dining out is primarily a social occasion. When asked, 'what do you like about eating out?', aspects other than the food were frequently considered. People said they enjoyed an occasion even when the food was poor; the company compensates for a disappointing meal. Social interaction is primary. Uma says, 'Normally I wouldn't want to go out but it's just my children, to be with them and spend time with them, you will go out of your way, because they want to go out'. Lara says, 'Well, it's nice to be with my family. It's nice to go out with the family.' Enid, who eats out infrequently, values the fact that 'we go with friends … and with our son and his girlfriend sometimes'. Atmosphere and excellent service are not the main objective when dining out, although an enchanting or even merely acceptable atmosphere does make for a better social occasion and is conducive to appropriate social interaction. The company and interaction around the dinner table are especially appreciated.

Interviewees wanted to facilitate the best possible and most suitable forms of social interaction with their companions. Tyler primarily wants to talk with his partner. He is less concerned about where that might be or what he might eat; he does consider the novelty of the venue and the food as criteria for choosing and judging restaurants, but these are secondary matters. Edward likes 'the event thing', as do others; Camilla is prepared to suffer a buffet restaurant when this is where her colleagues prefer to eat, as convenience and conviviality trump form and taste on such occasions; now too old for a Saturday night out drinking cocktails, Nadine likes to dine out with friends instead; and Enid appreciates the opportunity to socialise with her female friends without their husbands present. Edward also uses a restaurant meal as an opportunity to talk in a relaxed manner with his partner. Tristan values special occasion meals and the appeal of 'quality time' with his partner: 'when you eat at home, I think it's a bit more rushed. You're watching TV in the background or whatever. Quality time … you've not got your phone or the TV and you've got someone's full attention'. Meals with partners, although reducing as a proportion of all occasions, are more resistant to the tendency for the quality of the experience to decline (Table 7.2).

**Table 7.2** Characteristics of meal types with different companions in restaurants, 1995–2015 (column percentage)

| | Alone | | | Partner only | | | Friends only | | | Family only | | | Friends & family | | | All | | |
|---|---|---|---|---|---|---|---|---|---|---|---|---|---|---|---|---|---|---|
| | 1995 | 2015 | Sig | 1995 | 2015 | Sig | 1995 | 2015 | Sig | 1995 | 2015 | Sig | 1995 | 2015 | Sig | 1995 | 2015 | Sig |
| *Reason for eating out* | | | | | | ** | | | | | | | | | | | | ** |
| Special occasion | 0 | 0 | | 29 | 13 | | 17 | 11 | | 39 | 30 | | 43 | 38 | | 29 | 22 | |
| Quick/convenience | 95 | 80 | | 18 | 34 | | 21 | 22 | | 15 | 23 | | 6 | 10 | | 19 | 26 | |
| Just a social occasion | 5 | 16 | | 50 | 49 | | 61 | 66 | | 45 | 46 | | 46 | 52 | | 48 | 49 | |
| Other | 0 | 4 | | 2 | 4 | | 1 | 1 | | 1 | 1 | | 5 | 0 | | 4 | 3 | |
| *Number eating* | | | | | | | | | | | | | | | | | | |
| Ate alone | 100 | 100 | | – | – | | – | – | | – | – | | – | – | | 3 | 6 | |
| 2 | – | – | | 100 | 100 | | 39 | 52 | | 12 | 11 | | 0 | 0 | | 37 | 35 | |
| 3–4 | – | – | | – | – | | 33 | 26 | | 49 | 56 | | 44 | 39 | | 29 | 31 | |
| 5–9 | – | – | | – | – | | 16 | 14 | | 33 | 25 | | 36 | 37 | | 20 | 19 | |
| 10 people or more | – | – | | – | – | | 12 | 8 | | 6 | 8 | | 20 | 24 | | 11 | 9 | |
| *When took place* | | | | | | | | | | | | | | | | | | * |
| Within the last week | 50 | 62 | | 43 | 48 | | 44 | 50 | | 38 | 40 | | 40 | 48 | | 42 | 46 | |
| Within a fortnight | 5 | 13 | | 11 | 15 | | 14 | 15 | | 9 | 13 | | 9 | 11 | | 10 | 14 | |
| Within a month | 20 | 2 | | 16 | 15 | | 17 | 12 | | 17 | 19 | | 19 | 24 | | 17 | 16 | |
| More than a month ago | 25 | 22 | | 31 | 22 | | 24 | 23 | | 36 | 29 | | 33 | 17 | | 31 | 24 | |

*(Continued)*

**Table 7.2** Continued

| | Alone | | | Partner only | | | Friends only | | | Family only | | | Friends & family | | | All | | |
|---|---|---|---|---|---|---|---|---|---|---|---|---|---|---|---|---|---|---|
| | 1995 | 2015 | Sig | 1995 | 2015 | Sig | 1995 | 2015 | Sig | 1995 | 2015 | Sig | 1995 | 2015 | Sig | 1995 | 2015 | Sig |
| *Day of the week* | | | | | | | | | | | | | | | | | | |
| Weekend (Fri–Sun) | 20 | 31 | | 64 | 56 | | 60 | 52 | | 74 | 66 | | 73 | 66 | | 65 | 58 | ** |
| *Decided in advance* | | | | | | | | | | | | | | | | | | |
| Walking past | 85 | 56 | | 33 | 25 | | 34 | 35 | | 19 | 22 | * | 13 | 17 | | 27 | 27 | ** |
| One hour | 5 | 18 | | 14 | 19 | | 11 | 15 | | 10 | 16 | | 11 | 15 | | 11 | 17 | |
| On the day | 10 | 16 | | 23 | 26 | | 11 | 16 | | 19 | 21 | | 11 | 6 | | 16 | 19 | |
| Several weeks or more | 0 | 7 | | 8 | 3 | | 13 | 8 | | 15 | 6 | | 18 | 17 | | 14 | 7 | |
| *Duration* | | | | | | | | | | | | | | | | | | |
| 1 hour or less | 89 | 89 | | 22 | 30 | | 17 | 43 | *** | 20 | 30 | ** | 8 | 18 | * | 20 | 35 | *** |
| 1–2 hours | 11 | 9 | | 49 | 52 | | 51 | 42 | | 51 | 53 | | 36 | 49 | | 45 | 48 | |
| 2 or more hours | 0 | 2 | | 29 | 18 | | 32 | 16 | | 30 | 16 | | 56 | 32 | | 35 | 18 | |
| *Dressed up* | | | | | | | | | | | | | | | | | | |
| Yes | 0 | 7 | | 47 | 30 | ** | 25 | 13 | ** | 41 | 30 | * | 53 | 41 | | 39 | 26 | *** |
| *Courses included* | | | | | | | | | | | | | | | | | | |
| Starter | 16 | 16 | | 53 | 48 | | 47 | 35 | * | 51 | 38 | * | 62 | 42 | * | 52 | 39 | *** |
| Dessert | 21 | 11 | | 35 | 33 | | 32 | 18 | ** | 46 | 33 | ** | 55 | 46 | | 41 | 30 | *** |
| *Number of courses* | | | | | | | | | | | | | | | | | | |
| One course | 65 | 76 | | 36 | 34 | | 41 | 53 | | 36 | 44 | * | 24 | 28 | | 35 | 43 | *** |

**Table 7.2** Continued

| | Alone | | | Partner only | | | Friends only | | | Family only | | | Friends & family | | | All | | |
|---|---|---|---|---|---|---|---|---|---|---|---|---|---|---|---|---|---|---|
| | 1995 | 2015 | Sig | 1995 | 2015 | Sig | 1995 | 2015 | Sig | 1995 | 2015 | Sig | 1995 | 2015 | Sig | 1995 | 2015 | Sig |
| Two courses | 30 | 20 | | 36 | 39 | | 35 | 33 | | 26 | 32 | | 34 | 45 | | 32 | 35 | |
| Three or more courses | 5 | 4 | | 28 | 28 | | 24 | 14 | | 38 | 24 | | 43 | 27 | | 33 | 22 | |
| *Returning customer* | | | | | | | | | | | | | | | | | | |
| Been before | 63 | 80 | | 61 | 71 | | 68 | 59 | | 68 | 70 | | 48 | 66 | * | 62 | 67 | |
| Go again ('Very likely') | 42 | 69 | | 62 | 71 | | 60 | 54 | | 58 | 67 | ** | 46 | 68 | * | 55 | 64 | *** |
| *Costs shared* | | | | | | | | | | | | | | | | | | |
| Yes | 0 | 0 | | 14 | 27 | * | 72 | 74 | | 24 | 26 | | 56 | 49 | | 39 | 39 | |
| *Satisfaction ('Liked a lot')* | | | | | | | | | | | | | | | | | | |
| Food | 50 | 69 | | 87 | 83 | | 78 | 68 | * | 83 | 74 | * | 79 | 76 | | 81 | 72 | ** |
| Company | 25 | 43 | | 94 | 96 | | 92 | 85 | | 93 | 88 | | 96 | 93 | | 91 | 86 | |
| Decor | 10 | 38 | | 62 | 51 | | 54 | 36 | * | 63 | 54 | | 58 | 52 | | 57 | 48 | ** |
| Service | 35 | 56 | | 75 | 66 | | 56 | 47 | | 68 | 59 | | 68 | 63 | | 65 | 57 | ** |
| Conversation | | | | 82 | 90 | | 87 | 83 | | 81 | 77 | | 86 | 94 | | 82 | 79 | |
| Value for money | 40 | 56 | | 73 | 62 | | 64 | 54 | | 75 | 57 | ** | 70 | 54 | * | 69 | 56 | *** |
| Overall | 25 | 58 | * | 82 | 86 | | 84 | 71 | | 86 | 79 | | 88 | 85 | | 82 | 77 | ** |
| *Observations* | | | | | | | | | | | | | | | | | | |
| N= | 20 | 45 | | 134 | 119 | | 132 | 155 | | 167 | 250 | | 80 | 71 | | 585 | 723 | |

The treat for couples is often less the food than the opportunity to spend uninterrupted time together, as it is for others. Lara (quoted above) explains her excursions in terms of family, with the food an afterthought. *A fortiori*, Enid and Cheryl mostly do not like the food with which they are confronted in restaurants, but they still want to go out for the company. Everyone has some degree of concern about the food; it is never a total irrelevance. However, often the explanation of why an event took place in a particular venue begins from a statement of who was present. The presence of children explains why a pizza house or a carvery roast Sunday dinner is taken. Simon, for example, recounting his last meal:

> just a couple of weekends ago with the children when we took them out for a carvery, ... if it was just myself and my wife, we probably wouldn't go for a carvery just for ourselves, but it's because it's the ease on a Sunday afternoon ... you don't have to cook a roast ... and you know it's food the kids will eat.

Arlie also intimates in several ways that it is companionship and the pleasure derived from spending time with friends that endears her to restaurants. She recounts invitations from friends to various meals and it is clear that it really would not matter where the event took place but that the invitation and the occasion are to be cherished for their own sake. Eating with others, in her case almost always friends, is a major social and cultural opportunity.

The companions envisaged are the primary part of any justification of why a particular event took place where and when it did. People make special provision and take more or less care when planning an event with different categories of companions; partners, children and friends entail different approaches. Matching location to company is complex, a matter of social skill, requiring decisions about suitability, and a matter of considerable significance for some parts of the population. Cultural capital is mobilised, with the professional and managerial class most discriminating in its capacity to envisage alternatives and select for particular effects. Camilla is informative about the reasons for different purposes for different occasions.

> That would entirely depend on whether I'm bringing the children or not. If I'm bringing the children it has to be somewhere that serves food that I know they will eat but that is also fairly healthy, so there needs to be a balance there. So I would never take them to a fast-food restaurant, but equally there is no point taking them to somewhere where the food is too fancy or too healthy because they wouldn't eat it. But eating out with friends or grown-up family, I suppose it all depends on the occasion. If it's a treat then, yeah, we

would just go for what sounds like the most amazing fancy restaurant. If it's just about meeting up and a touch of convenience in there it would be where most people agree on meeting up, so it could be anywhere really.

Distinguishing occasions and companions, she is very clear about how the event has to meet a set of expectations, defined in terms of their social significance.

Table 7.2 shows some minor changes in who is likely to provide the desired companionship at the table in a restaurant. Warde and Martens (2000) pointed out that most meals out on commercial premises involve other family members, which is significant because it means that eating out does not entail that families stop eating together. Table 7.2 indicates that, on the last occasion, partners or family members were present as companions on at least 69 per cent of occasions, a substantial majority as in 1995 (71%). It also shows 6 per cent fewer occasions with only partners present, but a comparable increase in occasions with only family. This indicates that parents take their children out to eat more often, including younger children. This is part of the process of familiarisation whereby children become acclimatised to eating out at an early age and which serves to reduce its aura of exceptionalness.

The household structure affects with whom one eats out and, to a lesser extent, how often. Patterns of sociability depend on domestic arrangements. Figure 7.1 indicates the likely companions for people living in different types of household. Families usually eat out together. Parents with dependent children eat around half of their restaurant meals with children in tow and rarely eat out alone or only with their partner. Couples without children are the most likely by far to eat only with a partner. Those with partners, with or without children, rarely eat only with friends. People not living *en famille* are more likely to eat out alone, but by way of compensation do so more frequently, especially younger solos. Those not living in couples are also much more likely to eat out with friends. Of those who live alone, 15 per cent had their last restaurant meal alone, and of those who live with non-related adults, the figure was 10 per cent. The equivalent for each of the household types containing a couple was 2 per cent. This suggests reluctance on the part of family households to abandon the notion that, where possible, they should eat together.

Household structure – its formation rather than its size – both offers opportunities and imposes constraints. People make companions out of those who are most readily accessible. The underlying propensity for people living in different types of household to eat with particular categories of companion has changed very little. All ate out a little more

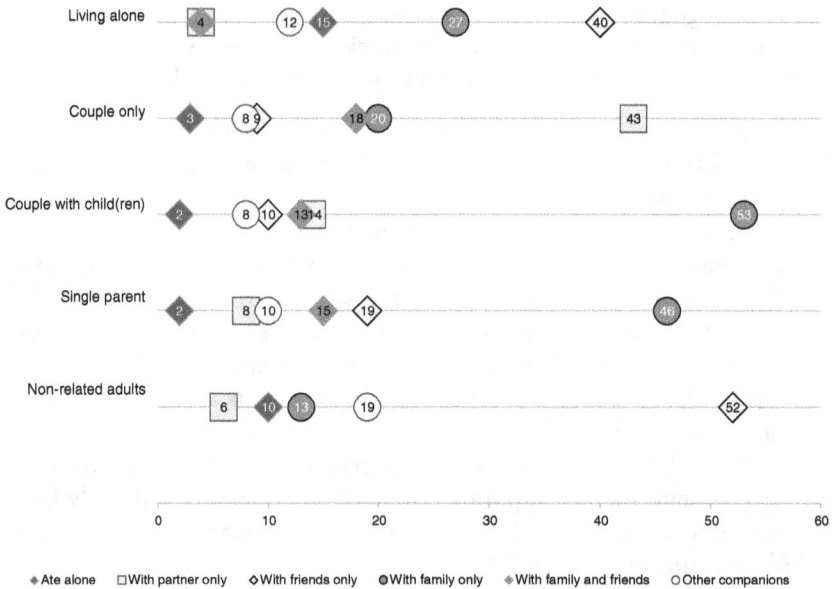

**Figure 7.1** Who was in attendance at the last meal occasion eaten at a restaurant, by household type, 2015 (percentage)

frequently, but the overall pattern of companionship remained constant, with age and life-course stage significantly affecting the propensity to eat out and the likely companions.

One significant change in practice is the rise in eating out alone (Table 7.2). The proportion of last meals out alone doubled between 1995 and 2015, although it still remains at only 6 per cent. In general people prefer not to eat alone in restaurants, especially women. Arlie, when asked if she would like to eat out more often, said 'I suppose if money was no object at all, probably, and if I could find enough people to eat with. That's one thing I don't like about eating out, is on my own, I don't like that at all. And I used to have to do it quite a lot when I was HR consultant. … it's something about being a single woman.' She continues by observing that sometimes it is no problem, for example at a pub lunch or on a train, 'But actually to go to a restaurant and eat on my own, no, I couldn't do it.' All interview discussion suggests that people expect to have company when eating in restaurants, except perhaps when away on business. Nevertheless, the aversion is decreasing as marked by a change in attitudes; whereas in 1995 only 14 per cent of respondents had disagreed with the proposition 'When I eat out I dislike eating alone', 20 per cent disagreed by 2015, with the proportion who reported 'strongly disagree' almost doubling. So, while no one positively prefers to dine without companions, the experience of eating alone has become a more acceptable and enjoyable experience since 1995.

Meals eaten alone epitomise the trends of regularisation and simplification. They are much more likely to be for reasons of convenience, to occur within the last week, on a weekday, lasting less than an hour, comprising one course and in a restaurant visited on a previous occasion (Table 7.2). Comparison with 1995 also offers some counter-indications, however, with fewer meals alone in 2015 taken on the spur of the moment. More are planned, occur at the weekend and are enjoyed a lot. In 1995 only a quarter of lone meals were liked a lot, a proportion rising to 58 per cent in 2015. To dine alone is becoming more attractive, although it remains much inferior to eating with friends and family.

## Procedures and interactions

### The 'work' of eating out

One of the great attractions of eating out is that it involves no domestic labour. The food is prepared by someone else, served by someone else and cleared up by someone else. There is another side to the equation when eating in the home of friends or family, for the saved effort will require subsequent recompense. By contrast, the commercial meal seems ideal for those who are tired or lazy. Nevertheless, the restaurant meal is not without its accompanying activities of preparation and measured performance. Elements of the occasion which are potentially problematic, and which require effort and attention, include a decision about where to go and when, the possible need to book in advance, time required for the personal care to make a credible public performance, time to travel from home to the destination, the requirement for tactful human relations management with companions and particularly serving staff, and the paying of the bill and awarding tips. (There is no such thing as an effort-free lunch!) Consideration of the sum of all these entailments is one reason given for not wanting to eat out more. These aspects of the event are not work in the sense of employment, and in some instances they are treated as positive features, but they do produce obligations which define the experience of eating out. Table 7.3 shows changes in some of the basic features of preparations for dining out.

There is a decline in joint decision-making. People in 2015 are more likely to have heard about the venue by word of mouth, in line with more people saying 'I often talk with others about eating out'. There is

**Table 7.3** Procedural features of eating out in a restaurant, 1995–2015 (percentage)

|  | 1995 | 2015 | Sig |
|---|---|---|---|
| *Who decided to eat in establishment* |  |  | ** |
| Me | 32 | 39 |  |
| My partner | 10 | 13 |  |
| Jointly with partner | 16 | 10 |  |
| Jointly with friend(s) | 13 | 10 |  |
| Jointly with family | 7 | 7 |  |
| My friend(s) | 8 | 9 |  |
| My family | 8 | 9 |  |
| Other | 7 | 5 |  |
| *How heard about establishment* |  |  | *** |
| Word of mouth | 45 | 57 |  |
| Noticed while passing | 33 | 27 |  |
| Always known about it | 11 | 6 |  |
| Taken there by someone | 4 | 3 |  |
| Other | 7 | 7 |  |
| *When decided to eat in establishment* |  |  | ** |
| Instant/was passing | 27 | 27 |  |
| About an hour before | 11 | 17 |  |
| That day | 16 | 19 |  |
| The day before | 8 | 7 |  |
| A few days before | 13 | 12 |  |
| A week before | 11 | 10 |  |
| Several weeks before | 9 | 5 |  |
| Longer than that | 5 | 3 |  |
| *Booked table in advance* |  |  | ** |
| Yes | 33 | 26 |  |
| *Dressed up for the occasion* |  |  | *** |
| Yes | 39 | 26 |  |
| *Mode of transport* |  |  | *** |
| On foot/walked | 17 | 28 |  |
| By bus | 7 | 9 |  |
| By train/underground | 5 | 6 |  |
| By taxi/minicab | 8 | 3 |  |
| By car/van | 61 | 52 |  |
| Other | 2 | 2 |  |
| *Costs shared* |  |  |  |
| Yes | 39 | 39 |  |

Note: Respondents between ages 16–65. *p < 0.05, **p < 0.01, ***p < 0.001

less advanced planning; the decision being taken on the day increased from 54 to 63 per cent and booking in advance reduced by 7 per cent. Only a quarter of respondents dressed up for the occasion, compared with 39 per cent in 1995, and people travel more on foot and less by car. A third of respondents in 2015 spent less than ten minutes travelling to the venue.

### Evaluating the restaurant experience: service and atmosphere

Once inside a restaurant the event is steered by the interaction between companions, staff and other customers. When asked what they liked or disliked about restaurants people responded mostly in terms of service, food and atmosphere. With the exception of two food enthusiasts who offered a dozen or more sentences weighing up abstractly the qualities of the organisation of restaurant regimes, most are not very articulate. Persistent grudges and memorable examples of disaster were the most common forms of expression, but they revolve around common themes.

People notice good service mostly in the breach, as mistakes or deficiencies obtrude, affecting interaction and atmosphere. Interviewees, when asked about service tend to give examples of unacceptable incidents or practices. The attitudes and behaviour of the waiting staff can sully the atmosphere and damage the quality of social interaction. Altogether nine interviewees had something negative to say specifically about the service. The adjectives used to characterise deficient service include: 'bad', 'not good', 'not right', too 'fast and furious', 'rushed', 'pressurising', 'slow', involving too much 'waiting', 'being ignored', 'forgetful', 'condescending', 'appalling', 'poorly trained', 'unapologetic', 'over-attentive', 'over-familiar', 'manipulative', 'sloppy or surly', 'slack', with 'a begrudging vibe', 'passive aggressive', and 'rude'. The common reservations about restaurant service fall into three categories: timing, attentiveness and crowding.

### Tempo

The tempo of meals in restaurants is largely determined by the staff and, depending on circumstances, they may appear slow by leaving unwanted protracted intervals between the stages involved, or unduly hasty. Nadine's first responses to a question about her discontents are 'Rudeness, waiting … feeling rushed'. The incident she recalls is a meal where 'mine came out ages after everyone else and they didn't say anything. … it was somewhere quite nice. But I think that's just really wrong, just really rude.' Failure to deliver everyone's food at the same time is a major mistake, testament to the power of the idea that everyone should eat together. Nicola detests 'waiting a long time for your meal'. By contrast, Arlie says 'I don't like feeling under pressure to finish my meal'. She continues that her preference is 'probably eating at my own pace and enjoying it with the company'. Stephen, Nicola, Nadine, Penny, Tristan and Simon also commented on the pace of meals.

*Attentiveness*

Penny says, 'I don't like it when they explain things on the menu and I don't like it when they're over-attentive'. Siobhan holds a contrasting grudge:

> One thing I hate which is unanimous across most restaurants is once you've had your main course you're forgotten. That's it. You can't get their attention to clear the plates or if you want the dessert menu that always seems to take massively long. You've had enough to eat; you maybe want dessert but ultimately you want to get out of there. It always seems to be a bit of a time lapse and that is a bit of a pain. It does seem hard to understand why they can't get it right. That's the only thing that's then quite irritating.

As Siobhan indicates, tempo and attentiveness intersect, the skills of waiting staff being to manage the flow of the meal in a way conducive to the preferences of the customer.

*Distance*

Restaurant organisation entails management of the relationships between groups of customers at different tables. This is a third source of disquiet. Pete finds noisy and drunken fellow customers offensive. Miranda also identifies noise as a problem:

> The only time I can remember a meal being spoiled was going to a very nice restaurant, it was an expensive restaurant. And the table next to us, it was about 10 people and they were all flight crew and they were so loud and raucous and about where and what. And you couldn't concentrate on your own conversation. And that, oh God, I wanted to clock the lot of them, but that's several years ago. I can't remember another meal being spoiled since.

Notably this occurred several years ago. Indeed, most accounts of disasters of this kind are long remembered, and therefore presumably infrequent. Overcrowding is also a problem. Tyler says of restaurants that 'though some of them are really big they tend to be cramped, and you can just hear too much and I just feel like I can't really enjoy my meal like that'. Christmas meals with large groups of diners present are mentioned (independently) twice as events with poor ambience. Too much noise, being too tightly packed together and unacceptable behaviour from other diners are the key problems.

Overall, people adjust their judgements in the light of context-specific expectations. Significantly, Arlie describes different occasions; one where the service was 'too fast and furious' and another where it was too 'slow'. At more expensive restaurants which promise refinement of food and ambience, higher standards of service are expected. Several interviewees were very clear that the combination of the characteristics of the venue and the purpose of the occasion required different criteria for evaluation. At relatively cheap chain restaurants other standards apply. Expectations are tempered by occasion and purpose, often in the context of value for money. Edward expressed a dislike of 'Things that are unfathomably expensive' – his example was a side order of chips. Lara was upset by a dish of steak and fries which was comparatively expensive but poorly presented and without any complementing garnishes. Others questioning value for money included Felicity, Miranda, Robert, Penny and Camilla.

If the interviewees are even roughly typical of British diners they are rarely unreasonable about what they have a right to expect, being on balance, according to their accounts, tolerant of imperfection. Many people will put up with mildly defective food. It is when compounded by staff ignoring indications that a customer is waiting too long, denying any fault, brushing over hints of dissatisfaction, or seeming to want to be somewhere else, that customers become irate. What is good or bad service is less a matter of personal judgement and more a set of shared expectations about what is appropriate to particular circumstances.

## Complaining

### Arlie's account

Arlie is a single woman, aged 70, living in London and retired from a lower managerial occupation in a company where she held a senior position. Asked if she complains she says 'Not often. Now and again.' She recounts two episodes, both long ago, one where the delivery of an initially mildly unsatisfactory dish escalated into a major incident, the other where shoddy general performance by the staff was effectively resolved.

> The last time was I was with a girlfriend, she was so angry. She didn't complain but she took the 12.5% service off the bill. And of course the

manager was over like a dose of salts, as you can imagine. But her service, it was … my food was fine and I had mine and it was okay … the service was a bit dilapidated. […] And they did not like it, they really did show off. They were all standing and looking at us in little groups. But her food had been … she'd ordered something, I think it was some sort of posh salad of some sort that had avocado in it and shrimp and something else. And when it came she said to me 'didn't it say on the menu avocado in it?' I said 'yes, it did, because I looked at that and nearly had it'. So she went 'excuse me, I don't seem to have any avocado'. 'Righto madam', so off he went. And they'd chopped half an avocado up and just plonked it on the top. So she looked at this and said 'do you think that's how it's supposed to be?' 'No, I don't actually', I said. She said 'oh well let's see how it tastes' and it was fine. And there was something else happened, I can't remember what it was, but that was the final straw, and she said 'right, I'm not paying them their service, blow it'. So she waited until the bill came and of course they always stick 12.5, or I think 15 maybe even at the Royal Academy on the bill, it makes a big difference. She said 'I'm awfully sorry, I'm not paying it'. She put her card down and said 'I will pay for that'. And of course the manager wasn't going to have two females telling him. But he met his match with Julie, she stuck to her guns.

And I went to tea at the Berkeley once, it was a few years back now, and the service was appalling. Everything was wrong from the word go. Our waiter changed half way, we waited forever for service. Then they couldn't find our coats. And when mine came back it was a brand new … I'd bought a new lightweight sheepskin and they'd broken the … they'd obviously hung it on the tab and not on the coat hanger. So I wrote to them and we got a free champagne tea and went back and took advantage of it. They were very apologetic. I was at work then and I actually wrote a letter while I was at work and said I was very embarrassed by the whole procedure, my colleagues that I was entertaining … I wasn't, they were paying for themselves, but that's what I said … and they came back, very apologetic and 'would you like to come back for tea?' […] It's usually a mess-up in the kitchen and the staff haven't been trained or something wrong some-where. I think if they'd apologised, said 'I'm awfully sorry, we realise things have not been up to scratch today, please let us buy you an extra glass of champagne' or something like that, we'd all have been perfectly happy. Instead of which it was just completely ignored, as if it wasn't hap-pening. And we were. We couldn't get the bill, we couldn't get extra tea. It was a nightmare, the whole thing. So I don't complain a lot but when I do, thinking about it, it seems to be service rather than the food.

The typical irritations about tempo, attentiveness and distance only occasionally lead to the explicit voicing of a complaint. In the survey, fewer people in 2015 than in 1995 agreed with the statement that 'If I was given an unsatisfactory meal I would complain'. In 1995, respondents declared that they certainly would complain, but in fact interviewees did so rarely (Warde and Martens, 2000: 177ff). In 2015 several interviewees said that they never complained despite unsatisfactory meals. A common explanation is that most infractions are not of such degree to justify formal complaint. People refrain from complaining lest it cause embarrassment and that 'making a fuss' spoils the atmosphere of the rest of the meal.

A few people make a habit of complaining and that is often a source of embarrassment and discomfort to others. Penny, who now will make complaints, says 'I didn't use to and I used to be mortified if one of my parents complained, I would be so embarrassed.' Pete remarks, 'My sister-in-law is the one to complain [...] I dread going out with her ... she could complain for England'. However, the majority of interviewees suggest they tend not to complain to the restaurant or waiting staff. Interviewees are more likely to express disappointment with particular events afterwards to their companions, acquaintances or an interviewer than they are to complain to the restaurant staff. As Edward says, apropos of an overcooked steak, 'It's not worth the fuss'. Interviewees are more likely to internally register their disappointment and vow never to return. In the catering industry, exit is a more frequent response than voice (Hirschman, 1982). Robert claims almost never to complain, and his main dislike is having food served cold. He says 'one's reaction then is, "I won't go there again".' Nicola says 'In fact, the way we complain is we don't go back', but also adds, as do others 'we don't complain probably as much as we should'. Miranda concludes a discussion about choice of restaurant by saying:

> I'm not a fussy eater but I do like nice things. I like things to be just so but that's like a bonus and if it's not 'just so' then so what? Maybe don't go there again. I sort of vote with my feet or my wallet. If you're giving bad service and you can't cook this stuff right then I'm not coming again, that's fine. But ultimately I think to be successful you have to produce good food.

Casual dining has offered more opportunities for less formal meals and has somewhat lowered expectations of the event. Often seen as opportunities to be fed while enjoying another social occasion or leisure activity, focus on the quality of food and level of service can be more relaxed.

Overall it is the interaction of service, food and the opportunity for conviviality with others at the table which matters. Dissatisfaction is comparatively rare and mostly minor. Probably there is a roughly even split between those who are dissatisfied with the food and those with aspects of ambience and service. Service is equally as important as the food, and must meet expectations of the occasion, the style of restaurant, the level of formality and the expectations of the guests. Interviewees seem to forgive poor food if the service is good, but less easily forget bad service. It would seem that restaurateurs who are losing customers should attend first to the quality of service. Tempo is critical; fast food should arrive quickly, fine food at a slower, suitable, and therefore negotiated pace. Ambience also matters; noise levels that facilitate conversation and spatial arrangements, which guarantee sufficient physical and social distance from staff and other customers are appreciated.

### Paying the bill

Cultures vary regarding how the bill in a restaurant is paid. Among the common options are: each diner will pay for exactly what he or she ate and drank; each diner will pay an equal share of the total bill; the same two options operate when especially couples, but also families, dine together – each household paying in proportion to its actual consumption, or each household taking an equal share; or, alternatively, one person (or household) taking responsibility for the whole cost of the meal. In the last of these scenarios, some obligation is usually incurred requiring the other parties to take their turn to finance a future equivalent event.

For meals not eaten alone, the costs of the bill were shared in two in five last occasions of eating out (42%). The bill is likely to be shared when eating out with friends (73% of bills with 'friends only' are divided). Sharing is least likely when eating with a partner (24% of occasions) or with family only (26%). Logistic regression models suggest that sociodemographic characteristics add nothing to the explanation; with whom people eat and how many people are present accounts for the variance in likelihood of splitting the bill.[2]

In three out of five commensal meals the bill was paid for by one person (58%).[3] It was most likely to be a man (50% of occasions) and much less likely to be a woman (21%). Some change is, however, apparent. Considering those meals at which only partners were present, the proportion sharing the bill increased from 14 per cent in 1995 to 24 per cent, with men paying reduced from 71 to 59 per cent, while women paying rose from 10 to 14 per cent.

It is difficult to calculate meaningfully the absolute costs of meals because of missing information and variation in party size. The cheapest

[2]   That is, when introduced as a set of independent variables they do not offer statistically significant improvement to the overall fit of the model (LR test) based on characteristics of the commensal group.
[3]   Obviously, 100 per cent of solo meals were paid for by the one person.

fifth of meals cost in total £20 or less, while the most expensive fifth cost £91 or more (the maximum being £780). Approximate estimation based on smaller group size of 'cost per head' suggests that a quarter of meals cost £8.50 per person or less, and the most expensive quarter cost £20 per person or more. Regression models show that having children in the household reduces the cost per person, while having a degree increases the amount. However, characteristics of the meal occasion explain more variance. More is spent when the meal lasts longer, occurs in the evening, is a business meal, involves more courses, a table has been booked in advance, wine is drunk, and a partner is the sole companion.[4]


## Content of last meals in restaurants, 2015

Even if company and conviviality are the primary considerations, the food served is always also significant. Available data does not allow precise comparison between 1995 and 2015. Despite counting ingredients and named dishes the margin for uninformative or erroneous classification is wide. Even giving a description of anything so complicated as a thousand individual meals in 2015 is taxing. Statements about apparent change should therefore be treated with caution. Nevertheless, some impressions of adjustments to the culinary map of England can be gleaned.


### Main course ingredients and dishes: change

One dimension of comparison concerns the ingredients contained in the main dish appearing on the restaurant table. Among heavily used items there was an increase in salad, bread, pasta, rice, fish, chicken and pork, while there was a decline in beef, potatoes and pastry. However, chicken had surpassed beef as the most popular meat.

The roast dinner exhibits continuity in cooking methods and presentation. The potatoes are almost always roasted, Yorkshire pudding is inevitably served with beef, with an accompanying medley of vegetables linked together with a gravy and the conventional relish – horseradish, mustard, mint sauce or apple sauce. Variation appears with seasonality, for example spring greens in place of winter cabbage. The smartest roast dinners are served with a 'jus', a reduction of wine and meat juices.

Potatoes remain the most common carbohydrate by far (appearing on 48% of main course plates) followed by bread (21%), rice (15%), pasta (8%), noodles (2%) and other carbohydrates (5%). The potato is

---

[4]   $R^2 = 0.444$

prepared in many ways and may be boiled, roasted, fried or mashed. The format widely considered characteristic of British cuisine – meat protein, vegetables and carbohydrate – survives. Nevertheless, methods of cooking, dressing and serving even the potato have undergone subtle transformation, while their role as an ingredient in cooked main meals remains. Side dishes of 'sautéed potatoes' or 'gratin dauphinoise' appear less frequently on menus than 'chips cooked three ways', 'crushed new potatoes', and 'cheesy' or 'garlic' mash, where flavours other than of milk and butter constitute innovation.

Alternatives to the potato are becoming more prevalent. Rice accompanies curries of South and East Asian origin, grilled kebab meats as well as roasted or grilled poultry flavoured with spices and marinades associated with the Caribbean and the Middle East, as well as fish dishes with Cantonese, Vietnamese and Thai influence. Dishes that incorporate rice more fully into the main element of the meal, such as Spanish paella, and Italian risotto, place meat as a peripheral ingredient. Commonly mentioned dishes that similarly decentre or even forego meat, without explicitly naming them as a vegetarian meal, are 'spaghetti carbonara', 'pasta with tomato sauce', 'prawn and vegetable stir fry' and 'margherita pizza'. In making space for novel cuisines, dishes containing pastry, such as flans, quiche and pie, have lost favour.

Restaurants mostly present food as composed dishes rather than a list of ingredients. Despite room for ambiguity, most main courses reported can be categorised as such. Accounts varied from the simple statement 'beef lasagne', 'vegetable dansak, mushroom rice', and 'roast pork, Yorkshire pudding/roast potatoes, cabbage, carrots and gravy' to 'mandarin fish in the shape of a squirrel'.

The detail provided in the survey is impossible to summarise in tabular form. Hundreds of ingredients are reported in multiple combinations. Impressions of dishes reported indicate that many comprise grilled meat, served not with a sauce but only accompaniments such as mustard, tomato ketchup or mayonnaise. These include 'mixed grills', which include different cuts of meat from at least two different animals, and were most typically served with potatoes, chips or rice, as well as salad and condiments. For example, Mediterranean variations of the mixed grill are reported, shish kebabs are mentioned, as well as dishes such as 'grilled chicken, rice salad', and 'chicken open grill, rice long grain, white rice boiled with butter, salad (huge) with tomatoes, cucumber, radishes, olives, onions with spiced red cabbage plus extra portion of butter rice'. There is a commensurate decline in meals that could be comfortably categorised as a meat or fish dish served with a sauce. Sauces popular in 1995, such as 'hollandaise' or 'peppercorn sauce', are making way for salad dressings made with olive oil, while roasted cherry tomatoes provide lubrication for grilled meats and fish.

**Table 7.4** Ten most popular main course dishes in a restaurant, 2015

| Rank | Dish | Percentage of restaurant mains |
|------|------|--------------------------------|
| 1 | South Asian curry | 10 |
| 2 | Burger | 9 |
| 3 | Steak | 8 |
| 4 | Roast dinner | 8 |
| 5 | Pasta | 8 |
| 6 | Fish & chips | 5 |
| 7 | Pizza | 5 |
| 8 | Chinese selection | 5 |
| 9 | Chicken & chips | 5 |
| 10 | Fish (not fried) | 4 |

Table 7.4 indicates the most popular dishes eaten by respondents in restaurants in 2015. Presented in this manner the range is limited and the content prosaic, although variations in construction and quality differentiate within the categories.

This table can be compared roughly with one reported by Warde and Martens (2000: 145). The greatest difference is in the decline of the roast meats; in 1995 they constituted approximately 25 per cent of main courses, almost three times greater than in 2015. Burgers and fish and chips also became three times more popular. Curry, steak, pasta and pizza, however, are eaten in much the same proportions as in 1995.

### Starters and desserts

Innovations in the content of starters and desserts are less pronounced (Figure 7.2). Common starters in 2015 include meat, fish and seafood items. There is a decline in the prevalence of soup, vegetable dishes and prawn cocktails. A firm favourite in 1995, the 'prawn cocktail', still appearing on sixteen occasions in 2015, is now supplemented by other seafood dishes,[5] although commonly described starters include grilled prawn or langoustines, squid or calamari served with lemon or a chilli dressing. 'Marie Rose' sauce gives way to a taste for umami – the savoury rather than the rich, creamy and sweet. Again, perhaps influenced by

[5]   The prawn cocktail is a sundae of prawns covered in a 'Marie Rose' sauce, of which there are variations, but primarily made from mayonnaise, tabasco sauce, Worcestershire sauce, lemon juice, and cayenne pepper, sitting upon a bed of iceberg or little gem lettuce, and dusted with paprika. Prawn cocktail was often served with buttered slices of wholemeal bread (untoasted). It is interesting to note that it was the one starter which statistically significantly changed in frequency between 1995 and 2015, being very popular when entertaining at home.

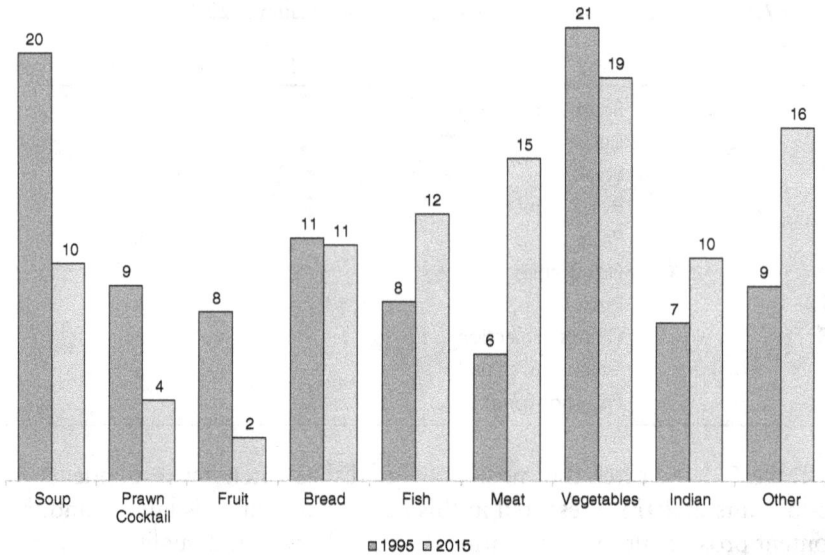

**Figure 7.2** Starters at last meal, 1995 and 2015
*Note:* Respondents between ages 16–65. Percentage of those who reported having a starter in 1995 (n = 407) and in 2015 (n = 346)

Southern Italy and the Middle and Far East, seafood is commonly reported as deep fried and served with a squeeze of fresh lemon juice, or grilled with a sweet chilli dipping sauce. Vegetable starters such as 'vegetable salad', 'grilled asparagus' and 'tomato and mozzarella salad' remain the most popular items, followed by meat and fish. Making an appearance in 2015 is the format of tapas and mezze, which comprise just less than 10 per cent of reported starters on the last occasion.

Desserts have changed the least. Ice cream remains the most popular choice. Pies, tarts and crumbles are still next in popularity, eaten on 63 occasions in 2015. They are followed by cakes, both with and without chocolate. Mousses and trifles come next, tailed by 'other' kinds of pudding, which overtake fruit as the next most popular selection. The category of 'other desserts' is relatively small, but now includes platters of mixed miniature desserts and some with their roots further afield such as 'special Turkish dessert', 'Indian sweets' and 'baklava'.

### Restaurant meals and menus

Typically, dishes are selected from a menu which is sub-divided to suggest different items for a sequence of courses. The possible permutations are many. Individual restaurants, however, offer a tiny proportion of the immense range of possible dishes suitable for each course. Menus thus, viewed from this perspective, are narrowly limited and loosely focused in accordance with conventional understandings of restaurant type and cuisine style. Menus reduce complexity and structure choice.

Some restaurants offer menus which are focused on a specific culinary style while the dishes in others are much more eclectic. Indian restaurants serve curries, but so do many other types of restaurant. One mark of the incorporation of 'foreign' dishes into the mainstream culinary culture is the extent to which they appear in establishments with eclectic menus. Consider the most popular dishes eaten out in restaurants on the last occasion (n = 821) and in what type of establishment they were served. Taking dishes eaten more than ten times in each venue, it appears that burgers, steak, curry and roast dinners are the most versatile. They are eaten in more than one type of venue. Curries are eaten in the widest variety of restaurant types – casual dining restaurants, bars, hotel restaurants, and fine dining establishments. Next in versatility is steak, eaten on the last occasion in casual dining, fine dining and hotel restaurants. Remembering that pubs and casual dining restaurants are the most frequented types of venue (around 60% of last meals) this suggests the high availability of eclectic or hybrid menus which in turn makes it possible for customers to eat a preferred dish in settings that they find most comfortable. So, while restaurants serving specialised foreign cuisines are now less likely than in the mid-twentieth century to put British dishes on their menus, more popular outlets have drawn down dishes associated with distant cuisines.

An impression of the diversity of meals and menus encountered in British restaurants can be obtained from the synoptic reports of last meals. Table 7.5 presents a dozen examples illustrating the similarities and differences between course structures, meal types and the purpose of the occasion. This is not, nor could it be, systematically representative of the full range of meals reported. However, even if not typical, each has properties similar to others in the sample, being neither exceptional nor eccentric.[6]

---

[6] The method of selection involved filtering one, two and three or more course meals, and then selecting examples which reflected differences by gender, city, occupational class, household income, and number of fellow diners present. The aim is to give some indication of how variety of foods and particular contexts might be aligned. These cannot be typical, but they are not exceptional insofar as there are other very similar examples in the data set.

**Table 7.5** Courses, contents and purpose illustrative of the last meal out, with socio-demographic characteristics of respondents, 2015

|  | Special occasion | Just a social occasion | Quick/ convenient | Business |
|---|---|---|---|---|
| 1 | **Main only** Rump steak with salad | **Main only** Mushroom pizza | **Main only** Haddock & chips with tartare sauce | **Main only** Lemon sole, with salad & chips |
|  | Type: Traditional steakhouse/ carvery | Type: A pizza house | Type: Casual dining | Type: Fine dining |
|  | Style: Traditional British | Style: Italian | Style: Traditional British | Style: Modern British |
|  | Female, 20s, Preston, Lower Managerial, White British. Eats out fortnightly. Taste: Popular. | Female, 50s, London, Higher Managerial, White British. Eats out fortnightly. Taste: Popular. | Female, 30s, London, Lower Managerial, White British. Eats out several times a week. Taste: Omnivore (H). | Male, 30s, Preston, Lower Supervisory, White British. Eats out monthly. Taste: Omnivore (L). |
| 2 | **Main** Roast beef & Yorkshire pudding with roast potatoes, gravy, carrots, parsnips & cabbage | **Starter** Halloumi, hummus & calamari with pitta bread | **Starter** Salad | **Starter** Steamed tofu, fried and raw fish, cold & cooked meats |
|  | **Dessert** Rhubarb crumble with custard | **Main** Spicy kleftiko lamb with potatoes | **Main** Pasta carbonara | **Main** Mutton, boiled rice & mandarin fish (in the shape of a squirrel) |
|  | Type: Gastropub | Type: Casual dining | Type: Casual dining | Type: Fine dining |
|  | Style: Traditional British | Style: Other Ethnic | Style: Italian | Style: Chinese |
|  | Male, 30s, Bristol, Lower Managerial, White British. Eats out monthly. Taste: Omnivore (H). | Male, 20s, London, Self-employed Own Account Worker, Mixed Ethnicity. Eats out once every 3 months. Taste: Popular and Uncommon. | Female, 30s, London, Lower Managerial, Asian. Eats out monthly. Taste: Popular and Uncommon. | Male, 40s, Preston, Higher Managerial, White British. Eats out once every 3 months. Taste: Popular and Uncommon. |

**Table 7.5** Continued

|   | Special occasion | Just a social occasion | Quick/ convenient | Business |
|---|---|---|---|---|
| 3 | **Starter** | **Starter** | **Starter** | **Starter** |
|   | Meat samosas | Smoked salmon | Soup | Beef spring rolls, octopus salad & shrimp ceviche |
|   | **Main** | **Main** | **Main** | **Main** |
|   | Lamb saag curry with mushroom pilau rice | Beef Wellington with carrots & spring greens | Rice cakes & dosa with lentil soup | Black cod, duck moja & pak choi |
|   | **Dessert** | **Dessert** | **Dessert** | **Dessert** |
|   | Cheesecake | Cake biscuits | Vanilla ice cream | Black Forest dessert |
|   | Type: Casual dining | Type: Fine dining | Type: Casual dining | Type: Fine dining |
|   | Style: Indian | Style: French | Style: Indian | Style: Fusion |
|   | Male, 30s, Preston, Lower Managerial, White British. Eats out once every 3 months. Taste: Popular and Uncommon. | Female, 40s, Preston, Intermediate Occupation, White British. Eats out monthly. Taste: Popular. | Male, 40s, London, Lower Managerial, Asian British. Eats out once every 3 months. Taste: Popular and Uncommon. | Female, 40s, London, Lower Managerial, White British. Eats out several times a week. Taste: Omnivore (H). |

The twelve meals display a considerable range, from the simple one-course quick meal to elaborate three-course meals. They indicate degree of fit between the purpose of the occasion, the company present and the social position of the respondent. These solutions to the question 'what can be eaten, where, and with a specific set of companions' make sense in the context of British norms and conventions. The range of foods is vast, but the formats much more limited. Curries, pizzas, pasta dishes, roast dinners and meat or fish with chips with a sauce are all eaten in a range of venues and can be matched to different types of occasion. The venue itself and the ambience thus created is an additional source of differentiation.

## The restaurant experience

Four outstanding features of dining in restaurants were identifiable in 1995. It was becoming increasingly diverse, it had a more regular and established place in most people's eating arrangements, it offered an experience different from home, and people of higher socio-economic status enjoyed more diverse and regular events (Warde and Martens, 2000). The survey in 2015 primarily suggests the reinforcement of tendencies already in train, as these key features of restaurant use have become further entrenched. Restaurants are moving in directions already set by 1995.

Performances have adapted. Eating out in restaurants occurs slightly more often and in different types of venue, in the process becoming rather less special as an experience. Events are somewhat simplified. Fewer courses, shorter meals and a larger proportion of quick and convenient episodes are key indicators of simplification. Greater frequency of eating out enhances its routine and regularised character. Despite more impromptu events, more people report having been before to the restaurant where they had eaten their last meal out, say more often that they expect to go again, and that they have eaten the dishes chosen on a previous occasion, implying that the food is not out of the ordinary. In addition, many aspects of the activity exhibit casualisation. Fewer special occasions are celebrated. Twice as many people are eating alone. The last occasion is more recent, fewer occur on Saturdays and more in mid-week early in the evening. Pre-booking has declined as has the time between deciding to eat and actually entering the restaurant.

Restaurant meals have become increasingly ordinary events, consistent with the diagnosis of the process of familiarisation suggested in Chapter 4. A substantial sector of the market is providing meals which do not require much investment of time, money or discernment on the part of the customer. Corroboration lies in the fact that almost 60 per cent of last meals were eaten in pubs or casual dining restaurants, locations often for simple, casual and affordable meals.[7] More people are more at ease in restaurant situations. Familiarisation makes people feel more comfortable and more in control of the experience of dining out. Nevertheless, a substantial proportion of events remain special, involving dressing up and eating several courses over an extended period of time, which do deliver great enjoyment, reflecting polarisation of provision within the market. Diversity of experience is increasing, apparent in the range of foods and cuisines consumed. People attend more types of restaurant offering more varied formats thus allowing greater exposure to and

---

[7]  Systematic comparison is impossible because casual dining restaurants were not identified as such in 1995. The term has become common only recently, as large chains have been established which deliver relatively cheap meals in a relatively informal setting.

sharing of dishes among companions as, for example, in East and South Asian restaurants or tapas bars. The experience of restaurants selling non-European cuisines has grown. Roast dinners are fewer, resulting in curry becoming the most popular-selling dish. The opportunities for more intense aesthetic engagement with places and foods have simultaneously become available. Diversification facilitates approaches to dining out steered by an aesthetic orientation which, as Part IV explores, offers possibilities for expression of social distinction and display of cultural capital.

# 8

# Organising eating

## Introduction

The previous three chapters outlined the main elements and features of eating, under the auspices of three different modes of delivery: the domestic, the communal and the commercial. This chapter compares and contrasts the behaviours in those three different modes and examines how people put the available options together in order to coordinate many different events. Through events separately and in their overall combination, people seek to meet functional, social and moral objectives and obligations. From the point of view of individuals this might be conceptualised as requiring a complex imaginary equation which computes costs of money, time, quality and personal reputation. Considerable variation between households should be anticipated, as the possible permutations permit vast variation. We therefore use some detailed vignettes of interviewees (using their survey responses as well as the testimonies from in-depth interviews) to show how each finds different solutions to the problem of permutating varied types of events to construct the platform for their eating arrangements. From these individual strategies, emerging as different solutions are implemented more or less frequently, a collective environment of food provisioning evolves. We explore how far these influences diffuse into the other modes of provision and what resistance to commodification is encountered. Household meals and domestic hospitality have intrinsic value, giving forms of satisfaction and gratification unobtainable under the terms of a contract in market exchange, and legitimated by long-standing normative justifications. People may be reluctant to forego such promised rewards.

## The appeal of eating out

One sign of resistance is displayed in answers to questions about whether people would like to eat out more. In the survey, respondents were asked 'Would you like to eat out more often?' to which 17 per cent agreed strongly, 28 per cent slightly, 22 per cent neither agreed nor disagreed, 22 per cent disagreed slightly, and 12 per cent disagreed strongly. To probe the reasons why people might differ and to establish the causes of the wide dispersion of answers in the survey, all thirty-one interviewees were asked the same question.

Reasons for wanting to eat out more include not only the reduction of labour but also enjoying intimate time with a partner and opportunities to eat with non-resident kin, especially children and grandchildren. Food variety and the opportunity to meet friends are also much valued, as is the relief from having to cook at home. Events are often welcomed as exceptions to mundane household routines. The sporadic nature of an event is essential for deriving pleasure from it. It is a 'treat' (Crispin), a more common indulgence than in 1995, but a treat nevertheless, and one which could never replace the meal at home. People want to eat out in order to be served, because they have not managed to do the food shopping, or simply because they want an excuse to dress up. Another primary reason is to escape the burdens of the labours of shopping, cooking, serving and clearing up at home. This, and opportunities for sociable social encounters, are maybe the most frequently cited reasons. However, no one declares that they want to eat out all the time. The interviews revealed a swathe of reasons for not wanting to eat out more. Eating out comes at a financial cost, and also takes more time than eating at home when taking into account dressing up and travelling to a restaurant some distance from home. Indeed, some note that eating out is more tiring than eating at home, for there is often more social interaction involved. People also mention considerations of health, food preferences, including allergies and foibles, disruption to daily domestic life, loss of a sense that eating out is a treat, the satisfaction of cooking, and a conviction that home food is superior in quality. The interviews revealed some of the ambivalence associated with solving the equation. To eat out more often would deprive people of the pleasure they take in being in their own home environment, and take away some element of control over the food they eat (valued for health and personal preference), and some people simply prefer to be at home as much as possible. Hence it would be wrong to underestimate the attachment to home and the satisfaction that people get from eating there. The academic literature gives many answers as to why the domestic hearth is valued, ones which vary in intensity and importance depending on the country and the sample under investigation. Absence of an alternative, caring for family members, economy, comfort, tradition, health, exercise of cooking skill, securing the integrity of the family are all aspects of an explanation. While eating is a universal human imperative, other important matters are at stake besides the content and quality of the food. The ideological figure of the proper family meal attributes benefits including love, care and comfort.[1]

The regular family meal has been a treasured ritual to which most families and most households still aspire. Its demise was announced repeatedly during the twentieth century but without sound enough evidence to publish its obituary. Its survival nevertheless exercises widespread fascination. It is often imagined that its greatest predators are market agents, especially the suppliers of meals out of the home, hence our concern with the connections between modes of provision.

## Women, work and the organisation of meals

When considering the overall balance in the ways in which meals may be accessed, issues of gender and women's work take centre stage. While women still do more cooking and take more responsibility for food, institutional arrangements for providing meals have changed in the last half century. More options exist for feeding family members, gender ideologies are somewhat transformed, notions of a fair and desirable division of labour and responsibility between partners have altered, as have expectations about accessing domestic and commercial provision.

Eating out offers distinctive benefits to some women in our sample. Those who cook regularly at home are particularly likely to feel relieved, if temporarily, of a burden when they eat out. Meals out represent a convenient way to feed oneself and others. They also offer other rewards. Eating out offers the opportunity for leisurely relaxation away from both domestic demands and the social obligations of hosting and reciprocity, alleviating the competition and anxiety around domestic entertaining that sometimes mars female friendships (Mellor et al., 2010). It gives women freedom from compromises often made in favour of the tastes

---

[1]    Warde and Martens (2000: 106) summarised the ideal as the 'coincidence of four elements – structured menu, mannered rituals, nuclear family companionship and housewifely provision'. That ideal was found to be strong in 1995, and in the UK it acts as a template – an ideal to which people aspire rather than universal behaviour.

and preferences of their partners and children (DeVault, 1991). Moreover, restaurants are relatively protected spaces where it is unusual for customers to be harassed by other clients. This may account for the significant increase in restaurant meals where there are only women at the table. It is not just that employed women have the financial resources to eat out more, nor that they seek to avoid cooking, but rather the acknowledgement that they deserve companionship and that a restaurant is a very congenial location for relaxed and uninterrupted conversation. The restaurant is becoming more central to the management of women's friendship networks outside of the home.

Visiting a restaurant is, however, only one of several measures that might be taken to relieve the pressure and ease the pain of burdensome domestic labour. Principal among these are the use of takeaway shops and pre-prepared dishes sold complete and requiring only reheating. Other less prevalent alternatives include eating meals in the workplace canteen, receiving meals as charity, free-riding on the reciprocal domestic hospitality system, and dropping by at someone's house and being fed *en passant*.

### Takeaway meals

Takeaway food is an important component of the British diet. Many shops sell ready-to-eat hot and cold foods which may then be eaten at home, in the office or the street. There have always been such establishments selling pies, fish and chips, fried British breakfast food, roasted chestnuts and sandwiches. Increasingly novel items, deriving from the street foods of other national culinary traditions, have become available, including burgers, fried chicken, kebabs, hot dogs, wraps, pizza, and latterly tacos and sushi. Also available since the 1950s have been complete dishes originating from Asian cuisines which can be carried out, especially Indian and Chinese.[2] Such pre-prepared food may be substantial, equivalent to a dish with several components which could be served in a restaurant (or at home as a cook-chilled or frozen dish) to substitute for a main meal.

In 2015, 44 per cent of respondents had at least one takeaway dish a week, and 8 per cent had more than two. Only 6 per cent had never had a takeaway during the previous year. Heavy use of the takeaway is associated with a less regular or routinised meal pattern; 52 per cent of

---

[2]   Although the size of the portions varies from a full meal to a light snack, the term takeaway tends to exclude small snacks and to apply to savoury rather than sweet items.

respondents claim to eat three meals a day compared with only 32 per cent of those who have more than two takeaway meals a week.

Interviews revealed the rationale for their greater or lesser use. For some it is largely a matter of conserving labour, of reducing the amount of time and effort in the kitchen at home, whether regularly or occasionally. One clear example is Lara who has several a week:

> I like different things, and I'm too lazy and too tired to cook for myself, to be honest. I do enjoy going out to eat food, because I haven't got to prepare it and cook it. [...] I'd eat out every day if I could afford to.[3]

Likewise for Luke, takeaways are the main alternative to cooking at home. He dislikes the formality of restaurants and mentions takeaway food being bought and eaten out and brought home, sometimes as part of domestic entertainment for his male friends. Takeaways play a significant role for Mal because of his very unpredictable work schedules; twelve-hour working days will be punctuated by takeaways and fast food of various kinds. For most people they are *predictably* occasional. They are a regular and casual treat for Tyler who goes to the local fish and chip shop when he and his partner have had a tiring day. Tiredness is a common justification. Enid explains that takeaways help by removing the obligation to make decisions: 'Sometimes you find that you've been shopping on a Friday and you come back and you just feel so tired you can't even entertain thinking what you're going to have, so we'll just say "oh we'll go to the fish and chip shop".' Others identify particular days of the week when they might regularly buy meals in. Thus Cheryl, on a Friday or Saturday, apparently about once a week, when her husband is working late, and especially if she has been looking after her granddaughter, will have fish and chips or a Chinese meal.[4] Siobhan and her family routinely buy a takeaway on a Friday evening, for both she and her partner work full-time and enjoy the reprieve from cooking as a start to the weekend. Karina purchases a takeaway on a Saturday, perhaps every other weekend, to enjoy the break from cooking. Douglas will order a takeaway because he works away from home and may not have

---

[3]  'I have the kebab, I have the Chinese, fish and chips, or a Nando's chicken ... Or sometimes we get a takeaway curry, because my granddaughter likes curry. That's the main sort of ones we have, really. Burgers and stuff. That's about the main things you get.' In the absence of sufficient funds to eat in restaurants, takeaways, including kebabs, Chinese, fish and chips, chicken, curry and burgers, play an important part in her food provisioning.

[4]  She says that he picks up the food on the way home, thinking that it saves her work. However, she says, 'I don't find it [preparing dinner] a lot of work but my – he seems to think it is.'

sufficiently stocked cupboards on his return. Nadine says, 'Saturday generally we will have a takeaway I suppose. Nine times out of ten …'. For others, a takeaway is more occasional and exceptional, although only Felicity explicitly avoids them entirely. She explains, 'I don't really use any takeaways or kebab places because I just don't know, I'm not quite sure where the meat is from.'

In general, people consider takeaways inferior to restaurant meals. Gerald, asked where he eats out, replies 'lots of places': 'The top of the range down to a takeaway. Well a takeaway is not eating out, is it?'. Few people consider consuming a takeaway as eating out, Crispin, for example, saying 'we eat out and we have takeaways'. Others say clearly that they would, in general, rather eat in a restaurant, including Jeff, Tristan, Karina, Lara and Penny. For Penny, who is very enthusiastic about food, the takeaway is something to be enjoyed, but about which she feels some level of guilt and suspicion, despite it being a regular feature of her routine in which it is considered equivalent to a supermarket cook-chill meal or a salad. Stephen ruefully remarks that because of his work schedule 'Some days you had to get a takeaway'. In addition, people with higher levels of education and who are in the service class have fewer takeaways, suggesting that this is not the most stylish or legitimate way to access commercial provision of cooked food.

Takeaways are sometimes used in emergencies but are mostly incorporated into household routines as part of a flexible pattern of domestic provision. However, they are only rarely in direct competition with restaurant meals. Indeed, those who frequently eat out in restaurants also consume more takeaways. We lack identical information on specific ethnic cuisines, but certainly fewer people abstain from ethnic takeaway food than in 1995.[5] This is probably another indicator of the overall greater acceptance among the population of tastes for foreign and ethnic foods and cuisines, although that does not by any means entail that everyone is eating everything. Of the genres of takeaway, only fish and chips has declined in popularity; in 1995, 19 per cent never purchased them, a figure rising to 26 per cent in 2015.

## Convenience and pre-prepared foods

The ready availability in supermarkets of fully pre-prepared meals, ones that require nothing other than removal of the packaging and the

---

[5]   In 1995 we asked only generically about ethnic takeaways and 27 per cent said they never ate any. In 2015 only 21 per cent of respondents said that they never ate any type of ethnic cuisine.

application of heat, is revolutionary for domestic provisioning. They allow people to eat meals of a kind and a quality equivalent to those supplied by the catering trade in their own homes and with minimal effort. Opinion varies on their merits. Some bemoan their role in the reduction of cooking from scratch, others are more welcoming, although often grudgingly, on account of concerns about both the healthiness and the moral rectitude of recourse to convenience products (Warde, 1997). Their spread is undeniable. Most households made some use of these products in 2015. Asked 'How often is a cooked, chilled or frozen ready meal served as a main meal in your home?', 28 per cent of respondents said 'never', 28 per cent said 'several times a week', and 11 per cent replied 'every day'. By contrast, asked 'How often is a main meal prepared in your home from fresh or basic ingredients?' 54 per cent responded 'every day' and a further 37 per cent, 'several times per week'. Ambiguities about what proportion of ingredients are fresh or basic aside,[6] the responses to the survey do not suggest the demise of extensive cooking at home, although they do indicate that ready meals constitute a substantial source of dinners at home.

As they have for a long time, domestic cooks adapt and build upon or around pre-prepared ingredients. Adding personal touches, or cooking fresh vegetables as accompaniments in part customises industrially produced food and imparts some semblance of being home-made. Thus, for example, Camilla talks about her handling of ready meals, justifying her choice in terms of sharing, health, body management and labour saving:

> I get them [ready meals] from Waitrose and I would almost always get an Indian ready meal, because we all like them and we can share the rice and it's just a bit easier. But I always steam lots of broccoli with it. When I'm trying to be very healthy I just have a whole head of a broccoli that I've steamed and the curry, and no rice for instance. Or I'll have a vegetarian curry with just the broccoli, to try and sort of balance it a little bit.

Ready meals may be seen as expensive, indeed, they result from commercial organisations adding value through extra processing in order to make greater profit. While they vary significantly in price, the same

---

[6]   These questions are somewhat ambiguous, as a great many of the ingredients used when 'cooking from scratch' are processed, cut to a convenient size, cleaned, etc. It often does not require many strictly-speaking fresh and entirely unprocessed items to be used to create the illusion of cooking from scratch.

dish cooked at home from component ingredients of equivalent quality would usually be cheaper. Economy favours home-cooking. So too does concern about control over ingredients. There is always suspicion that the manufacturer will use lower quality ingredients, perhaps use more parts of the animal, add water, or use fillers by replacing the prime ingredients with cheaper substitutes. Some ready meals approach toxicity but others, often more expensive, contain only ingredients recommended in domestic cookbooks. Additionally, there is a symbolic dimension, associated with the emotional consideration of care represented by home-cooking, which casts suspicion. Reticence about offering ready meals to guests reflects the symbolic capacity for home-cooking to mark social relationships of mutual respect and care for others, absent when a meal is purchased without the addition of love. So, while home-cooked meals may be neither technically superior nor better in taste (some ready meals are superb), an entrenched predilection (or prejudice) that meals should be cooked by someone who is in a personal relationship with the diner, in the past almost always a woman,[7] still persists. Currently, this equating of personal sacrifice and emotional connection is becoming diluted, probably not because the emotional connection is broken but because of the perceived economies or efficiencies to be gained from separating the point of preparation from the point of consumption. The time–space coordinates of the preparation and the consumption of a meal are further loosened.

Most people do not think the ready meal to be the equivalent of a restaurant meal and some prejudice persists against using them for domestic hospitality. Nevertheless, they do get used for that purpose, as sometimes do takeaways. In most situations these are considered inferior options, more a safety valve than a special treat. Along with takeaways, ready meals play a role in restructuring the gender order. Declining amounts of labour expended at the point of preparation are part of the explanation for the reduction in the absolute amount of time that women spend cooking. Commercial provision is an important driver of change as more available options potentially disrupt the status quo. In this regard, although the restaurant is especially visible because it eliminates responsibility for several types of labour, it is doubtful if eating out is the main cause of change.

---

[7]   Now it is maybe mostly the case with respect to mothers' relationships with children when love and sacrifice of time and effort lie at the core of the equation about how to provide meals.

## Getting household performances to dovetail: questions of balance

Given the various alternatives, how do people decide which to use on which occasions? No doubt they do not think about it very hard; their solutions are routinised, regularised and habituated. Nevertheless, even small shifts in their permutation might have extensive effects on future modes of provision. What can be said about the combination of these many sources of dinner?

Figure 8.1 shows the correlation between how frequently respondents access different modes of provision and sources of dishes and meals. A positive relationship exists between the frequency of restaurant visits and meals as a guest of friends and kin, and also household dinners; the more of each one, the more of each of the others. The different types of eating out are also associated positively with eating takeaway food. Figure 8.1 confirms that eating out opportunities cumulate; frequent eating out in restaurants, as a guest, as well as with hosting, are positively associated with each other, as is buying more

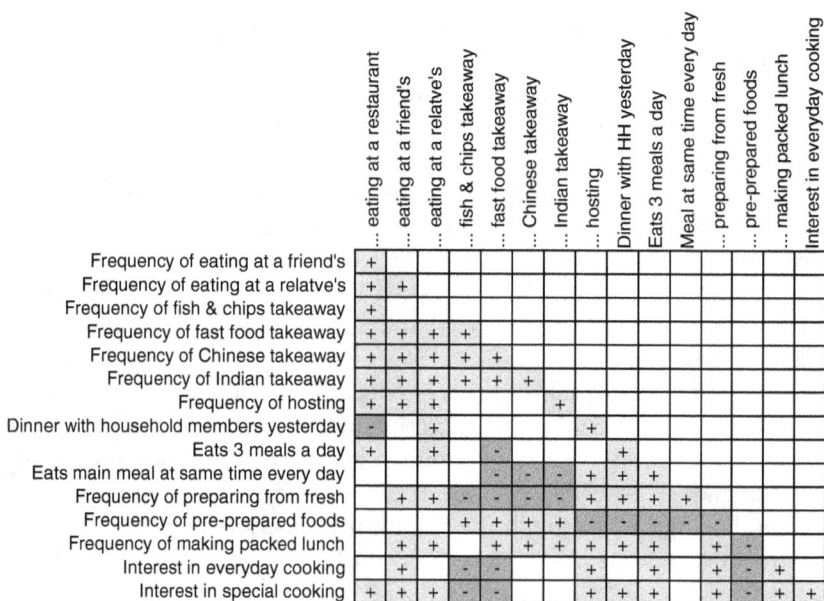

| | ...eating at a restaurant | ...eating at a friend's | ...eating at a relative's | ...fish & chips takeaway | ...fast food takeaway | ...Chinese takeaway | ...Indian takeaway | ...hosting | ...Dinner with HH yesterday | ...Eats 3 meals a day | ...Meal at same time every day | ...preparing from fresh | ...pre-prepared foods | ...making packed lunch | ...Interest in everyday cooking |
|---|---|---|---|---|---|---|---|---|---|---|---|---|---|---|---|
| Frequency of eating at a friend's | + | | | | | | | | | | | | | | |
| Frequency of eating at a relatve's | + | + | | | | | | | | | | | | | |
| Frequency of fish & chips takeaway | + | | | | | | | | | | | | | | |
| Frequency of fast food takeaway | + | + | + | + | | | | | | | | | | | |
| Frequency of Chinese takeaway | + | + | + | + | + | | | | | | | | | | |
| Frequency of Indian takeaway | + | + | + | + | + | + | | | | | | | | | |
| Frequency of hosting | + | + | + | | | + | | | | | | | | | |
| Dinner with household members yesterday | - | + | | | | | | + | | | | | | | |
| Eats 3 meals a day | + | + | | | | | | | + | | | | | | |
| Eats main meal at same time every day | | | | | | | | - | + | + | | | | | |
| Frequency of preparing from fresh | | + | + | - | - | - | - | - | + | + | + | | | | |
| Frequency of pre-prepared foods | | | + | + | + | + | | - | - | | - | - | | | |
| Frequency of making packed lunch | | + | + | | + | + | + | | + | + | + | + | | - | |
| Interest in everyday cooking | | + | | - | - | | | | + | | + | + | - | | + |
| Interest in special cooking | + | + | + | - | - | | | | + | + | + | + | - | + | + |

**Figure 8.1** Correlations between different elements of practice in the procurement and preparation of meals, 2015

*Note:* Vertical labels are abbreviated. Light shaded cells indicate statistically significant positive correlation while dark shaded cells indicate statistically significant negative association

takeaways.[8] Opportunities to access cooked dishes from outside the home cumulate for some people, while others are relatively deprived overall. Patterns of association are more or less identical in 1995 and in 2015 with one exception; in 1995 no association existed between eating more frequent household meals and eating less often in restaurants.

Those who more frequently eat dinner at home are likely also to entertain, visit kin, prepare packed lunches and to cook from scratch rather than using pre-prepared dishes. Figure 8.1 identifies a divide between tendencies to cook dinner from scratch as against greater use of part-prepared dishes. The former was associated positively with almost all activities, except for the use of takeaway food. Those cooking from scratch eat out a lot, play host, follow a regular meal pattern and express interest in cooking. By contrast, regular use of part-prepared dishes is negatively associated with frequency of household dinners, regular meals, playing the role of host, and interest in cooking and food shopping, but positively associated with frequent use of all types of takeaway food. The reason for the difference is probably attributable to greater dependence on commercial services by some groups and its knock-on consequences for modes of domestic provision. It perhaps presages an emergent pattern, differentiated by cohort, in the organisation of eating regimes in which younger people are reappraising domestic self-provisioning.

## Organising eating: the case of Nadine

Nadine illustrates how market, communal and household modes of provision are combined in the face of the obligations of everyday life. The temporal sequencing of her household routines serves to meet social commitments and the demands of paid and unpaid labour while still deriving pleasure and enjoyment from eating. Catching up over a meal serves several purposes: the opportunity to socialise, to stay in touch with friends, to meet one's care work obligations while also feeding oneself. Different modes of provision enable the meeting of different obligations, offering solutions at the crossing point of many daily practices.

Nadine is a professional woman in her thirties who lives in Bristol with her husband. At the time of interview, she was expecting their first child. Her last main meal out was 'just a social occasion' at the home of a relative (grandparents) where she ate melon, and a chicken broth soup

---

[8]   The exception to this generalisation is fish and chips, which seems to have a singular symbolic significance.

with pasta to start, followed by chicken served with a mixture of oven roasted and boiled vegetables, including mushrooms, carrots, spinach, green beans and salad. She had a stewed apple and raisin pudding for dessert.

Present at the follow-up interview was her husband, Steven. Their accounts together paint a picture of the continuum of events shaping repertoires of eating. Familial meals, both at the homes of relatives and out in restaurants, are a regular occurrence for Nadine. With both sets of parents living nearby, they are most likely to eat with each other on a Sunday afternoon, where they are mostly entertained by Nadine's mother. This she does not classify as eating out. At other times, they meet in a restaurant or pub carvery such as the 'Harvester'.[9] These are considered 'routine' occasions and thus are not occasions afforded the label 'eating out'. They eat with family in this way once every couple of months but go out by themselves approximately once a fortnight.

The frequency and choice of restaurant is guided by the purpose of the meal, which itself appears to be guided by the expectations and regular commitment to fulfil the obligations required of social relationships, on balance with 'whatever takes our fancy that night'. They have the family meal at Harvester's once a month, the meal out as a couple at a Michelin-starred restaurant twice or perhaps three times a year, and the more regularised meeting with different sets of friends, each at a range of restaurant types serving a variety of styles of cuisine. Where and what they eat when dining out is situated in relation to all other meals eaten in a given week, as well as other temporal demands upon the day.

In contrast to family occasions, where simple food is eaten in simple surroundings, she and her partner define 'eating out' as an entirely different sort of affair. A finer atmosphere than typically offered by a pub carvery or grill restaurant is anticipated by reading reviews online and following friends and public figures on Twitter. Examples of successful adventures include their visits to establishments operating under the brand of Marco Pierre White and Tom Kerridge, celebrity chefs known for their interpretations of British and French cuisine. Each time they travel abroad on holiday, Nadine and Steven also seek out a Michelin-starred restaurant, which requires them to conduct research, discuss, decide and make a reservation sometimes months in advance of the anticipated occasion.

---

[9]    The Harvester chain is known for its freshly grilled meats and buffet-style fresh salad bar, upon which there is no limit imposed for the visiting diner.

Eating out and eating in at the homes of others are occasions meeting a range of formality, company, and expectation. Each are balanced according to the purpose, options available, preferences and budget. Eating at the homes of their friends is somewhat suspect because some make too much use of ready-prepared ingredients; they mention an occasion where frozen potato wedges were cooked and served without apology. Nadine now tries to ensure that she remains in control of domestic gatherings with this particular group of friends, often by hosting them herself.

At home, Nadine takes sole responsibility for preparing their dinners. She prefers to cook simple dishes; 'if it takes longer than half an hour during the week, we're not having it'. Pasta, rice dishes, and chicken with new potatoes, are examples given. Despite suggesting a purist commitment to simple dishes prepared from scratch, they also use pre-prepared and cook-chill ingredients to buffer interruptions to their routine. Indeed, a ready meal was in the oven awaiting the end of the interview.

Market, communal and household modes of provision are thus mixed, matched and balanced according to the varied obligations of daily life. Routines share common features, with market modes providing solutions to the problems in the sequencing of activities, such as commitments to friends and family, recreation or attending prolonged meetings at work. Yet, meals out are not merely a solution to practical problems, for great pleasure is derived from impromptu, special and regularised social meals alike. Variety of purpose also affects entertaining and being a guest at someone else's home, with occasions ranging from an invitation to an informal family event, and buffets, to friendly and elaborate home-cooked meals.

## The dishes people order when eating in different modes

Foods eaten across all three modes of provision further illustrate the social and structural patterning of food selection. The limited variety reported, and the ease with which dishes can be gathered into categories, suggest patterns and rules shaping the dishes served to guests and those presented on restaurant menus. As Figure 8.2 shows, the most popular dishes to serve to guests in one's home (based on the reported meal eaten at someone else's home on the last occasion) are curry, closely followed by roast dinners. These two comprised 34 per cent of all such occasions. Pasta dishes comprised a further 9 per cent. Thus, three types of dish appeared on approaching half of all occasions. Baked or grilled fish, various forms of chicken dish, casseroles and

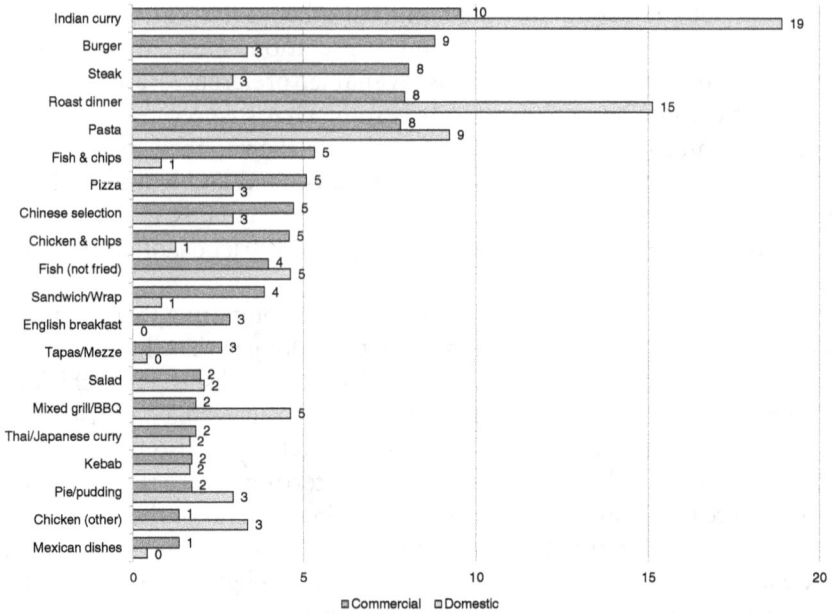

**Figure 8.2** Dishes served in commercial and domestic settings on the last occasion (percentage)
*Note:* Data sorted by popularity of dish in commercial setting. Top 20 dishes in a commercial setting displayed. All dishes listed in survey data (n = 1044); dishes represented in above figure (n = 893)

mixed grilled meat dishes (presumably reflecting the popularity of the barbecue in Britain) were also popular, each accounting for another 5 per cent. Dishes in restaurants were more varied, with five types (curry, burgers, steaks, roast dinners and pasta) accounting more or less equally for 44 per cent. Some dishes are more or less equally likely to appear in the home and in the restaurant, for instance pasta and grilled or baked fish. However, curry and roast dinners are almost twice as likely to be eaten as a guest in someone's home than in a restaurant. The dishes which are left to the commercial kitchen include fried fish and chips (which in Britain are served in both restaurants and in take-away form) and steaks (which are almost three times more likely to be in a restaurant). Burgers are also three times more likely to appear in a restaurant. Some items, which are comparatively new and requiring of skills that are uncommon in the British population, such as sushi, or are new in their manner of presentation, as for example tapas and mezze, have only market identities. The variety of restaurant dishes was significantly greater and the difference sufficiently strong to suggest that the informal dinner parties of 2015 mostly do not mimic restaurant provision.

The reasons are several, but not hard to fathom. Restaurants have chefs with skills and knowledge associated with a wide variety of culinary traditions, and the stock and equipment to accomplish dishes which are beyond the practical capacity of most domestic cooks. Restaurants have better recourse to a greater variety of ingredients, herbs and spices, as well as techniques, skills, labour power, and equipment not usually found in the domestic kitchen. The chargrilled meats described require specialist grills, tandoor ovens, and coal or wood-fired indoor barbecues. Obtaining the same result indoors at home would likely make for an uncomfortable meal with lingering smells, which probably explains why foods served with fried chipped potatoes occur much more often in commercial settings. Other dishes are complicated to the point that, as Edward remarked, if made at home 'your kitchen would be a complete bomb site'. Hence, eating out offers the opportunity to indulge tastes not usually ventured in the home. While many dishes are transferable between different modes, conventions and practical constraints mean that burgers are eaten out of the home on casual, impromptu and social occasions, while roast meats and curries are the staples of contemporary hosts. All in all, eating out seems to have a diffuse and rather mild direct effect upon domestic menus. That is not to deny indirect influence. Patently, supermarkets copy restaurant dishes in their frozen and cook-chill ranges. Professional chefs communicate widely through television, magazines and websites, although, as is often said about cookbooks, their messages may have more effect on the imagination than practice.

## The importance of (saving) time

Achieving a suitable balance between modes of provision requires temporal organisation. Arranging to be in the same place at the same time with the right companions is often difficult (Southerton, 2006). It is easier if a large proportion of the population eat at the same hours of the day, but evidence suggests that meals have a reduced propensity to partition activity at the population level.[10] Studies show that peaks in the

---

[10] Zerubavel (1981) remarks on the importance of meals as devices for partitioning the day into functionally different discrete segments in which different types of activity occur. Rotenberg (1981) gives a classic demonstration of the way in which the Viennese day in the nineteenth century was divided up among most of the population by five different types of daily eating occasion.

**Table 8.1** Meals eaten with a household member the previous day, weekdays and weekends, 2015 (percentage)

|            | Weekday | Weekend |
|------------|---------|---------|
| Breakfast  | 42      | 56      |
| Lunch      | 29      | 60      |
| Dinner     | 72      | 79      |

Excludes one-person households (weekday n = 706; weekend n = 174)

times at which the British population eats have flattened out in recent decades (Shove et al., 2009; Yates and Warde, 2015; Paddock et al., 2017). Studies such as that of Brannen et al. (2013) indicate that for many households the imperatives of jobs, school and social obligations prevent them from eating together as much as they would like. However, Sullivan and Gershuny (2018) suggest that the difficulties are no greater in 2015 than in 2000 insofar as there is no increase in pressure to engage in more activities in more rapid succession.

Aligning preferred companions and the timing of meals is one factor conditioning calculations about use of convenience foods and commercial venues. In general, predictable mealtimes make it easier for family members to plan to eat together, as props of the daily schedule which call all together with only occasional exceptions. Conversely, mealtimes may have to be constantly negotiated to accommodate flexible commitments of individual household members, in which case they are less likely to be fixtures in the daily schedule. Thus, how often people eat with co-residents (Table 8.1) indicates the integrating capacities of family meals under pressure from opportunities to eat out.

An interesting question is whether other activities take priority over the shared meal, and whether those are within the control of family members. Preferring a visit to the gym over dinner with the family is different from being away travelling for work purposes. Correlation and regression analysis shows that those who eat out frequently are likely also to go more often to the cinema, the pub, keep-fit activities, the theatre and to museums.[11] Being generally popular recreational activities, rather than instances of legitimate or high culture, this confirms that dining out is

[11] There is no statistically significant correlation between frequency of eating out and the other activities inquired about, such as playing or watching sport, opera and ballet, orchestral concerts, rock concerts and visiting night clubs. The regression equation, in which belonging to the service class and having more income were the other statistically significant variables, explained 31 per cent of the variance.

now an ordinary and normal pastime, a prominent element in an active cultural portfolio. While on every occasion it precludes a household meal, it is unlikely to be a specific cause of fewer household meals.

Another conditioning factor is disruption in the temporal regularity of meals. The majority of interviewees talk as if they have regularised eating habits. They readily give accounts of what they usually do, while admitting to exceptions. No doubt contingent events always result in exceptions to routine, but perhaps they occur more frequently now. Most studies suggest that the British meal pattern is built around three meals a day (breakfast, lunch and dinner). A recent survey of the meal patterns of the British population conducted in 2012 reported that on the day prior to the survey, 80 per cent had eaten three meals and also that 'A very large majority of people (approaching 90%) claim to have a regular pattern, mostly of three meals per day. Only one person in ten report that on the days of the survey they had diverged from their normal practice.' (Yates and Warde, 2018: 113). One of the more surprising results of our survey is therefore that, when directly asked the question 'Do you usually eat three meals per day', only 52 per cent of respondents agreed. Younger people, those in higher professional occupations, female and living outside London were *more* likely to agree.

Moreover, only 41 per cent replied affirmatively when asked, 'Do you usually eat your main meal at the same time of day on weekdays?'. This question indicates individual rhythms and the regularity involved in eating patterns and an estimate of personalised disruption and de-routinisation. This question was not asked in 1995, but it seems likely that this figure of 41 per cent is lower than it would have been fifty years ago, or even twenty years ago. Those who claim to eat their main meal at the same time every day tend to be older, with dependent or adult children in the household, to be full-time homemakers and employed in intermediate and own account occupations. A positive correlation exists between taking three meals each day and eating the main meal at a regular time (Figure 8.1).

We cannot, however, determine definitively whether de-routinisation occurs because of events beyond household control, or whether there is a normative shift which de-sanctifies the family meal. People may have the same values and objectives in 2015 as earlier but face greater obstacles to eating meals together.

## Effects of the growth of eating out on other modes of provision

The catering trade is a visible force of commodification and one heavily subject to the logic of innovation and competition, and thus might be thought to be a prime mover in changes to the pattern of food habits and a major source of dynamism and disruption. Restaurants cultivate and exploit the aesthetic qualities of eating. By deploying intricate visual presentation of food on the plate, fashions in service delivery and the interior design of dining rooms, the catering industry is constantly adjusting appearances and performances in their efforts to attract customers. The spread of restaurants stimulates greater interest in food, cooking and eating, particularly through celebrity chefs and the trickle-down effect through mass media of the awareness of variety and options (Ashley et al., 2004; Parasecoli, 2008; Naccarato and Lebesco, 2012; Rousseau, 2012). Mass and social media are, maybe indirectly, responsible for introducing new foodstuffs and new concepts for dishes to a wide population, although it seems likely that cookbooks, holidays, migrants (foreign settlers and transient chefs) and supermarket ready meals have a greater impact. Novel ideas and aesthetic standards of taste and design affect people differently. Some food enthusiasts seek to imitate restaurant menus at home, perhaps especially when entertaining guests. However, most of the dishes cooked and served are little affected, witness different menus at domestic hospitality events. Dining out also, as we go on to show in Part IV, provides knowledge and ammunition for performances of distinction, as manifest through competitive cooking in the realm of domestic hospitality as well as in expressions of taste for authentic and exotic cuisines at restaurants.

Eating out in restaurants has not affected the frequency of domestic hospitality. A couple of interviewees noted that they now go with friends to restaurants, whereas previously they would have organised domestic events. However, the stock of hosts and the flow of domestic hospitality has not declined. The stock is replenished by younger people who, sometimes, use different means. The burden of serving guests at home diminishes as the acceptability of takeaways and prepared foods increases. Despite the formal dinner party as a mannered event continuing to erode, domestic hospitality has changed little overall. Domestic hospitality events are highly appreciated and a source of fun, a symptom of their being restricted to a defined social circle of mostly like-minded associates. There is evidence of divergence in the numbers of people present, their timing at weekends, and in the degree to which they meet with satisfaction. As in the restaurant, meals have speeded up. However typical menus are not convergent.

One major attraction of eating out is that it reduces domestic labour, but other innovations probably have done more to reduce the time, effort, drudgery and cost of eating at home. Takeaways and convenience cook-chill meals, which can be eaten without pomp and ceremony in the home, subject to the rituals of relations of a family meal or a dinner party, are in much more regular use and are efficient alternatives to cooking from scratch daily. Food preparation is moving out of the domestic kitchen, but slowly. It has a long history; buying bread from a commercial baker or tinned ingredients from a grocer are long-established means to eliminate domestic preparation, but cooking at home and eating meals with the family are not terminally challenged. Of eligible respondents, 74 per cent ate an evening meal with at least one other family member on the day before the survey, a decline of 11 per cent since 1995. No positive evidence of the abandonment of the *ideal* of the family meal exists, but the frequency of eating breakfast and lunch with family members is distinctly low and declining.

Dissensus over wanting to eat out more often implies much variation within the population, some having clear preferences for eating at home whenever possible while others avail themselves of opportunities provided by the market. The marginal decline in the frequency of family dinners and a slight increase in the number of meals eaten out have thus become associated (Figure 8.1). Changing patterns primarily reflect pressures upon and the preoccupations of women. Women remain pivotal to the societal system of provision in terms of time devoted to labour, responsibility and cooking (Jackson et al., 2018). Commodification alters the constraints upon them. This is not immediately apparent, as dining out *behaviour* does not vary greatly by gender. Gender inequalities are much more visible in the domestic sphere. However, although not caused by restaurants per se, more improvisation, greater awareness of alternatives, and the use of takeaways in hospitality situations symbolise general adjustment to commodification. The subtext is the encroachment of options seen to be 'convenient' because they require not only less labour but also less planning; the decision to eat in a restaurant or cafe was made within the hour in 44 per cent of cases. Normalisation, informalisation and de-routinisation go hand in hand, both causes and effects of gradual adjustments in practices over time and between modes.

# Part IV

# Diversification

# 9

# Regard for variety

## Introduction

This chapter explores the pursuit of variety. It is widely agreed that in cultural matters broad experience is a worthwhile and commendable objective, and that there is some honour, as well as personal satisfaction and pleasure, from avoiding mere repetition and conservative observance of local tradition. Searching for new and different cultural items and forms is part of the spirit of modernity and a fundamental prop of consumer culture which requires the constant refreshing and refurbishing of the material bases of living (Campbell, 1987; Featherstone, 1991; Slater, 1997; Baudrillard, 1998; Sassatelli, 2007; Lury, 1996).

Chapter 4 identified changes in dispositions and orientations, noting a strengthening of a prevalent disposition towards exploration and greater novelty. This chapter examines further how people value and develop new tastes. This underpins a trend towards diversification, one which counteracts simplification, casualisation and regularisation. More regular eating out offers opportunities for greater sophistication, gastronomic adventures, and widening of the range of experience that the casual restaurant and a quick one-course meal is unable to deliver. The consequent divergence in experience, and its uneven distribution in the population, counteracts the tendency towards familiarisation. Differences within the population are illustrated by close examination of the orientations of interviewees towards variety when eating out. How this is represented in aggregate behaviour is examined through the survey results about how people incorporate foreign styles of cuisine into their personal repertoires. Chapter 3 showed that cuisine style remains symbolically significant, in that it produces greater *social* group differentiation than frequency or type of establishment. People combine styles, and the resulting portfolios form typical patterns. Hence, social groups differ in what they include and what they avoid. We distinguish popular, uncommon and exclusive blocs of taste. The social foundations for these patterns are identified, showing that gender, class, ethnic and age differences underpin attachment to taste blocs. These patterns will subsequently be interpreted in Chapter 10 in the light of debates about cultural omnivorousness, distinction and cosmopolitanism, through an examination of how people traverse the different blocs.

## Diversification: restaurants and the pursuit of variety

Eating is mostly habitual, both in the practical sense of how it is done and what is actually consumed. Eating out away from home is rather less routine than household meals. It is an opportunity to eat new foods and new dishes whose availability is determined by someone other than the household provider and offers a potential source of diverse tastes, both sensory and aesthetic. The extent to which eating out serves this latter function is variable. Some people are more adventurous than others. Experimentation may be challenging. Harvesting the pleasures and achievements of novelty is not always easy. It is often said that children are conservative in their tastes; they must learn to eat many foods and they typically have favourites and items that they refuse. Adults are often no less selective and avoid some foods on grounds of religion and nutrition, but also unfamiliarity and revulsion. Combinations of textures, flavours and tastes are represented, with a little justification, as bases of distinct national and regional cuisines. For example, Darmon and Warde (2016) found among Anglo-French couples typical aversions; the French to strong and spicy items such as curry and the texture of porridge, the English to sweet breakfasts and bloody meat. Of course not everyone born in a geographical region shares exactly the same tastes or preferences. To talk of a national cuisine is to mark foods or dishes which have special symbolic value and are ranked as suitable for ritual occasions and to emphasise combinations of items which are disproportionately consumed when compared in aggregate with other populations.

Restaurants and takeaway outlets often branding themselves as purveyors of specific national, and latterly also regional, cuisines, have had increasing influence on the mind and on the plate. The concatenation of a transformation in the manner of meal supply as a result of people coming to eat out for pleasure, people having greater contact with foreign cuisines during holidays abroad, and groups of migrants bringing with them established preferences and a capacity and incentive to run catering outlets which would sell the dishes of their country of origin, has had an impact on most of the developed world. Britain was perhaps in the vanguard. Panayi (2008) discerned a revolution in British food in the 1960s, the decade when national cuisines were invented for commercial and tourist purposes. Before then there were dishes in British cookery books and in restaurants which derived from identifiable foreign culinary traditions, but they were not considered to belong to an integrated or geographically distinctly separate foreign cuisine, for example Indian, Italian, or Chinese. Arguably, a false impression of the coherence and distinctiveness of discrete culinary traditions has arisen from greater professionally inspired reflectiveness about food and an aesthetic and commercial concern to attribute symbolic meaning to what is made and sold. Aestheticisation coincided with sections of the population beginning to welcome cuisines from further afield, marking greater internationalist sentiment, as well as increased international trade, in the period after the Second World War.

Burnett (2004), Driver (1983), Hardyment (1995) and Panayi (2008) present a chronology of the arrival of Chinese and Indian cuisine in the years after the Second World War. Burnett, like Panayi, thinks of this as part of a revolution. There was a further distinct wave as North American fast food proliferated in the 1980s (Ribbat, 2017). Gradually, restaurants selling other cuisines, previously sparsely present only in London until the last quarter of the twentieth century, spread across the United Kingdom. Response to the Indian and Chinese wave is instructive. Four phases of the incorporation of tastes for these unfamiliar cuisines can be detected (Warde, 2000). Britons experienced such cuisines unevenly; different parts of the population would be at different stages of this process of incorporation, and many would still avoid altogether outlets advertised as selling Oriental cuisine. The British population gradually became familiar with new culinary traditions; curry was probably no less strange and scarcely less unacceptable to a majority of the British population in the 1950s (Buettner, 2008) than is the idea of eating dishes whose protein content is insects (House, 2019). Only in later phases has it become de rigueur to want 'authentic' regional cuisines from afar.

## Culinary adventurousness

We have made passing reference to evidence suggesting that between 1995 and 2015 ways of eating away from home have been directed by a positive evaluation of diversity. This section demonstrates how practices have diverged in a manner consistent with, and driven by, the pursuit of variety. We focus on the orientation towards exploration, a very pronounced shared orientation which intensified between 1995 and 2015. Increasingly, experimentation is applauded and conservatism deplored.

There is considerable evidence of a growth of interest in food, availability and awareness of more types of food, more varied cuisine on offer, more publicity and discussion of food, aestheticisation and, overall, an increase in diversity. Table 9.1 indicates that people are increasingly inquisitive about food and willing to adopt innovations in culinary culture. More people say that they get excited about going to a new place, hinting at greater adventurousness and appreciation of novelty. Seven per cent fewer people assent to the proposition 'I am suspicious of foods that I do not know'. More people talk often about eating out, learn about food from restaurants and acquire knowledge from eating out abroad. This interest extends, for example, to more positive evaluation and greater tolerance for vegetarian meals. The embracing of unfamiliar foods and attendance at restaurants which sell foreign cuisines indicates that these dispositions are put into practice, forming cultural repertoires of eating (Lamont, 1992, 2000). Akin to Cappeliez and Johnston's (2013) suggestion that cosmopolitan consumption of culture

**Table 9.1** The growth of interest in food, 1995–2015 (row percentage)

| | Strongly agree | Slightly agree | Neither agree nor disagree | Slightly disagree | Strongly disagree |
|---|---|---|---|---|---|
| | I get excited about eating out at new places | | | | |
| 1995 | 13 | 28 | 20 | 23 | 16 |
| 2015 | 31 | 36 | 18 | 9 | 6 |
| | I often talk with others about eating out | | | | |
| 1995 | 15 | 35 | 16 | 20 | 14 |
| 2015 | 20 | 39 | 19 | 13 | 8 |
| | I have learned about food through eating out | | | | |
| 1995 | 15 | 36 | 12 | 22 | 15 |
| 2015 | 21 | 42 | 14 | 13 | 11 |
| | I eat things now that I learned about on holiday abroad | | | | |
| 1995 | 14 | 21 | 14 | 20 | 31 |
| 2015 | 19 | 33 | 19 | 12 | 16 |
| | I like eating out because it means I do not have to prepare the meal myself | | | | |
| 1995 | 49 | 20 | 13 | 10 | 8 |
| 2015 | 29 | 33 | 17 | 12 | 9 |

*Note:* Respondents between ages 16–65

and cuisine maps onto three modes of engagement – a knowledge-focused connoisseur mode, a pragmatic mode and a tentative mode – the form and extent to which individuals subscribe to an exploratory orientation varies considerably, as can be seen from the testimonies of four of our interviewees, Penny, Arlie, Cheryl and Pete.

### Penny: culinary explorer

Penny is a senior manager in the private sector in her mid-thirties and living alone in London. She eats out weekly and proclaims herself 'obsessed' with food. In the previous year she had visited six of the fourteen types of restaurant spanning nine of the thirteen cuisine styles. She chases new food experiences, both exclusive and prosaic. Her answers in the survey reveal a very strong disposition towards adventurousness. Thus she wants to eat out more, is less concerned with health when eating out, finishes her dinner always, doesn't like the meals she eats at home, doesn't think that home is best, likes to dress up, finds eating out good value for money, feels comfortable anywhere, is excited about new places, often talks about eating out, has learned from eating out in restaurants, and is not suspicious of unfamiliar food.

Speaking at interview about how she decides where to eat, she sees the broadening of her food horizons as a project rather than an accident: 'for me, it's all about what I've tried'. Penny's motto is that people should try everything and eliminate nothing prior to actually experiencing it. One might decide that one dislikes a particular food once it has been tried, but not to try is, like her young cousins, to be boring. She says,

> It's always nice to try new things. I think it's important. [...] And I think it helps you be less picky and also gives you topics of conversation to bring up with people. I mean, my cousins, I don't think they tried fish until they were 12 or 14, and they already had preconceived ideas about what they liked and what their parents liked and it was fed down to them. They were all incredibly fussy until they got to their late teens, and pretty boring for just eating veg and chocolate sponge for ten years of your life, but each to your own, you know.

She expresses breezy and unreserved neo-philiac tendencies which are indulged both at home in London and when travelling. She explains that

> [travel] broadened my horizons. I would never be one of these people that says, I don't like that, if I haven't tried it. I would always try something before I say that. And yes, there are things that I didn't particularly like. I would never eat jellyfish again; that was horrendous, or eyeball again, no thanks. Yes, I'm always willing to try ... I think if you go on holiday and

you're going to the Caribbean or Mauritius or wherever, that gives you the chance to try local cuisine. You can get it from a chap in the road or in an amazing – you know, I think there's more variety there, you get to see what the locals enjoy; you get to see how they cater for westerners' taste and all of that. There's a really exotic mix. Yes, I think when you're in a new country, if you want to learn about the culture and the history, food is such a big part … I think it's always important to have a nice range, just to broaden your horizons and taste buds. You might try something that you've never heard of before and it might be one of your favourite things. It might be a taste explosion and you didn't realise how good something can be.

She seeks and wants wholeheartedly new gustatory experiences, which she thinks she has attained: 'I'd say I'm pretty happy with my palate, but I know what I like and, like I said, I'm always looking for new things to try.' She views adventurousness and the extension of the breadth of her knowledge and repertoire very positively. Such excited and aesthetically charged engagement with the trappings of eating well is typical of only a small minority. However, it illustrates a culturally highly regarded approach to food and eating out, prioritising variety, adventurousness and attention to detail, which finds echoes in the testimonies of other, less enthusiastic, members of the middle class.

### Arlie: ambivalent responses to diversification

Many other people expect to be adventurous and to explore the varied possibilities presented by a global market. Probably a much more common account comes from Arlie, aged late sixties, living in London and retired from a senior managerial position in a large corporation, who is somewhat ambivalent about exotic food, determined to try, but with trepidation.

I'm a little bit more adventurous [than I used to be]. I'm not saying I'm as good as my friend, Alice. She would have had a go … she likes street food. Have you seen them on television where they walk and they cook the food in front of them and I'm like I don't know what that is they're cooking, is it starlings or what is it? I'm sure it wouldn't hurt you, it's up here [indicates the head] rather than here [the stomach]. So I have got better. And I will try things like dim sum. We went to a dim sum restaurant and we tried all sorts of different flavours. One or two of them, even Alice said 'I don't like this'. But others we were 'oh, I like this'. But then again they were tastes that we recognised, like shrimp and crab and chicken, whereas other foods that they do … I don't know, it might be cat or dog, you just don't know. The first time I ever went to Hong Kong we ended up in a burger bar. Because I said to Pam I must never tell anybody this because they'd be horrified. It was the only place where we recognised the food.

This confirms the desirability of experimenting and seeking maximum variety of experience. Yet such adventurousness is understood to be challenging, riven with the possibility of visceral disgust. Arlie sees value and status in being open to the variety made possible by the culinary cultures of more distant countries. She expresses personal satisfaction at her growth in knowledge and accumulation of experiences which can be communicated to others; one suspects that this would not be the first time that these stories had been recounted in conversation. Her declaration acknowledges the sway of common attitudes towards purity and taboos regarding some foods, while recognising the positive significance of unusual flavours. It also references a commonly held prejudice against street food. Some practical flexibility is required, for instance to accommodate street food and overcome apprehension that it may be inferior in quality or uncomfortable to consume in a public arena. The connection between travel and exploration in food is affirmed. Arlie clearly thinks that *others* expect her to be adventurous; she says 'I have got better'. When she apologises for eating a burger in Hong Kong she implies that shame is involved in not being open to novel and unfamiliar experiences. The elements of an ideal approach lurk in this quotation, including appreciation of variety, the desire to extend the range of experience and to extend knowledge of different foods and settings. Arlie, despite some ambivalence, wishes to explore culinary alternatives. Others are more resistant.

### Cheryl: constricted variety

At the other end of a continuum of practical engagement and range of experience is Cheryl. In her mid-sixties and living in Bristol, she reports having eaten only in restaurants serving traditional British cuisine during the last year. She scores most highly of all the interviewees on the scale measuring caution regarding new foods and dishes. Discussing what she eats in restaurants – she mentions omelettes, Sunday roast, local belly pork, scampi and burgers – she says 'we do a wide variety. I mean we don't just go to restaurants'. Elaborating, she mentions McDonalds, kebabs, fish and chips, and Chinese and Indian takeaway shops. (It might be noted that she has an Italian husband who has a broad range of tastes, so the use of 'we' may obscure the extent of her personal limits because they go out to eat together. She says he often finishes the dishes she has ordered for herself.) She does not eat spices, an avoidance attributed to a medical condition, but she also admits to being fussy and often not eating everything she is served in a restaurant. Elaborating, Cheryl says of her limited tastes, 'It's my own fault for not liking things' and, apropos of foreign holidays, she declares 'I am not very adventurous'. Asked one of the stock questions in the interviews 'Are you a foodie', she replies 'No. There's too much I don't like and too much I would not try.' So, in practice, even she, while observing a very restricted menu, genuflects towards the ideal of variety. Cheryl accepts the importance of adventurousness. She both apologises for her limitations and cites examples of how she does achieve variety. If personally rather unenthusiastically, she endorses the general expectation that variety will be valued positively and that it is important to have some practical understanding of the practice of eating out which will make possible excursions to a restaurant. She clearly also has sufficient practical knowledge to get by in situations where she does eat out and, in tandem with her husband, makes such occasions acceptable and manageable. Moreover, she eats out fairly often without reported social discomfort (in the survey she reported that she feels comfortable in any type of restaurant) and, having been the household's sole cook during her long marriage, she has a general practical knowledge of foods. One reason why overall practice changes slowly is because people like Cheryl are very cautious and adopt a conservative approach to dining out, seeking to minimise such occasions or choosing similar dishes on every occasion.

### Pete: routine contentment

Finally, consider Pete, who lives in the outskirts of east London. He is 55 years old, divorced, and earns between 40 and 65 thousand pounds per annum. He is upwardly mobile into the service class, works as a communications engineer and does not have a degree. His tastes are traditional and limited. Pete eats out regularly but has encountered only three types of cuisine in the past year: traditional British, Chinese and American. His cultural activities involve going to the pub, playing sport, and visiting a museum occasionally. He never goes to the ballet, opera, or any of the more 'highbrow' forms. He prepares fresh food several times a week and is very interested in food and cooking.

Pete says, 'When you go out, I like to have a decent meal'. He describes such meals as centred on meat and dishes which are conventionally British. He talks fondly of 'something nice like a steak or something, or chicken and ribs or something like that'. He recounts experiences of trying new dishes, some of which are more exotic, although probably of the sort which Johnston and Baumann (2010) would describe as 'socially near' – a bite of the exotic in recognisable form (hooks, 1992; Huggan, 2001). He has recently come across Mexican fajitas, for example, served in 'tapas' style. These Pete considers a 'snack' and 'not quite a meal, you know'. He likes curry occasionally and says he would like to *try* a Greek restaurant, as he's been to Cyprus a few times. He playfully mentions that he's threatening his sister-in-law and brother with their next meal out being in a Greek restaurant. He likes 'Italian and pasta and stuff' and has 'even started over the last few years eating a lot more seafood' as part of an effort to lose weight. To this end, he also eats vegetables, and tries not to eat 'rubbish', but states that people 'have to have a bit of junk food every now and then'. However, his regular behaviour is less diverse.

At interview, Pete mentions several restaurants regularly frequented with friends and family: Harvester, Beefeater, Brewer's Fayre, Wetherspoons, carvery restaurants, the golf club restaurant and Cafe Rouge. These establishments are mostly national chains and franchises which sell traditional British dishes in amalgamation with more contemporary naturalised international items. Menus include 'chicken tikka curry', 'grilled gammon steak', 'breaded wholetail scampi', and 'lasagne', as well as burgers and a range of starters and desserts. Pete's meals usually involve a single course, with no lingering, although the event may be prolonged by enjoying a drink before and after the meal, without needing to vacate a table for other diners. He seeks value for money, in balance with quality, freshness and taste, and prompt delivery (20–25 minutes is long enough to wait for food to arrive after it's been ordered). He enjoys the food and it is considered a treat not to have to prepare it himself. Nevertheless, the company of his close friends, and the opportunity to 'get out of the house' are the primary benefits making eating out an anticipated pleasure. Despite having relatively narrow preferences, Pete declares, like almost everyone else, that he tries different foods and different restaurants. Sharing the dominant discourse in which exploration is applauded and conservatism deplored or pitied, he exemplifies another variant on interpretations of exploration, experimentation and adventure.

## Avenues of adventurousness

If Penny is determinedly open to novelty on every occasion and others less inclined to radical experimentation, most still pursue variety and see holidays as a source of culinary education. Many who do not seek foreign restaurants on a regular basis in the UK make a point of eating foods associated with the countries of destination on holidays. Simon says about travelling abroad, 'I try to see what their main meal is', although that may not always meet with approval. In the case of Croatia, he notes 'one day we had some sort of cabbage and potatoes and it was awful. You get a spicy German sausage, but you get bored of that after a while.' Nicola is another who welcomes new experiences, but is not committed to it as a principle. She says

> I think if I'm paying for something ... I like to try something that I haven't had before. And I would, in a perfect world I would go to, you know a different restaurant each time I went out and I would try something different. But you have to be sensible about that.

Others present themselves as open to exploring novel foods despite being, in practice, much more constrained and inhibited. Sometimes this is because the risk of disappointment is too great, understandably a more common condition for those with limited funds to spend on eating out. Lara, a woman in her mid-sixties, talked positively of an experience of a 'world buffet' at a restaurant in London:

> There's all different types of little curry things, so you could try different little spoonfuls of everything, like ... They did lots of various little Chinese things, and you could just have a spoonful, as much as you want. I wasn't greedy, I just had a little bit of everything and tried it, so you get to know what you like and what you don't like. Because some of the foods could be too hot, too spicy for me, and I think sometimes if it's too spicy it kills all the flavours. [...] You don't feel so bad because you've got other food you can eat if you don't like that one, you can leave it. [...] It's a good idea, I think, to get used to different flavours. They do the traditional, steak and chips and stuff, I think, or they did. I do like a place like that [...] where you can just eat a little bit of what you fancy ... Because you pay a lot of money for food when you go out, and if you don't like it you feel cheated.

This is a very hesitant affirmation of the principle that one should 'get to know what you like and what you don't like' hedged round by caution. And why not? It is perfectly understandable that people restrict themselves to what they know they like. However, novelty has such a prominent place in the ideology of consumer culture that even the least adventurous need to imagine their behaviour to be exploratory.

### Explaining the allure of variety: exposure to different styles of cuisine

A good source of evidence of exposure to variety comes from reports about eating in restaurants serving different styles of cuisine. New commercial outlets in Britain over the last fifty years have given routine access to new and diverse foods. Alongside familiarisation, the period 1995–2015 has seen significant diversification of opportunity for experiencing culinary traditions from afar. The frequency with which respondents had been to restaurants selling particular styles of cuisine within the previous year and on the last occasion is shown in Figure 3.1 (p. 42). In this section we develop the analysis of the social and symbolic significance of these styles.

The social and political connotations of the apparent status-conferring properties of 'ethnic' food are an increasing source of interest among scholars. The designation ethnic is problematic for several reasons. Ethnic food is always the property of a distant culture, one not of one's own birthplace, considered part of a culinary tradition attributed to a social group, region, society or nation-state (often imagined), which honours different principles of taste and uses specific ingredients in distinctive combinations (Ahn et al., 2011). The foodways or culinary systems of the majority ethnic group within a society are never described as ethnic by its citizens by birth. Nor, it would seem, do ethnic minority groups in any society identify the mainstream tastes of the ethnic majority as 'ethnic'. Ethnic cuisine is thus not a singular descriptor of a manner of cooking but a marker of a sociocultural relationship between a local majority and distantiated minorities.

Applying the qualifier 'ethnic' to food, cuisine or cooking has recently become politically controversial. Terms such as foreign, ethnic and exotic carry overtones of Orientalism, associated with recent imperial and colonial domination, that frames mainstream food culture from the point of view of the white majority, a process through which unfamiliar cuisines are framed as 'other', thus peripheral and extraneous (Said, 1978; Guthman, 2011; Heldke, 2003; Slocum, 2007; Oleschuk, 2017). Ray (2016) makes a distinction between 'foreign' and 'ethnic' restaurants, the former already partially assimilated or having a positive culinary reputation (French and Japanese), the latter less well integrated, often cheap and associated with poor ethnic minorities (Chinese, Vietnamese, Mexican). This suggests something of a continuum between highly regarded foreign and less well regarded ethnic restaurants, both identified relative to the American mainstream. Some foreign cuisines are celebrated (and maybe thought superior to the mainstream) while others are denigrated. Some arrive with a migrant community and may be nurtured initially within that community in locales where it is spatially concentrated. Others (in some countries) flourish irrespective of whether an associated migrant or ethnic community is resident, which is a testament to the capacity for global mobility of cultural products of all kinds. The US provides the best laboratory to date for examining such processes, notwithstanding the uniqueness of its experience, and it shows the relationship between the prevalence and rank of ethnic restaurants and the presence of local migrant communities to be highly variable (Zelinsky, 1985; Park, 1997). Some types of ethnic restaurant flourish only where there is a kindred ethnic minority presence in support, but others are not so dependent. Par excellence, the persistence of French cuisine in French restaurants is not dependent upon French citizens or the French-born to be living locally for the capacity to sell French dishes.

Chapter 3 indicated the range of experience of different 'foreign' cuisines. Those simple frequency counts can be enhanced by examining the social characteristics of the clientele of different restaurant styles. Different cuisines attract different clientele. Examining each of the styles separately shows, for example, that customers of French restaurants are disproportionately white men, with service class connections and the highest level of household income. Modern British food is consumed by child-free white respondents who are currently in the service class. The clientele of restaurants serving Italian food is more likely to include university graduates, also white, with moderate and especially high household incomes, and with a very strong habit of eating out a lot. Indian cuisine is interesting in that it appeals very much to the young, and to men, but also to those with service class connections. Also, the more frequently a person eats out the more they will try Indian food. Vegetarian cuisine is preferred by youngish, child-free, non-working-class people, living in London or Bristol who, most significantly, have university degrees. Space prohibits further examples, but note that some cuisines attract the youngest cohorts (Indian, Japanese and Thai), a few disproportionately attract university graduates (Japanese, other ethnic, vegetarian, Italian and Thai), while service class connections are significant for a similar number (Indian, modern British, French, Japanese, other ethnic and vegetarian). Income also often matters, but not at all for modern British, Indian, vegetarian or American.[1] It might be concluded that a person's social characteristics, trajectory through the life course as well as economic resources influence the propensity to select among types of cuisine.

While the characteristics of people experiencing each cuisine separately is interesting, how they combine them is more revealing. Do, for example, those who eat in French restaurants also go to Indian and American venues? Patterns emerged when PCA was used to reduce the

[1]    Of course income is also relevant to how often people go out to eat in the first place so its effect, as with age effects especially, are contained within measures of frequency of eating out which are also included in these equations.

**Table 9.2** Three-component solution from principal component analysis of cuisine styles of restaurants visited in last twelve months, 2015 (oblique promax rotation)

|  | Component 1: Uncommon | Component 2: Popular | Component 3: Exclusive |
|---|---|---|---|
| *Variance* | 2.708 | 1.376 | 1.209 |
| *Proportion* | 0.246 | 0.125 | 0.110 |
| *Rotated components* | | | |
| Traditional British | −0.218 | **0.677** | 0.043 |
| Indian | **0.368** | 0.042 | −0.174 |
| Chinese | 0.224 | **0.318** | −0.230 |
| Japanese | **0.431** | −0.109 | 0.119 |
| Thai | **0.443** | −0.083 | 0.072 |
| Italian | 0.078 | **0.319** | 0.294 |
| French | 0.211 | 0.113 | **0.383** |
| American | 0.047 | **0.501** | −0.153 |
| Other ethnic | **0.370** | 0.048 | −0.017 |
| Vegetarian | **0.483** | −0.299 | −0.072 |
| Modern British | −0.026 | −0.027 | **0.796** |

Note: $\rho = 0.4916$. Bold typeface items indicate highest loadings across factors (<−0.3 & >0.3)

eleven specific cuisine styles into a smaller set of meaningful 'blocs of taste', effectively grouping together preferences for different cuisine styles.[2] PCA suggests a three-component solution, which comprised a taste for the *uncommon* (Factor 1: vegetarian, Thai, Japanese, other ethnic and Indian), the *popular* (Factor 2: traditional British, American, Italian and Chinese), and the *exclusive* cuisines (Factor 3: modern British and French).[3]

Table 9.2 indicates the weightings of each cuisine style on three blocs of preferences showing how tastes converge. The labels for the three blocs of taste reflect our interpretation of the symbolic meanings of cuisine types in contemporary Britain. The first component contains the

[2]   This technique produces factors in sequence according to the amount of the total sample variance they account for. To ease interpretation, PCA was followed by oblique promax rotation, which allows for correlation between the different factors identified, using eigenvalues 1 as extraction criteria.

[3]   Only respondents who reported eating out at least once in the last year, and therefore had experience of at least one cuisine style, were included in the analysis (n = 1034).

rarer and more arcane foreign cuisines which, with the exception of Indian, are relatively recent additions to the UK repertoire. They are, again with the exception of Indian, not very widely patronised.[4] Their exceptional nature offers opportunities for the expression of social distinction. The second group, where the style with the strongest loading is traditional British, includes the most popular styles which are well known, well established, and in their locally adapted forms supply relatively unchallenging food. Most respondents have eaten in restaurants serving one of more of these cuisines. The third component bears just two items, modern British and French. These are relatively expensive, often delivered in formal settings and, according to the gastronomic evaluation of British food guides, carry greatest prestige. The classification parallels other fields of cultural consumption where genres are hierarchically ranked in terms of rarity, excellence or innovativeness.

Table 9.2 also illuminates aspects of the hierarchy of styles in the UK today. Some cuisines are homogeneous, but the most popular ones have many different types of outlet at different levels of the market. Italian cuisine almost crosses the threshold (0.3) for inclusion in the exclusive bloc, indicating that Italian restaurants feature strongly among upmarket venues as well as offering popular provision. The negative loading for vegetarian restaurants on the popular factor also almost passes the threshold, positioning them at the opposite pole to the popular. The loadings on the uncommon component indicate the meaningfulness of the association between cuisines and ethnic identity, such that the foreignness of cuisines is a source of shared evaluation. The four cuisines which weigh little or negatively on the uncommon factor are the two British styles; American, which has similarities with British fare and has already become naturalised; and Italian, which has been co-opted into popular taste through pizza and pasta venues. So, apart from the anomaly of the vegetarian restaurant, which still seems alien to many, the first component has a positive loading for all the named foreign and ethnic styles of cuisine.

Table 9.3 indicates the social characteristics associated with strong attachment to the three blocs of taste. It shows that as almost everyone eats at some places serving the popular cuisines, the clientele of that bloc of venues is not heavily socially marked. The most powerful predictor is majority ethnic identification. That being white British enhances this

---

4   'Other kinds of cuisine' is the residual category which includes a large number of different styles whose overall moderate popularity is a statistical artefact of aggregation. The category is nevertheless also symbolically significant because it is probably the most indicative of tastes for exceptional and unfamiliar cuisines.

**Table 9.3** Bases of common, popular and exclusive blocs of taste, 2015 (logistic regression)

| | Uncommon | Popular | Exclusive |
|---|---|---|---|
| *Sex* | | | |
| Male | −0.017 | −0.277 | 0.092 |
| Female | 0.000 | 0.000 | 0.000 |
| *Age* | | | |
| Age | 0.081** | −0.002 | 0.088* |
| Age² | −0.001*** | 0.000 | −0.001* |
| *Ethnicity* | | | |
| White British | −0.253 | 0.958*** | 0.511* |
| *Children* | | | |
| Child(ren) in household | −0.210 | −0.228 | −0.494* |
| *Education* | | | |
| No degree | 0.000 | 0.000 | 0.000 |
| Degree | 0.771*** | 0.313 | 0.438* |
| *Class mobility* | | | |
| Stable service class | 0.929** | 0.397 | 2.629*** |
| Upwardly mobile into service class | 0.746* | −0.283 | 2.587*** |
| Downwardly mobile from service class | 0.915** | −0.060 | 1.953* |
| Other (Sideways mobile) | 0.406 | 0.292 | 1.697* |
| Stable working class | 0.000 | 0.000 | 0.000 |
| Unknown | −0.072 | −0.758* | 2.055** |
| *Equivalised household income* | | | |
| Highest | 0.281 | 1.008** | 0.560* |
| Middle | 0.302 | 0.522 | 0.152 |
| Lowest | 0.000 | 0.000 | 0.000 |
| Unknown | −0.072 | −0.758* | 2.055** |
| *City* | | | |
| London | 0.772*** | −0.008 | 0.801*** |
| Preston | 0.000 | 0.000 | 0.000 |
| Bristol | 0.300 | 0.260 | 0.416 |
| *Frequency* | | | |
| Frequency of eating out in a restaurant | 0.368*** | 0.327*** | 0.432*** |
| Constant | −3.164*** | −0.007 | −8.606*** |
| | | | |
| *Observations* | 1034 | 1034 | 1034 |
| Pseudo $R^2$ | 0.185 | 0.142 | 0.185 |

*p < 0.05, **p < 0.01, ***p < 0.001

propensity indicates a mixture of exclusion on social and culinary grounds. The concentration of the white British population in the popular bloc is partly a technical artefact of Indian cuisine not belonging to the popular cluster; some of the ethnic minority population avoid most venues except Indian, and a sizeable proportion of the white British population never go to Indian restaurants. In addition, the financial capacity of those with the highest level of income allows eating often in popular and ubiquitous venues specialising in selling traditional British, American and Italian cuisine.

The exclusive restaurants, serving French and modern British cuisine, appeal to a distinctive clientele. Its most striking feature is its class composition. Every class trajectory is significantly more likely to use these styles of outlet than members of the stable working class. These, the most prestigious of outlets, which appear disproportionately often in fine dining restaurant guides such as Michelin or the Good Food Guide, are uncongenial to people with a persisting working-class habitus. The clientele is heavily skewed to current members of the service class; the stable service class and the upwardly mobile are disproportionately present. Living in London has a strong effect too. Several other variables are weakly significant, namely identifying as white British, education, income, being older and having no dependent children.

Taste for the uncommon is also associated with privileged social position. Those who go to restaurants in the uncommon bloc are characterised most significantly by having a degree. Experience of service class habitus or culture – whether stable in the service class, upwardly mobile into it or downwardly mobile from it – bequeaths a propensity to visit more arcane ethnic restaurants. Consumers of the uncommon are neither the very young nor the elderly and live disproportionately in London. Identifying as white has no impact on preferences for uncommon cuisines. This is most immediately a result of the positive preferences of ethnic minorities for restaurants in this cluster but also perhaps identifies a sector within the service class with cosmopolitan dispositions. People well positioned through their possession of economic, cultural and social assets have a taste for uncommon cuisines or at least feel a need to contain them within their culinary portfolio. This does not necessarily mean that it is their favourite, neither that they eat it very regularly, or that they eat all of the cuisines available. However, it does mean that they have eaten several such cuisines in the last twelve months and that they are aware of the symbolic significance of variety in taste. A taste for the uncommon corresponds to class position and is associated very powerfully with level of educational qualification. Note that gender is insignificant, as is, very unusually, ethnicity.

## Other indicators of variety

If cuisine style is particularly redolent of the search for variety there are other indications too. Signals include the types of restaurant (fast food, fine dining, pubs), the formats of meals served (tapas, mezze, buffets, carveries), the ingredients, the service, as well as differences in interior decoration and atmospheres cultivated by restaurateurs (from tablecloths and candlelight to repurposed industrial spaces with exposed brickwork and open kitchens). Just as wide engagement in the consumption of cuisine styles corresponds with higher social rank, so too does diversity along these further dimensions. Pearlman (2013) examines carefully the way in which restaurant interiors have been designed and redesigned in recent times. Alternative interiors allow different categories of diner to feel both comfortable and distinguished. The place in which a person eats itself says something about the diner and the meal. White tablecloths have retreated, as have gingham checks. The bare simplicity of minimalism means something different from the textiles, wall hangings or pictures of others. The availability of foods in different contexts is part of the enlargement and diversification of the market, creating options allowing a potentially better fit between population segments (youth, ethnic minorities, subcultural conviction groups) and congenial contexts.

Simon refers to 'straightforward' meals with his friends in curry houses which he frequents when the occasion demands an informal and rowdier scene. By contrast, Simon speaks of a gastropub located within an historic building, which provides the ideal atmosphere and mood for a fortnightly date with his girlfriend. The service here is smoother, more gentle, and provides a setting for conversation and for attention to ingredients and presentation.

How interviewees describe and locate the curry house suggests that its casual atmosphere in part arises from markers of differentiation such as format, service and decor. Dishes representing what Bourdieu (1984) called abundant and elastic meals, of meat or vegetables in a sauce, spooned onto the plate by the diner rather than a server, accompanied by bowls of rice or naan bread, offer opportunities to share, making for more communal and informal meals. Hot flannels provided at the end of the meal assume that hands would be used for parts of the meal; bread will be torn by hand and used to mop up sauces from one's own plate or common bowls. Absence of embarrassment about food spilled on the tablecloth indicates relaxation of table manners and orderliness (Mennell, 1985).

More or less serious and formal arrangements for eating are fostered by different restaurant environments. Dining areas in traditional pubs, casual dining franchises and chains offer informal settings which are frequented and favoured by interviewees regardless of social rank. The atmosphere can range from cosy to the more functional design and lay-out of a cafe. Camilla makes use of the leisure centre cafe with her two daughters and visits buffet restaurants with colleagues. She also dines in Michelin-starred restaurants, settings for experiencing and learning about the distinctive and novel gastronomic traditions and innovations. These typically entail not only finer ingredients put together in ways rarely ventured at home, but are recognisable by the service, the decor, and the meal format. Variety thus pertains not only to the style of cui-sine, but the supporting services of front of house, sommeliers and care-fully dressed waiting staff. Customers appreciate types of service commensurate with their own preferences. Miranda, Nicola, Stephen and Simon, among others, enjoy the friendly service of the local pub and the more specialist treatment afforded by the bistro and brasserie, but avoid venues where they might encounter a sommelier or be expected to work through a long and fussy menu. Even within one style of cuisine, one can find the variation of these types of restaurant marked by their differences in atmosphere and service. The more privileged have access to and make use of a wide range, while others have limited experience.

## Conclusion

Propelled by the imperative to be adventurous (or maybe to be more adventurous than they used to be – a frequent comment from interview-ees) most people make variety a criterion when deciding where to go and what to eat. The expectation of an exploratory orientation towards food is confirmed by the apologetic tone of those who perceive them-selves as limited in the breadth of their tastes. Approaches to diversity and variety, while appealing to all, are envisaged in different ways by different people. Some, likely to be of high socio-economic status, have a broad repertoire and wide experience. While wide experience in itself does not necessarily signify or entail exceptional interest in food or eat-ing out, food is an object of considerable enthusiasm for at least a minority of this group. It is a topic of conversation, to be judged in a reflective manner, and involving conscious decisions. Even omnivores with limited enthusiasm acquire more-than-average knowledge about food and its varieties.

The increasing availability of restaurants of cuisines from around the world is a contemporary feature of the UK restaurant trade. Globalisa-tion and commodification together have had marked and rapid effects on the foodstuffs purveyed in Britain. The capacity of 'foreign' food to act as a marker of distinction is not impaired by the sharp fall in the avoidance of ethnic restaurants since 1995. Generally, people of higher socio-economic status consume a greater range of ethnic cuisine. The highly educated specifically seek out a greater range and sample the rarer species; the clientele of Japanese and Thai restaurants, for example, are distinguished by their high levels of institutional cultural capital. The social foundations of the uncommon bloc (Table 9.3) leave little doubt that taste for ethnic cuisine is symbolically significant and a mark of elevated social position. There is a social compulsion to pursue variety. Unusual, often 'ethnic', foods provide the means to display specialised and arcane knowledge about ingredients, techniques and flavour principles, potential sources for conversation about the exotic and the authentic.

# 10

## Aesthetics, enthusiasm and culinary omnivorousness

### Introduction: variety and taste

Variety entails selection; some items and activities are embraced, others declined. Eating out requires selection among venues and menus. On average, respondents select thirty venues in a year and eat two courses, quite sufficient to entrench patterns of behaviour and sediment distinctive tastes. Reasons for selection were discussed in Chapter 4. Practical and instrumental issues of price, accessibility, time constraints and convenience pertain. Other considerations are more matters of taste, when the quality of food or suitability of a venue and its menu for a specific occasion are paramount. Aesthetic judgement can be exercised over categories of foodstuffs, presentation of dishes, quality of ingredients, technical cooking skill, decor and context, service, the characteristics of the other customers, and much more.

Art and ease are not mutually exclusive. Individuals sometimes prioritise one, sometimes the other, with each entering into most decisions; price is not irrelevant in fine dining nor taste preferences when opting between fast-food chains. However, some people pay frequent and scrupulous attention to aesthetic matters.

### The aesthetic moment

Scholarly consensus decrees that in recent decades aestheticisation has affected many aspects of the selection and circulation of commodities (Haug, 1986; Ferry, 1990; McCracken, 1990; Lash and Urry, 1994; Firat et al., 1995). The effect on culinary matters is profound. This is partly an effect of the expansion of the culture industries. Marketing, advertising and culture journalism operate to influence purchasing decisions on the basis of the aesthetic quality of competing products.

Not that aesthetics are the sole criterion for their recommendations; consistency, price and accessibility are also grounds for competition between commercial organisations. Promotion of commodities in terms of aesthetic merit has accelerated since the 1980s (Haug, 1986). Encouragement of knowing and talking about style and taste is a second factor. Many people, explicitly or tacitly, recognise that taste is an expression of self-identity. Consumer choice is assumed to be a domain where personal judgement is freely exercised and where the tastes revealed will be subjected to judgement by others. Consumption is a realm of judgements of taste and judgements upon judgements of taste (Warde, 2008).

Aestheticisation facilitates and fuels enthusiasm. While food is essential to bodily reproduction, it can also be elevated to a focal interest of daily life. Like many other human activities, it can become the object of obsessive concern, its features reflected upon, judged, discussed, and experimented with (Stebbins, 1992; Arsel and Bean, 2012). An aesthetic disposition can be applied to ordinary activities; practical activities such as home-making, self-adornment, hobbies and pastimes, and most manual and creative occupations can be approached as art. Distinctive aesthetic approaches can be identified as people put together a combination of items, over time, sequentially, about which they can offer justification if required. Some things are judged better than others, are more appropriate for a particular occasion, or are effective in combination together. Sequences of outings, each with many attributes, form a larger picture disclosing features of lifestyle and social position.

The complex compound practice of eating can be subjected to extensive and critical reflection, a potentiality realised by people popularly referred to as 'foodies'. It is a term widely used in the UK now which belies precise definition but implies exceptional enthusiasm in culinary matters. The term 'foodie' arose in almost all the interviews, sometimes introduced spontaneously by the interviewee, sometimes by the interviewer. Only a few failed to recognise the term. When asked if they themselves were foodies the majority said no, two were ambivalent, and seven wholeheartedly embraced the label. Interestingly, the self-confessed foodies were all women.

Differences emerge around the valence of the term. Whether being a foodie is a matter of congratulation or censure is controversial. A quarter of the interviewees hold an unequivocally positive attitude (unsurprisingly including most of those who deem themselves foodies). They see foodies as 'cultured' and 'refined', appreciating aesthetic and experiential aspects of eating and cooking, and making the most of opportunities for breadth of experience. Being a foodie is an achieved status.

Another quarter are equally unequivocally negative. Foodies are referred to as 'pretentious', 'gourmets' or 'food snobs', exhibiting an unseemly degree of concern, even obsession, with food, and overvaluing its decorative and obscure elements.[1] Those who are adamantly critical are all men, often older, who take a utilitarian approach to eating, preferring 'volume' to finesse and liking unembellished dishes. Robert for example says, 'I think we are lucky to be able to eat at all and the idea of incredibly elaborate preparations being made passes me by. Food is not a recreation for me, it's a pleasure but it's a necessity.'

Valence judgements aside, a common understanding of the term emerges from discussion of whether or not they, or sometimes other people of their acquaintance, are foodies. A foodie is someone with a good deal of specialised knowledge, an appreciation of the unusual and a passionate interest in eating and cooking.[2]

The most authoritative scholarly examination of the foodie syndrome is the work of Johnston and Baumann (2010) which, having traced new aesthetic approaches to food and eating in gourmet periodicals in the US in 2004, interviewed a sample of thirty self-confessed foodies. Frames of exoticism and authenticity form two central qualities which shape foodie discourse. Authenticity appeals to geographic specificity, simplicity, personal connection and history, deciphered through reference to the origin of ingredients, such as olive oil and balsamic vinegars, and celebration of the simplicity of unschooled cookery. Successful engagement with authentic foods demands some specialised gastronomic knowledge (most commonly obtained from professional food writing), usually accompanied by a conviction that authentic foods are finer than their industrially produced counterparts. Exotic foods, by contrast, are framed as exciting and unusual, giving opportunities to break food norms and transgress mainstream taste profiles. Achieved via foreign foods and cuisines, exoticism is at its most distinctive when the socially distant is combined with the norm-breaking. The opposite, a taste for the familiar and normal, is the preference for socially near and popular foods.

Presenting themselves as adventurous and even obsessed explorers with a sensory and sensual relationship with food, foodies avidly evaluate food, with each meal an opportunity to assess the quality of the food and the experience – judgements which they may share with friends and strangers online though blogs and other social media platforms. However, while they have wide-ranging tastes, they do not like everything indiscriminately. Their analysis suggests that such considerations – part of

---

[1]   The rest fall between, with equal proportions tending to be positive or negative.
[2]   Foodies normally cook, or at least understand the technical aspects of cooking.

what may appear to be an open, democratic and omnivorous engagement with diverse food cultures – serve as a means of conferring status
and reproducing privilege. 'Foodyism' is a statement of social position
and an expression of cultural capital which exhibits class effects consistent with the diagnosis of the cultural omnivore thesis through appropriation of variety and by appreciation of both apparently modest and
unpretentious street food and haute cuisine.

The rest of this chapter teases out the relationship between aestheticisation, enthusiasm and the cultural omnivore orientation. In the next
section we identify a segment of the population of high socio-economic
status who, in respect of their exposure to different cuisine styles, display culinary omnivorousness. We then analyse some of the important
differences among the fifteen interviewees who exhibit omnivorous
behaviour. The degree to which they experience variety of cuisines is one
such difference, and their voraciousness provides a pretext for returning
to the survey one last time to examine significant differences between
'major' and 'minor' omnivores. The penultimate section, after a short
interlude discussing the measurement of class, compares models which
predict major and minor omnivore status, in order to examine the relationship between distinction and enthusiasm and their significance for
divisions within the service class. We conclude by reiterating the symbi-
otic relationship between divergence in supply, the regard for variety
and the increased role of aesthetic judgement in food practices.

## Variety and omnivorousness

A central topic of cultural sociology, the issue of variety became more
important in the context of debates about the implosion of high culture
(Peterson and Kern, 1996). The cultural omnivore thesis predicts that
some groups in the population will enjoy a greater variety of experience
than others, and that this occurs in particular combinations. The thesis
maintains that, in recent decades, people of high socio-economic status
have tended to display knowledge, liking and participation of a wide
variety of cultural activities and genres, and that this is the foremost
contemporary way to exhibit distinction. The basic contention is that
whereas in the mid-twentieth century distinction was expressed through
mastery of high culture (of opera, classical music, modern literature,
etc.), a sole focus on forms of legitimate culture has come to be seen as
narrow and snobbish, and that any display of cultural competence
requires the incorporation of elements of popular culture. The most
profitable disposition of cultural capital requires command of forms on

both sides of the boundary between high and popular cultures (Peterson and Kern, 1996; Peterson, 1997; Bennett et al., 2009). The thesis anticipates that, if dining out is a field where symbolic messages about cultural taste and social rank circulate, people of high status will embrace variety in available goods and practices (Warde et al., 1999).

### Cultural omnivorousness: the foundations of restricted, modal and omnivore repertoires

The likelihood that those acquainted with 'exclusive' cuisine styles will also eat the other styles is a rigorous criterion for identifying an omnivorous disposition, because it involves bridging cultural categories or genres with hierarchically disparate reputations. Table 9.2 (p. 171) shows that exposure to different cuisine styles clusters into three blocs. The restaurants visited by respondents in the last twelve months could all have lain within a single bloc or, alternatively, in any two, or in all three. Three blocs permit seven combinations. Very few people (1%) eat only in exclusive venues, suggesting that old forms of snobbery are minimal. Eight per cent eat only uncommon cuisines, notable because they are disproportionately non-white British respondents. A substantial proportion (28%) have only eaten in restaurants selling popular cuisines. Of three possible dual combinations only that of 'popular and uncommon' contains many respondents (37%). Finally, 18 per cent of respondents have eaten in at least one venue in each category.

We examine the socio-economic characteristics of each the three largest groups.[3] The first group contains people who had only eaten *popular* cuisines, the second and largest combines the *popular* and *uncommon*, the third had eaten in all three categories.[4] If the restaurants in each group offer symbolically different types of experience, then to span all three might be seen as obeying a social imperative to explore variety and to express an eclectic or omnivorous disposition. The groups, which are not real social groups but rather repertoires of practice, we will call *restricted, modal* and *omnivore*.

---

[3]  n = 841. We exclude the remaining four categories from analysis due to low cell counts.

[4]  Note that the calculation is based on whether people have eaten in one or more restaurants in a given bloc, so it is possible to register as an omnivore by eating in only three restaurants during the last year if each was from a different bloc.

The key characteristics of the *restricted* group, who had eaten only popular cuisines, can be gleaned from Table 9.3 (second column, p. 173). The clientele of this category of restaurants, ordinary places which most people visit sometimes, is socially indistinct, with the exception of a disproportionate *absence* of people who identify as other than white British. Respondents who eat only in these outlets have limited experience of culinary variety, hence the designation 'restricted'.

The differences between the restricted group and the other two are shown in a multinomial regression model (Table 10.1). The modal group, the most numerous, who attend both uncommon and popular

**Table 10.1** Restricted, modal and omnivore patterns of taste, 2015 (multinomial logistic regression)

|  | Restricted (base) | Modal | Omnivore |
|---|---|---|---|
| *Sex* | | | |
| Male | | 0.006 | 0.283 |
| Female | | 0.000 | 0.000 |
| *Age* | | | |
| Age | | 0.084* | 0.194*** |
| Age² | | −0.001** | −0.002*** |
| *Ethnicity* | | | |
| White British | | −0.238 | 0.463 |
| Other ethnic | | 0.000 | 0.000 |
| *Child(ren) in household* | | | |
| Adult only household (16 and over) | | 0.000 | 0.000 |
| Children in household (under 16s) | | −0.346 | −0.636* |
| *Education* | | | |
| Degree or higher | | 0.734*** | 1.252*** |
| Less than degree level | | 0.000 | 0.000 |
| *Social mobility* | | | |
| Stable service class | | 0.659 | 3.112** |
| Upwardly mobile into service class | | 0.849* | 3.192** |
| Downwardly mobile from service class | | 1.084** | 2.867** |
| Other (sideways mobile between intermed) | | 0.512 | 1.833 |
| Stable working class | | 0.000 | 0.000 |
| Unknown | | 0.138 | 2.394* |
| *Equivalised household income (tertiles)* | | | |
| Highest | | 0.071 | 0.787* |
| Middle | | 0.254 | 0.575 |

(Continued)

**Table 10.1** Continued

|                          | Restricted (base) | Modal      | Omnivore    |
|--------------------------|:-----------------:|:----------:|:-----------:|
| Lowest                   |                   | 0.000      | 0.000       |
| Unknown                  |                   | 0.365      | 0.937*      |
| *City*                   |                   |            |             |
| London                   |                   | 0.586*     | 1.858***    |
| Bristol                  |                   | 0.120      | 1.092***    |
| Preston                  |                   | 0.000      | 0.000       |
| *Frequency of eating out*|                   |            |             |
| Frequency of eating out  |                   | 0.360***   | 0.920***    |
| Constant                 |                   | −3.265***  | −13.371***  |
| Obs                      | 841               |            |             |
| Pseudo R$^2$             | 0.207             |            |             |

*p < 0.05, **p < 0.01, ***p < 0.001

restaurants are, when compared with the referent group, much more likely to eat out frequently and especially to hold degree level qualifications. They are a little older on average but not elderly, have experienced social mobility, and live in London. The modal group has a weak class profile and is less socially distinguished by class than the omnivore group. Education and class of origin distinguish them from the restricted group, but this is not the domain of the stable service class. The weak positive effect from living in London is presumably due to the greater ease of access to restaurants serving congenial uncommon cuisines. Ethnic identity has no effect because uncommon cuisines are equally popular with ethnic minorities and the ethnic majority population.

Omnivores, regardless of the extent of their experience, differ from the restricted referent group on a greater number of dimensions: they are more concentrated in the middle age categories, better educated, especially likely to live in London or Bristol, eat out more frequently, have greater experience of the service class and have the highest level of income. The omnivore group is of higher socio-economic status than either of the others, with class trajectory being especially significant.

The evidence is consistent with the cultural omnivore thesis. Just fewer than one in five respondents display an omnivorous orientation, crossing hierarchical boundaries between popular, uncommon and exclusive venues. Taste for variety remains greatest among people in higher social positions. People of higher social rank most heavily patronise restaurants serving the most highly ranked cuisines. Among these, taste for the uncommon ostensibly confers distinction. Having a degree-level qualification is an especially powerful predictor of the use of a range of ethnic restaurants. In line with Bourdieusian expectations, those with the highest levels of institutional cultural capital distinguish themselves by their permutations among foreign cuisines. Class position and taste are mutually adjusted with preferences within a hierarchy of cuisines running parallel to social rank.

## Meeting omnivores

Of the thirty-one interviewees, fifteen fall into the category of omnivore.[5] Of these, some are men, some women, and they vary by age, location and domestic circumstances. A large majority hold a degree, have service class connections and identify as white British. By our definition, culinary omnivores have recently visited restaurants selling exclusive, uncommon and popular cuisines, thus exhibiting considerable variety of culinary experience. Aware from the literature that not all omnivores are the same (Ollivier, 2008; Ollivier et al., 2008; Warde et al., 2008), we looked for internal heterogeneity within the group.

Dining out offers great opportunity for experiencing and exercising judgement about a wide variety of features and has always attracted people, usually men in the past, who approach food from an aesthetic point of view. The interviewee best representing and reflecting such concerns is Edward. His answers in the survey put him in the category of omnivore and we describe his practices in some detail before comparing his behaviour with that of other omnivorous interviewees.

### Portrait of an enthusiast: Edward

'I'm not a fussy eater but I do like nice things.'

Edward has a substantial household income, a university degree, a service class occupation in the culture industries, no dependent children, and lives in inner London. He exhibits omnivorous food-related behaviours, not only eating out frequently in restaurants and at the home of friends, entertaining others, appreciating prolonged meals and liking formality in its place. He is also interested in food shopping and in reading recipes.

---

[5]  As pointed out in Chapter 2, the criteria for selection of interviewees was slanted towards respondents with a declared interest in food, hence the disproportionate number of omnivores.

Although he does eat fast food and Chinese and Indian takeaways, he 'never' buys from fish and chip shops, nor did he visit a casual dining restaurant or eat bar food in the twelve months prior to survey.

Edward thus has experience of a wide range of different places and different foods. He mentions in his interview having eaten tapas, street food, sliders, 'free from',[6] nose-to-tail, buffets, English breakfast, roast Sunday lunch, 'unbelievably delicious' Chinese spicy cuisine, burgers, fried chicken, steak and chips, chitterlings, deconstructed stew, avocado and cocoa powder, poached chicken, melanzane and Vietnamese rolls. He makes basic omnivore claims: 'I like to try everything' and 'I am happy with anything'. He also asserts that he has no wish to impose his opinions or tastes on others. Remarking that 'to be successful [a restaurant will] have to produce good food', apropos of a popular chain he says,

> Lots of people like bad coffee. And I don't care, that's up to them. And it's only bad to me as well, that's just my opinion, [and therefore] I won't go. I'm not going to judge someone for liking something I don't like.

This tolerance is associated with an adventurous and open disposition involving experimentation and connoisseurship. He tries the same dish in different restaurants, or even in the same restaurant, in order to conduct comparative taste tests; the example he gives is a Chinese soup.

Edward talks of the authentic, the exceptional and the unusual. He recognises authenticity in relation to both local and foreign cuisine. For example, he describes fondly regular breakfasts with his father in 'a real workers' cafe' and he is mildly perturbed by a local Chinese chef who has 'tweaked it for an English palate'. Critical judgement is applied to all aspects of the restaurant experience, standards of service, atmosphere, menu construction and cooking. He knows how the food should be cooked and served, and avoids dishes he might prepare better himself. He detects pretension, distinguishes a 'fad' from the truly delicious, and identifies tricks that restaurants use to make more profit. He appears very knowledgeable and well capable of differentiating between occasions, and matching locations and menus to suit. He gets genuine pleasure and satisfaction from the rhythms of a meal where he can enjoy 'nice service and nice wine', sit with company for two or three hours, eating a sequence of interesting dishes. He notes that

> it's really nice to have good service and stuff like that because you're going out, you're inevitably going to be paying a good amount of money, so it

---

6   Concern about allergies has resulted in food providers advertising foods and dishes which do not contain certain ingredients such as gluten, milk and nuts.

makes sense that the whole experience is nice. [...] my wife, she likes it to be a special occasion. I just like the food. Well I like the special occasion as well but I specifically like to eat things that I'm definitely not capable of cooking.

Some dishes he would not attempt, because of lack of required techniques or equipment, or because they would cause too much mess or smoke. He thus makes judgements not only by comparing restaurants but also by comparing what is eaten out to what he prepares at home.

Edward is informed by discussions with friends and restaurant critics. He trusts the reviews of Giles Coren, Jay Rayner and Grace Dent. If a restaurant nearby receives a good review he will visit. He is, however, wary of recommendations, conscious that he might not share the tastes of a particular reviewer. He says that he would hate to spend '£300 or £400 for a meal, which is definitely not something we'd be doing regularly' and be 'massively disappointed'. He is wary of recommendations from friends which may involve some posturing. He notes that sometimes 'people want to tell you that they've been there as much as go there themselves ... Fine. I've probably done the same thing.'

He has a routinised and regularised way to combine eating in and eating out. He describes weekday dinners with his wife as occasions guided by their concern for healthy eating. Cutting down on red meat – citing explicitly ethical, cost and environmental reasons – is one aspect of his search for a 'healthier' diet. He is reducing consumption of gluten and has been experimenting with recipes from clean-eating mogul 'Deliciously Ella' and 'Hemsley and Hemsley', which he and his wife used to make 'courgetti' with their the newly purchased 'spiraliser'.

Edward distances himself slightly from the label of 'foodie', primarily because he has some friends whom he thinks more deserve the label. He considers the term a compliment rather than a criticism, and sees connoisseurship as admirable. His friends are 'real' foodies with a 'real intricate knowledge', 'and love of very specific food niches', whereas he positions himself as simply liking it 'when it's really good'. Nevertheless, he admits that 'a lot of my friends are foodies so probably I feel pressure to try and give them something that will maybe impress them'. Meeting their expectations does not always come easily to Edward, despite his high level of competence, knowledge and experience in the culinary field.

Edward is very active in other cultural fields, has an active family life with his wife and wider kin, and an absorbing and time-consuming job.[7]

---

[7]  The survey shows that culinary omnivorousness is associated with cultural omnivorousness more generally. Those who consume many kinds of cuisine also participate extensively in a wide range of other cultural activities.

He obtains variety across a broad canvas, exhibits a sense of assurance, which barely wavers, about performances based on reflection, routine, research, and a wide knowledge based in practice as well as reading. Edward displays the dispositions and experience definitive of a cultural omnivore and a contemporary food enthusiast.

### Other omnivores

Edward's enthusiasm is both broad and deep and includes an exceptional level of aesthetic reflection. Among omnivores we detect four lines of fracture. The first is that some omnivores show little aesthetic appreciation. Douglas, for example, has the social attributes of a voracious omnivore; he is single, in his thirties, living in London, a doctor with service class parents. He eats out a great deal in a wide variety of venues because unpredictable arrangements around work mean that he frequently needs to eat away from home. He sees those occasions as opportunities to meet his friends but he is largely indifferent to the aesthetics of the food. Robert, a retired teacher, is another very little interested in epicurean matters. However, while disdaining 'the idea of incredibly elaborate preparations' and declaring that 'food is not a recreation', he nevertheless belongs to a social circle which guarantees extensive experience of dining out.

By contrast with Douglas and Robert, who are omnivores almost by accident, others are interested, engaged and widely experienced. Penny, encountered earlier (pp. 163–164), is an example of someone highly enthusiastic about food, particularly eating out but not very reflective and critical about the quality of food delivered. Nor does she carry over her strong interest in the variety and quality of food into the domestic arena; she cooks very little at home and confesses to being neither skilled nor much interested. Relatively limited cooking skills and shortage of time mean that many omnivores eat fairly simple or ordinary domestic meals. This is also true of Arlie, Nicola and Lara who, like many other women with primary responsibility for preparing domestic meals, are reluctant to lavish extensive attention or thought on day-to-day domestic cookery and restrict their enthusiasm to eating out occasions. Indeed, among our interviewees, those most skilled and dedicated to cookery were not omnivores and did not eat out expansively.

Domestic obligations to family, to partners and especially to children, do not divide people by disposition necessarily, but do affect patterns of behaviour. Several of the omnivores – all women – refer to themselves as foodies, in a manner connoting less aesthetic connoisseurship than straightforward enjoyment of food eaten out and especially the social pleasures of the occasion. Apparently Siobhan and Camilla would adopt distinctive and more elaborate profiles while eating out were it not for their childcare responsibilities. Siobhan says that her practice has evolved to suit the needs of her children who cannot reliably be taken to more formal dining environments because they might dirty tablecloths and cause mischief, but also such establishments do little to cater to the restricted palates of small children. Circumstances restrict the breadth and depth of her engagement in epicurean dining, but her dispositions include a range of types and styles of cuisine, from the kind of informal restaurant that allows for children, such as chain Italian restaurants and gastropubs, to the finest of dining establishments.

Money is another constraint. Omnivores are financially relatively affluent but some, like Luke, are at the beginning of their careers and strapped for cash. He claims to have never had much money but to enjoy food immensely. When asked what kinds of establishment he frequents, he responds: 'all sorts really, yeah and absolutely anything. There's quite a few good, like, falafel and wrap kind of places in Bristol that I love to go to. There's a lot of variety here and then just anything I suppose, burgers, pizzas.' He rarely patronises the exclusive cuisine styles and restaurant types because of his limited income, although his social network brings him opportunities to eat in fashionable London restaurants such as Moro which serve 'uncommon' cuisines. He has social and cultural capital – his parents once owned and ran a restaurant and he grew up engaged with food and cooking – which guides him through diverse options. Currently he experiments with creative vegetarian cooking and he finds fresh and interesting food in Bristol, such as a Korean–European fusion organic cafe where he can eat a three-course set menu for as little as £12.50. His limited budget does not prevent him from exploring a wide variety of ethnic eateries in Bristol.

Hence, one can have omnivorous experience without being enthusiastic about eating out or showing connoisseur tendencies. One can be enthusiastic while lacking the resources of time or money which permit extensive engagement in dining out. One can be immersed in critical appreciation of restaurant culture without taking its lessons or inspiration into the domestic kitchen. In addition, a further dimension of difference, highly germane to the debate about cultural omnivorousness, is the absolute range of culinary experience encountered. Edward, Siobhan, Penny, Douglas, Tristan, Luke and Nadine have experienced more different styles than the others, and we designate them '*major* omnivores'. They are not homogenous in their behaviours, although except for Douglas they are enthusiastic and evidently appreciative of their breadth of engagement.

In the next section we return to the survey data to identify the distinctive characteristics and behaviour of major omnivores, differentiating between those with more experiences of cuisine style in the last year and those with fewer.

## Omnivorousness and class

### *Approaches to class*

The conceptualisation, theorisation and measurement of class remain contentious in sociological analysis. One dispute concerns the relative merits of employment aggregate and assets approaches (Savage et al., 2005; Crompton, 2008). The former operationalise class solely in terms of economic position (e.g. Erikson and Goldthorpe, 1992; Rose and Pevalin, 2003; Weeden and Grusky, 2005). The latter, most often in Bourdieusian fashion, consider in addition cultural and social 'capitals, assets and resources' (CARs) (Bourdieu, 1984; Bennett et al., 2009; Savage et al., 2005). Up to this point in the analysis a single measure of social class has been used – intergenerational trajectory – constructed on the basis of the reported occupations of respondents and the principal earner in their household of origin at minimum school leaving age. However, the survey posed many other questions to respondents regarding their resources in order to take into account determinants of cultural practice which asset-based theories identify as foundations of differential class experience. Survey questions about household income, cultural participation and social connections were employed to construct CARs models. The models comprise a core set of control variables – sex, age, ethnic identity, presence of dependent children, having a partner, and city of residence. Class position is operationalised as household income (five levels), having a degree, rate of cultural participation, rank of social connections, mothers and/or fathers having highbrow cultural interests (classical music, art, reading) and length of time living in the current city. Rate of cultural participation is a composite measure of the frequency of participation in various cultural and recreational activities including sport, the use of pubs, cinema, concerts and religious meetings. Status of social connection uses the position generator technique (Lin, 2001) to estimate the mean status of acquaintances in difference occupations as calibrated by the Cambridge scale (Stewart et al., 1980). Each of these independent variables predicts some aspects of the dining out experience and, taken together, they comprise an effective and parsimonious bank of variables to account for behaviour. Many points of methodological interest arise to fascinate experts in social stratification, but for present purposes we seek only to contrast two operational definitions of class, intergenerational trajectory and a reduced assets version.

One way to demonstrate the power of these different operational schemes for class is to look at how they compare when trying to explain specific phenomena. We therefore take a final look at the issue of omnivorousness by using, in tandem, the information drawn from the trajectory and the assets models to draw some analytic conclusions. A more nuanced understanding of the impulse for dining out is obtained by combining the results from each.

### Major and minor omnivores: statistical profiles

Culinary omnivores, defined by their proclivity for visiting popular, uncommon and exclusive restaurants, comprise 18 per cent of the survey population. Some had eaten only a few of the twelve available styles listed in the survey, while others had eaten in most. We partition the omnivores into two groups on the basis of the total number of styles experienced, which is consistent with the convention that omnivorousness may be measured by both the volume and the composition of items of appropriate symbolic significance. These were defined as low volume, 'minor', omnivores (n ≤ 6 styles) and high volume, 'major', omnivores (n ≥ 7 styles).[8] The division among the omnivores was designed to isolate two potentially separate sources of motivation, one lying in social distinction, the other in gastronomic enthusiasm. If heavy involvement means enthusiasm it might correlate with other food behaviours.

Table 10.2 shows that, when compared with other groups, major omnivores make distinctive arrangements for dining out. Compared with the other three groups, they eat out more frequently in restaurants and with friends. On the last outing reported, more of their restaurant meals were 'just a social occasion' and they lasted longer (59% lasted more than two hours). They judge restaurants more harshly; fewer said that they 'very much enjoyed' the food, the service, value for money or the occasion overall. Only 72 per cent very much enjoyed the occasion overall, compared with 78 per cent of those who had only eaten popular cuisines, and 81 per cent of those in the modal and minor omnivore categories. They were also more prone to complain. They are much more likely to have learned about the place visited last from a colleague and very much more likely to have been taken there by someone else. They show greater devotion and greater culinary discrimination as well as having greater breadth of experience. Their appropriation and appreciation of dining out is distinctive.

As regards their orientation, major omnivores display exceptional interest in all aspects of food and eating. They eat more than average takeaways, make heavy use of pre-prepared food and cook more often

---

[8]  This was the chosen cut-off point as half the omnivores reported six or fewer cuisine styles and the remaining half reported seven or more cuisine styles.

**Table 10.2** Culinary omnivorousness and procedures in dining out, 2015 (column percentage)

| | Restricted | Modal | Minor omnivore | Major omnivore |
|---|---|---|---|---|
| *Frequency of eating out* | | | | |
| Several times a week | 3 | 5 | 7 | 23 |
| Once a week | 9 | 17 | 17 | 30 |
| *Frequency of eating at a friend's* | | | | |
| Once a fortnight | 5 | 8 | 10 | 22 |
| Once a month | 13 | 25 | 24 | 34 |
| *Frequency of eating at a relative's* | | | | |
| Once a month | 17 | 24 | 20 | 28 |
| Once every 3 months | 19 | 24 | 28 | 22 |
| Never | 23 | 13 | 14 | 9 |
| *Attitudes: Agree* | | | | |
| Choose things I don't eat at home | 68 | 80 | 91 | 92 |
| Complain if meal unsatisfactory | 71 | 73 | 80 | 84 |
| Get excited about going to eat at a new place | 52 | 74 | 70 | 87 |
| Often talk with others about eating out | 47 | 67 | 64 | 78 |
| **Last occasion** | | | | |
| *Reason for last meal out* | | | | |
| Special occasion | 28 | 22 | 17 | 14 |
| Just a social occasion | 43 | 50 | 50 | 57 |
| *Meal duration* | | | | |
| Less than an hour | 7 | 7 | 0 | 1 |
| 2–3 hours | 49 | 46 | 50 | 59 |
| *Eaten similar dish before…* | | | | |
| …while eating out | 84 | 86 | 77 | 82 |
| …at home | 71 | 63 | 50 | 67 |
| *Ate last meal…* | | | | |
| With family only | 41 | 34 | 26 | 23 |
| With friends only | 20 | 23 | 21 | 28 |
| *Very much enjoyed the…* | | | | |
| Company | 87 | 87 | 94 | 86 |
| Conversation | 73 | 81 | 89 | 85 |
| Food | 76 | 74 | 76 | 65 |
| Decor | 52 | 49 | 39 | 46 |
| Service | 62 | 60 | 59 | 46 |

**Table 10.2** Continued

|  | Restricted | Modal | Minor omnivore | Major omnivore |
|---|---|---|---|---|
| Value for money | 63 | 57 | 56 | 47 |
| Overall | 78 | 81 | 80 | 72 |
| *How receives recommendations* | | | | |
| From friends | 62 | 80 | 85 | 88 |
| From colleagues | 22 | 39 | 35 | 60 |
| Taken there by someone else | 23 | 33 | 41 | 61 |

*Note:* All 2015 respondents. Total observations (n = 841) as analysis excludes respondents where data are missing (n = 21), or 'inactive' (n = 66) or have 'other' types of taste (n = 173)

daily from scratch. The only measured activity on which they fall beneath the rest is in the purchase of takeaway fish and chips. They are more likely than the other groups to agree that they complain when dissatisfied, get excited about going to a new place, and 'often talk with others about eating out'. They are very adventurous and not at all cautious. All omnivores feel comfortable in any type of restaurant and seek out foods which they would not eat at home, but major omnivores appreciate, in addition, eating in formal surroundings, for example liking to dress up for the occasion and preferring there to be no children present, suggesting a seriously attentive approach to dining out.

Major omnivores also show a distinctive orientation to food and eating within the home (Table 10.3). They are more likely to host guests at home (92%, compared with 64% of the restricted group), to shop for groceries several times a week (45%, compared with 32%), to visit independent food stores (61%, compared with 23%) and to say that they are very interested in reading recipes, using recipes, everyday cooking and, most strikingly, special occasion cooking. Thus 63 per cent of major omnivores were very interested in 'special occasion cooking' compared with 42 per cent of minor omnivores, 37 per cent of the modal group and 26 per cent of the restricted group.

Major omnivores, in addition, have distinctive routines including being more likely than any other group to eat three meals a day, usually consuming five portions of fruit and vegetables a day, making use of leftovers and seeking to limit meat consumption. In every instance, the major omnivore is at the extreme, being more likely to act in accordance with current understandings of best practice, as indicated by official guidelines, cultural intermediary recommendation and nutritional orthodoxy. The implication is that they are not only deeply concerned

**Table 10.3** Culinary omnivorousness, domestic routines and dietary preoccupations, 2015 (column percentage)

| | Restricted | Modal | Minor omnivore | Major omnivore |
|---|---|---|---|---|
| *Hosting* | | | | |
| Hosts guests at home | 64 | 82 | 85 | 92 |
| Hosts family (of those that host) | 84 | 75 | 73 | 74 |
| Hosts friends (of those that host) | 64 | 82 | 85 | 94 |
| *Frequency of grocery shopping* | | | | |
| Several times a week | 32 | 36 | 41 | 45 |
| Once a week | 49 | 46 | 41 | 32 |
| *Frequency of online grocery shopping* | | | | |
| Once a week | 2 | 7 | 8 | 13 |
| Never | 78 | 66 | 65 | 49 |
| *Visits independent food stores* | | | | |
| Yes | 23 | 37 | 43 | 61 |
| *Very interested in…* | | | | |
| …reading recipes | 14 | 19 | 22 | 28 |
| …using recipes | 12 | 18 | 21 | 30 |
| …everyday cooking | 26 | 28 | 31 | 39 |
| …special occasion cooking | 26 | 37 | 42 | 63 |
| *Food behaviours* | | | | |
| Limit meat consumption | 17 | 26 | 27 | 36 |
| Eat three meals a day | 46 | 56 | 52 | 66 |
| Five a day of fruit and vegetables | 42 | 49 | 64 | 69 |
| Use up leftovers | 58 | 74 | 84 | 84 |
| *Dietary requirements (last year)* | | | | |
| Vegetarian | 5 | 11 | 6 | 10 |
| Vegan | 0 | 3 | 2 | 5 |
| Pescatarian | 1 | 4 | 7 | 7 |
| Gluten-free | 2 | 3 | 3 | 8 |
| Lactose-free | 1 | 3 | 5 | 9 |

*Note:* All 2015 respondents. Total observations (n = 841) as analysis excludes respondents where data are missing (n = 21), or are 'inactive' (n = 66), or have 'other' types of taste (n = 173)

about the aesthetic aspects of eating and dining out but also with matters of health. Perhaps counter-intuitively (if the model indicates a gastronomically aesthetic interest in eating) they are more likely than average to follow vegan, vegetarian, pescatarian, gluten-free and lactose-free diets. A battery of questions about special dietary practices presented eight types of special diet to respondents and 59 per cent of major omnivores were following one or other, a higher proportion than any other group.[9] We thus conclude that major omnivores exhibit a high level of enthusiasm, but is this the pursuit of social distinction?

Table 10.4 shows models of omnivore status comparing the class trajectory and the CARs versions. The trajectory model (the left-hand panel) explains slightly less variance but offers in broad terms a very similar interpretation of the social foundations of membership of the four categories. Compared with the restricted group, major omnivores are more likely to be middle-aged, have no dependent children, have a degree, have high household income, live in London or Bristol, and have strong service class connections. Minor omnivores are slightly less distinguished, less homogeneous in age, not differentiated by income, more defined by having a degree, and less by class pedigree. They are especially likely to be upwardly mobile into the service class. Compared with the major omnivores they are a little more likely to have children in the household and are less wealthy, making it possible that they have similar potential but are currently restricted in their public participation by their material and domestic circumstances.

The CARs model (right-hand panel), measuring assets rather than employment classes, has similar features but with subtle substantive differences. The comparison between major omnivores and the restricted group (the base category) differs little from the employment class model, but comparing them with the minor omnivores offers interesting nuances. The role played by social and cultural capital is barely significant in explaining minor omnivore status, for which having a degree (and living in London) is the strongest predictor. Age is weakly significant, and, intriguingly, having a father with highbrow cultural pastimes has a moderately strong significant effect. The profile of the major omnivore can be drawn more graphically, however. High levels of all three types of capital are indicated. Major omnivores participate heavily in other cultural activities; they are culturally voracious. They have

---

[9]   In these matters minor omnivores were closer to them than any other. The main exception was the three meals per day pattern that 66 per cent of major omnivores observed, compared with 56 per cent of the modal group but only 52 per cent of the minor omnivores.

**Table 10.4** Multinomial logistic regression of omnivore characteristics, comparing class trajectory and asset models, 2015

| | Class trajectory | | | | Asset model | | | |
|---|---|---|---|---|---|---|---|---|
| | (base) | Modal | Minor omnivore | Major omnivore | (base) | Modal | Minor omnivore | Major omnivore |
| *Sex* | | | | | | | | |
| Male | | 0.012 | 0.051 | 0.462 | | -0.012 | 0.015 | 0.358 |
| *Age* | | | | | | | | |
| Age | | 0.081* | 0.168** | 0.314*** | | 0.090* | 0.161* | 0.311*** |
| Age$^2$ | | -0.001** | -0.002** | -0.004*** | | -0.001** | -0.002* | -0.004*** |
| *Ethnicity* | | | | | | | | |
| White British | | -0.269 | 0.250 | 0.647 | | -0.290 | 0.120 | 0.686 |
| *Children* | | | | | | | | |
| Child(ren) in household | | -0.360 | -0.641 | -0.913* | | -0.281 | -0.433 | -0.510 |
| *Education* | | | | | | | | |
| Has a degree | | 0.802*** | 1.397*** | 1.156*** | | 0.537* | 1.230*** | 0.811* |
| *Household gross income per annum* | | | | | | | | |
| Under £15,000 | | 0.000 | 0.000 | 0.000 | | 0.000 | 0.000 | 0.000 |
| £15,000–£29,999 | | 0.511 | -0.231 | 1.255 | | 0.416 | -0.482 | 1.244 |
| £30,000–£49,999 | | 0.461 | 0.800 | 2.133* | | 0.339 | 0.551 | 2.052* |
| £50,000–£77,999 | | 0.283 | -0.167 | 1.431 | | 0.127 | -0.384 | 1.080 |
| £78,000 or more | | 0.472 | 1.201 | 3.246*** | | 0.314 | 0.852 | 2.814** |
| Unknown | | 0.576* | 0.434 | 2.358** | | 0.431 | 0.050 | 2.303** |
| *City* | | | | | | | | |
| London | | 0.568* | 1.542*** | 2.359*** | | 0.553* | 1.558*** | 2.223*** |
| Preston | | 0.000 | 0.000 | 0.000 | | 0.000 | 0.000 | 0.000 |
| Bristol | | 0.115 | 0.907* | 1.342** | | 0.068 | 0.818* | 1.014* |

**Table 10.4** Continued

|  | Class trajectory | | | | Asset model | | | |
|---|---|---|---|---|---|---|---|---|
|  | (base) | Modal | Minor omnivore | Major omnivore | (base) | Modal | Minor omnivore | Major omnivore |
| *Cohabitation* | | | | | | | | |
| With partner | | | | | | 0.051 | 0.100 | 0.094 |
| *Social contacts* | | | | | | | | |
| Position (mean) | | | | | | 0.019 | 0.044* | 0.064*** |
| *Cultural participation* | | | | | | | | |
| Rate of participation (adj. volume) | | | | | | 0.057* | 0.076 | 0.192*** |
| *Parental influence* | | | | | | | | |
| Mother: Highbrow interests | | | | | | 0.342 | 0.321 | 0.399 |
| Father: Highbrow interests | | | | | | 0.550** | 0.977** | 0.415 |
| *Resident* | | | | | | | | |
| Years in current city | | | | | | -0.007 | -0.001 | -0.031* |
| *Class mobility* | | | | | | | | |
| Stable service class | | 0.261 | 1.104* | 2.153*** | | | | |
| Upwardly mobile into service | | 0.477 | 1.512*** | 1.928*** | | | | |
| Downwardly mobile from service | | 0.692* | 0.629 | 2.244*** | | | | |
| No service class experience | | 0.000 | 0.000 | 0.000 | | | | |
| Unknown | | -0.290 | 0.064 | 1.524* | | | | |
| *Frequency of eating out* | | | | | | | | |
| At a restaurant | | 0.365*** | 0.707*** | 1.211*** | | 0.293*** | 0.611*** | 1.043*** |
| Constant | | -3.095*** | -10.368*** | -17.976*** | | -3.551*** | -10.609*** | -18.210*** |
| Observations | | | | 830 | | | | 830 |
| Adjusted R$^2$ | | | | 0.219 | | | | 0.232 |

Note: All 2015 respondents; *p < 0.05, **p < 0.01, ***p < 0.001

higher household incomes. Their social contacts – some of whom they will eat with – are of high socio-economic status. If social capital is profitable then they will benefit accordingly. Once these features are taken into account, the effect of holding a degree diminishes, implying a different disposition of assets when compared with the minor omnivores. Major omnivores are also from a younger cohort and are more recently geographically mobile, mostly into London. By these indicators, major omnivores exhibit high levels of social distinction and are well positioned to profit in terms of reputation and material reward.

The two different operational measures of class emphasise different mechanisms for the acquisition and reproduction of class privilege and capture the effects of both primary and secondary socialisation. The role of habitus of family of origin is marked in the employment class models, while the current disposition of assets, capturing the effects of post-educational experience, is more prominent in the CARs model. No theorist of class would deny that these are both relevant mechanisms in explaining persistent material and cultural inequalities, but different measurement devices highlight different dimensions.

For many purposes this division within the group of omnivores is unimportant. In the context of the English population as a whole, minor omnivores are socially privileged in much the same way as the major ones. In most respects the group behaves in ways closest to the major omnivores, especially alike with respect to domestic cooking and shopping.[10] However, they are little different from the modal group in respect of procedures within the restaurant, especially in their lower level of participation.

Major and minor omnivores, despite both being disproportionately drawn from the service class, divide between one fraction with a greater volume of social, cultural and economic capital, and another, the minor group, who have a habitus marked by high cultural capital but are currently less well endowed with other types of capital. This in part arises from the way in which their everyday lives are organised and constrained. The differences, however, remain intriguing, both substantively, as evidence of divisions within the service class, and methodologically, because they are brought to light by different ways of operationalising class. Major omnivores apparently convert education and background into a way of life in which dining out, and the pursuit of variety, play a significant part in marking high status. Dining out is shared with other people of high rank (i.e. with high social capital) who are probably just

[10]   Minor omnivores are more fastidious with respect to reduction of waste and avoiding snacking.

as confident in their own good taste and who collude in the definition of good taste. So, if the pursuit of variety, familiarisation and validation of dining out is common across most of the population, this group may be playing a pivotal role in constituting those criteria as legitimate taste. Rich households in London, who have high cultural and social capital, are best able to define excellence in this area of the cultural field. Along the way they put their stamp on the practice which can, if required, be converted into a claim to social superiority.

### Summary: class and omnivorousness

All models confirm that culinary omnivorousness is associated with the privileges of class, income and education. Being second-generation service class is an especially significant factor underpinning a prestigious and varied pattern of eating out. Those of higher socio-economic status adopt an omnivorous orientation but while not all are exceptionally interested in food, on aggregate major omnivores are both exceptionally enthusiastic and socially privileged.[11] Enthusiasm is not itself entirely homogeneous, for while it will involve elements of both, a distinction exists between aesthetic and ludic orientations, between strength of orientations of connoisseurship and playfulness. Some omnivores seem primarily attracted to novelty, seeking out new experiences, typically of exotic and unusual foods and flavours, while others adopt an epicurean approach, gnomic rather than ludic, driven less by the exceptional and exotic, but rather subjecting all, not just exceptional, food experiences to critical judgement.

### Conclusion

Diversity and variety, while of universal appeal, are envisaged in different ways by different people. Some people have a broad repertoire and wide experience, and they are likely to be of high socio-economic status. Wide experience in itself does not necessarily signify or entail exceptional interest in food or dining out, although it will always provide resources for talk, reflection and judgement; those with major omnivore

---

[11] It is interesting, although no form of disconfirmation, that the seven major omnivores among our interviewees are heterogeneous, with one who was decidedly not an enthusiast and another with a young family. They nevertheless conform sufficiently closely to the ideal type to attribute individual divergence to normal errors and sample selection.

experience inevitably acquire greater-than-average knowledge. However, for many omnivores, food is an object of considerable enthusiasm. As in all cultural domains, some people seek primarily the internal goods that a practice can deliver irrespective of any external benefit accruing from recognition by others. Enthusiasm does not *necessarily* coincide with a search for distinction but in practice it often does. Nevertheless, while some omnivores are exceptionally concerned about the aesthetic quality of food, they are *no less* concerned with the sociable and commensal aspects of eating together with others.

Omnivorous behaviour might be considered legitimate not only because promoted by the service class, although variety clearly charms the best-established sections of the professional and managerial class, but also because others share the definition of how to eat well. Not everyone can, nor would they want to, emulate enthusiasts' practices, but no counter-definition or alternative model exists. Negative reactions to the term foodie indicate that over-exuberance is controversial and capable of causing resentment, and thus not endorsed unconditionally, but the importance of variety and adventure pervades the whole population.

# 11

## Landscape of variety

### Introduction

Variety is appreciated for its own sake and also appropriated for making hierarchical social statements. However, looked at overall, it makes for a very diverse landscape, with many alternatives; hence restaurants have different clienteles and different groups perform identity in different ways. Less an instantiation of a postmodern heaven, rather more a structured platform of eating out where meaning and aesthetic value can be internalised and communicated.

This chapter begins by looking at expressions of social divisions other than class. We describe the clientele of different types of restaurant which attract differentially the young and the old, men and women, and different ethnic minority groups. An interesting case is the Indian restaurant and we explore further its role, its clientele, the British habit of 'going for a curry' and the role of curry in the domestic sphere. Not a highly esteemed dish but widely and popularly consumed, curry can no longer readily be described as 'foreign'. Fast food, the epitome of mass consumption, is also popular and relatively uniform in presentation. We consider interviewee reactions and how, as it is incorporated into almost everyone's repertoire, it becomes established and its reputation recovers. We then examine vegetarianism and veganism, practices once considered as alternative, and finally discuss innovations in formats for the presentation of food in restaurants.

### Exploring social divisions

We have not commented much on social divisions other than class and ethnicity. One of the most unusual features of dining out as a form of elite entertainment and participation is the few indications of differences between men and women. Gender registers as a strong differentiating factor in relation to domestic food preparation and consequently in orientations towards dining out as relief from the obligations of domestic labour. Otherwise gender disparities are found only occasionally. One instance is the use of wine bars and bistros. Wine bars emerged relatively recently but by 2015 were widely distributed in urban areas; 26 per cent of respondents had dined out in a wine bar / bistro in the last year. Clients exhibit high levels of all three types of asset (cultural participation, social connections and high levels of economic resource). Customers are also likely to be white British, have no dependent children and be in the middle age groups. At a lower level of significance they are also likely to have a degree and to be female. In this model the effects of assets are strong. In an equivalent occupational class model, class trajectory was a powerful factor, primarily because the working class avoid wine bars.[1] Age, being white British, and having no children are equally strong factors, but gender is not significant.

The clientele of Indian restaurants contrasts very sharply with that of wine bars, one feature being the over-representation of men. The asset model indicates that extensive cultural participation along with age are powerful predictors, but otherwise only two minor effects can be detected – having the highest level of income and having a mother with interests in high culture. Ethnicity, social capital, education and household composition were all insignificant. The occupational class measures gave the same result, with service class connections replacing cultural capital in the model.

The propensity to patronise fine dining establishments has yet another profile. The assets model indicates that only social capital, cultural capital and having a household income greater than £30,000 per annum are significant.[2] Sex, age, education, household structure and city are insignificant, as is ethnicity. Hence, we can deduce that fine dining appeals to ethnic minorities to the same degree as to the white British. The white tablecloth has perhaps lost its symbolic relevance in a context of the informalisation of habits among the ethnic majority, while its intimations of luxury or formality resonate more among minorities. Perhaps we might deduce that among ethnic minorities distinction is still obtained more by conspicuous display rather than through the combination of variety and informality preferred by the white British. As regards fine dining, possession of key assets outweighs educational qualifications and the cultural practices of family of origin.

[1]    pseudo $R^2$ = 0.23
[2]    All are relevant at the 0.001 level of significance.

The fine dining restaurant – not a term very commonly used in contemporary British discussion – was presented as one of fourteen *types* of restaurant that respondents may have visited. As shown in Chapter 3, access to multiple types is socially differentiated, with ethnic minorities, the poorest households and the less well educated relatively restricted in access. The CARs model[3] of number of types attended shows once again that cultural and social capital are powerful predictors, as is household income above £30,000 per annum. Sex, household composition and educational qualifications are insignificant. Having dependent children becomes significant once other assets are taken into account, and the highbrow interests of fathers emerges as a factor, suggesting that capital endowment from the family of origin has an effect. Ethnic identification, however, remains statistically significant at the highest level suggesting strongly that the avoidance of some types of restaurant, for whatever reasons, is the major basis of exclusion of ethnic minorities in England.

Another factor which we repeatedly identify as significant in explaining variation in behaviour is city of residence. While it does not matter in relation to predicting frequency of eating out in restaurants,[4] it does matter in most aspects of the experience of variety. Experience of uncommon and exclusive restaurants and registering as an omnivore is much more likely in London than elsewhere, even after controlling for other social characteristics. So, while the population of London is richer, better educated and of higher socio-economic status than that in the other cities there is an additional independent effect of living in the metropolis. A greater variety of provision results from more commercial opportunities in an area which is large and densely populated. It is hence no accident that more of our omnivorous interviewees lived in London. However, there is also probably an ecological effect; if a lot of people eat out with wide variety, they have a demonstration effect on others, as friends get brought along to different types of location and acquaintances are told about varied visits. In London more people are more often guests of friends and less frequent guests of family than in the other cities. In this, as in most experiences, London is the antithesis of Preston, with Bristol falling between the two. Bristol, more similar to Preston in 1995, had become more like London by 2015, even after taking into account the social profile of the population, implying that indeed the nature of local provision is the key to city differences. In addition, length of residence in a city is also sometimes significant,

[3]  pseudoR$^2$ = 0.35
[4]  Nor does it make any difference to the number of different types of restaurant the respondents visit.

with those who have lived locally for a shorter period making more use of the variety of commercial eating out options.

Life-course stage also has an effect. Age directly affects behaviour, although its complex relationship with cohort and household structure, especially the presence of dependent children, makes interpretation difficult. The young eat out more frequently, but in a less varied manner. The elderly also eat out in a less varied way. Those who have children participate less frequently in visits to both commercial and communal events, and their access to a variety of styles is more limited. The difficulty of making practical arrangements for a family to eat out, and the expense, along with the limited tastes of some children are the most likely reasons for restriction. So, life-course phase, alongside class, education, gender and geographical location, has consequences for eating out, as does ethnicity.

## Ethnic groups and ethnic cuisine

Access to greater variety, as indicated by experience of many types and styles of restaurant is a privilege enjoyed by those identifying as white British. As shown in Chapter 10, ethnic cuisine plays a significant role in the display of distinction; experience of foreign cuisines among the majority ethnic group in Britain conveys status, and the rarer and more arcane genres attract those endowed with high cultural, economic and social capital. What, however, of the behaviour of the minority ethnic groups themselves?

### Measuring ethnicity: ethnicity as a variable

Net migration figures suggest increased ethnic diversity of the British population over the last twenty years (ONS, 2017). In both 1995 and 2015, respondents' ethnicity was identified by asking, 'To which of these (ethnic) groups do you consider you belong?' In line with official classificatory practices (ONS) nine response alternatives were offered in 1995 and nineteen in 2015. Both additional response items (e.g. options to identify as multiple/mixed ethnicities) and disaggregated response alternatives (e.g. identifying national /regional origin within the identification as 'white') were offered in 2015 compared with 1995.

The expansion of response alternatives enabled the substantive exploration of ethnicity and cuisine styles but the limitations of the data in 1995 prohibit quantitative analysis to establish changes in the tastes of non-white British groups. Instead, we contextualise the findings from

2015 within other research concerned with the changing landscape of taste, the increased diversity of the population, and the relationship between them.

The ethnic composition of the survey samples in 1995 and 2015 differs. Notable differences exist between the three cities and there is some significant change between the two dates. In 1995, 80 per cent of the London sample was white, compared with 96 per cent of Bristol. The ethnic minorities in London were roughly equal between Asian/Asian British, Black/Black British and Other (non-white) groups. In Preston most of the 9 per cent non-white population were Asian, while there was no Asian presence in Bristol. By 2015 London had become a very multicultural city with less than two thirds (65%) of the population white, the Asian population comprising 17 per cent, Black, 10 per cent and 'other ethnic', 9 per cent. Using the more refined breakdown of minorities available from the 2015 survey, a bare majority (52%) identified as white British, there was a substantial white Other presence (one sixth of the sample, 16%), with the same proportion of Asian residents and 9 per cent Black. Bristol was three quarters white British, with the white Other group the next largest section (9%) and roughly equal proportions of Mixed, Asian and Black groups making up the remainder. In Preston, 81 per cent identified as white British, 11 per cent as Asian and 4 per cent as white Other.

### Ethnic minority group tastes

Preferences vary by ethnic group. Asian and British Asians are very much more likely to use Indian restaurants than any other group. They were making comparatively little use in 2015 of traditional or modern British, Chinese, Thai, French or other ethnic cuisines. The Asian population avoids pubs, restaurants attached to pubs and wine bar/bistro types of establishment. Black minority ethnic groups are more likely than any other group to visit American and Chinese restaurants and to avoid traditional and modern British, Italian and Indian. There are minor differences in 2015 between white British and white Other, the latter avoiding traditional and modern British cuisine but being significantly more highly represented in Japanese, French and other ethnic restaurants and also making more use of restaurants in hotels and fine dining establishments. The white Other group thus seem disproportionately attracted to prestigious cuisines and settings.

Bivariate correlations indicate that ethnic minority identification is associated with a number of apparent disadvantages. In 1995 on many measures of privilege (assuming that opportunities to eat out often and in different places were special and a treat), the Black group was most disadvantaged, eating out less frequently and in a narrower variety of places. By 2015 it was in a very similar position to the Asian population, although still at a disadvantage in relation to white groups. Among the more interesting features is a decline in the proportion of the Asian population eating dinner at home with other household members. In 1995, 97 per cent reported eating dinner the previous day with co-resident kin, compared with 85 per cent of white and 83 per cent of Black groups. By 2015 the figures were, respectively, 82 per cent, 72 per cent and 82 per cent.

The more refined measures in 2015 allow a focus on the intersection of ethnicity and class. In most multivariate statistical models the core variable distinguishing white British from other ethnic designations predicts significant differences in behaviour. This is true of, for example, frequency of eating out in a restaurant, access to a wide variety of types of restaurant and styles of cuisine, being omnivorous, and holding exploratory orientations towards eating out.

Frequency of eating out is a threshold which underpins other differentiating behaviours. Black groups eat out much less frequently than whites; if eating out at least once a fortnight is the yardstick for regular eating out, then the rate for Black/Black British is less than half that of the white population (20% compared with 42%), with the Asian population reporting 30 per cent. Thus, frequency of eating out in a restaurant is significantly skewed in favour of the white groups. That does not hold for dining at the homes of friends where there is no ethnic effect. The weak measured effect for eating with kin is presumably due to temporary and more recent migrants having fewer accessible kinsfolk to visit. Greatest ethnic inequality occurs in public space and the marketplace.

Ethnic identity is a significant factor behind attendance at some, but not all, types and styles of restaurant. The prominence of the white British is marked in wine bars, in-store restaurants, coffee shops and cafes, steakhouses, pub bars and pub restaurants, but not in other types of venue. The importance of ethnicity in relation to styles of cuisine is highly significant in respect of traditional British and modern British, more weakly relevant to Italian, Thai and French, and not at all significant for the remainder. Thus, the clientele of some venues will be marked by the lack of ethnic mix, the reasons being various but including availability of alcohol, forms of meat consumption and aspects of traditional locations for sociability.

White British respondents are advantaged with respect to many esteemed aspects of dining out. However, when examined in detail, ethnic difference is absent in some circumstances, including eating at a friend's house, fine dining, French cuisine and fast food. In one symbolically significant case – the number having eaten during the previous year in a restaurant serving Indian cuisine – white British respondents were under-represented. This does not mean that they never go, or that they feel any sense of exclusion, rather that Indian food proves exceptionally attractive to the South Asian members of the sample; 70 per cent had eaten in an Indian restaurant in the last year compared with 46 per cent of white Britons. Inspection at this level of detail suggests that it is more the absence from some types of restaurant rather than a dislike of styles of cuisine that marks ethnic differentiation.

The better our measures of class, the less strong is the ethnic effect. Rarely is that effect eliminated, although that happens with some CARs models, implying intersection between class position and ethnic identity with some minorities disadvantaged by both class and ethnic identity. This suggests that a well-designed measure of class qualifies the independent effect of ethnic identity by revealing mechanisms lying behind the diverse experiences of ethnic groups. Of course, it does not imply that the association between ethnicity and (dis)advantage is spurious, for the bivariate analysis indicates very significant differences in experience between ethnic minorities and the majority ethnic group.

## The story of curry

Curry is popular in the UK. It is primarily associated with South Asian cuisine and Indian restaurants and takeaways, though people reported East Asian versions as well. Respondents reported that, on the last occasion out, both in restaurants and in other people's homes, curry was the most popular of all dishes; 10 per cent of last restaurant meals were described as curry (equal in popularity with roast dinners) and on 19 per cent of last occasions of domestic hospitality, curry was served. Curry was the most popular dish ordered in a restaurant in 2015 (equal with roast meat dinners) and it was the most popular dish served to guests in the process of entertaining at home. Curry is reported by survey respondents to have been eaten in several different types of restaurant including casual dining restaurants, pub venues and fine dining restaurants. Indian restaurants are the third most commonly attended; 44 per cent of respondents said that they had eaten in an Indian restaurant in the last year (and 60% had bought a meal from an Indian takeaway shop). Of main courses eaten on the last occasion in an Indian restaurant, 84 per cent was a curry dish. The wide range of Indian frozen and cook-chill meals in British supermarkets also adds to the impression that curry is a mainstay of the British diet.

There is a close connection between identifying as South Asian, eating in Indian restaurants (69% of our respondents in this community had eaten in an Indian restaurant in the last year) and reporting eating curry (46% of last main dishes recorded). It was at the core of descriptions of domestic meals, domestic entertaining and to a lesser extent eating in restaurants, in the interviews with people with South Asian connections. However, the proportion of South Asians in our sample was only 11 per cent, indicating that most users of Indian outlets and most eaters of curry were not themselves South Asian.

Curry has long played a role in the British diet. It exemplifies how colonial connections and selective migration patterns result in the different distributions of 'ethnic' restaurants in European countries. While it is dangerous to assume that this is the sole or even main explanation of its current popularity relative to other cuisine types, it has had a presence in some households and restaurants in Britain since the late nineteenth century. It became widespread in the 1960s (Driver, 1983; Buettner, 2008; Panayi, 2008). Use of Indian takeaways increased by 50 per cent between 1995 and 2015 and the number of curries reported as the last main course in a restaurant increased by 25 per cent. It also became more common as a domestic dish; just less than half of interviewees mentioned in passing that curry is a dish prepared and served at home. A homely and traditional dish for major ethnic minorities in contemporary Britain, it is also widely popular and increasingly mundane among respondents describing their ethnic identity as 'white British'.

The changing acceptability of curry is to some degree a consequence of differences in population. The major increase in curries consumed away from home is in the context of domestic hospitality, where it appeared twice as often. The increase for white British at someone else's home, however, was even greater – 150 per cent – an increase from 6 per cent to 14 per cent of all events. The marginal increase in consumption of curry in restaurants shows no difference in rate between the white British and other ethnic groups. Aside from South Asians, those identifying as white British were more likely than any of the other four ethnic groups to eat in Indian restaurants or use Indian takeaways. Those most likely to eat curry in a restaurant were South Asian and middle-aged, with a significant increase in men between 1995 and 2015. Those with a cautious orientation avoided curry in 1995, among whom the white British were well represented. By 2015 the cautious were more likely to eat curry, a consequence of the white British population abandoning their fear or dislike of it. Curry, once a challenging food widely avoided in Britain, offers a good example of the dialectical process of diversification and normalisation which operates through the extended commodification of food services and especially the catering trade.

Cultural globalisation, with both its homogenising and its localising consequences, has been carried on the winds of international commercial circulation of commodities. Ingredients and recipes, migrant populations and international corporations have spread at an increasingly fast rate in the last few decades with a significant influence upon tastes, meals and service provision. This could result in most places across the globe becoming similar. However, cuisines exhibit very considerable path dependence when diffusing across national territories. England sports a very large number of cuisines, through restaurants and supermarkets and specialist grocers, but its particular mix refracts its history of imperial rule. Most visitors can tell that they are in England rather than France, Finland or the US.

## Fast food

Fast food constitutes a rather ill-defined set of commercial products. However, it is a form of commercial provision used to save time and labour, about which there is much misdirected anxiety, primarily due to its association with the perceived decline of home-cooked meals (Meah and Watson, 2011). Its suppliers almost always allow people to eat on the premises, in basic surroundings, while also having a significant takeaway trade. Their common features include the sale of a large volume of a narrow range of uniform products amenable to preparation using limited cooking techniques (typically frying or grilling) which can be cooked quickly on demand. They lie on the cusp between the simple cafe/restaurant and the takeaway shop. They are also characterised by a highly routinised labour process which requires no intervention on the part of skilled cooks and no table service. If any single operation symbolises industrialised, manufactured, uniform, mass catering, it is the burger bar, although similar organisational techniques are now used to sell fried chicken, kebabs, falafel and the like.

The content of what is sold is often disparaged. In many British minds, McDonald's is the model of the fast-food restaurant, for which the company has suffered ignominy as many people identify it as the exemplar of poor, mass-produced food. McDonald's has figured for political campaigners as the doyen of the fast-food industry, and many people over the last thirty years have expressed opinions about the attractiveness of a Big Mac. The political campaigns have almost certainly provided an excellent form of free advertising for the company, compensating for problems of corporate image requiring the attention of management (Klein, 2000; Schlosser, 2012). The success of these firms is some indication of the acceptability of fast food among a large swathe of the population. Others, however, object to the industrialised, mass-produced, uniformity of the product, are suspicious of the cooking process and the produce used, and are disappointed that the dish is not tailored to the tastes and requirements of the individual who is purchasing it (Leidner, 1993). These reservations are most common among the middle class.

We did not ask interviewees about fast food explicitly but several of them mentioned it, mostly when explaining what sorts of restaurant they liked or disliked. Lara and Luke were positive, although probably well aware of the relative lowly reputation of fast-food restaurants. As Lara put it,

> McDonald's is quite tasty. I know a lot of people think it's crappy food, but it's got flavour to it. The Big Macs have, anyway. And I like the Filet O' Fish ones, they're nice. But I'm not keen on chicken burgers much. But I do think McDonald's is reasonable for the price.

Luke much liked the unpretentiousness of such places, as they require none of the 'formality of going to a restaurant'. One measure of this was his assertion that 'I wouldn't go to a restaurant on my own but I would go to a fast-food place'. For others the informality was viewed negatively. Felicity, who incidentally reveals the difficulty of defining the boundaries of fast food, says

> I quite like intimate restaurants and stuff, not too busy but not too quiet. I'm not a huge fan of Nando's and that kind of thing, which is just quick, it's fast food but it's not, so I like more restaurant service type places, if that makes sense?

When asked 'what do you think gives it that fast-food feel?' she explains,

> It's so big and you kind of go and there are no waiters and you go and order, it's a bit like McDonald's or whatever, and you get to sit down, although you do in McDonald's. I don't know, it just has that feel about it, the mass-produced thing, there's quite a limited menu, although it is quite big, they know exactly what's coming in, there is nothing very unusual for them to cook.

Douglas was not averse to fast food itself, but, like Felicity, did not much favour the associated service regime. Explaining why, he says that he 'wouldn't sit in and eat a McDonalds in the restaurant. I'd only be grabbing a burger on the way past' he says:

> It's not relaxing and actually if I'm going to get some food I'm going to get some proper food not just a McDonald's or a Burger King or whatever.

Though they taste very nice, so on the way somewhere if I'm grabbing
something I will do but I won't sit down. It's probably a bit busy in the
turnover and if it's just me on a table of four and someone sits down next
to you it's going to be awkward and all this sort of stuff.

Nor is Penny averse to the food on occasion: 'Sometimes I want a pizza
or a hotdog and chips or burger. I want something greasy and calorie-
laden.' So fast food has become part of the British food scene for most
people and indeed only Pete was unremittingly critical: 'I'm not too keen
on all of this stuff and I'm not too keen on McDonald's'. When asked
why, he says:

I think it's about everything. I don't think the food is very good quality and
you're shovelled in and shovelled out, you know. That's having a snack to
me, that isn't a meal to me or having something to eat, that's just a snack.
If you're desperate you go in there and get it, that's it, but that's about it.
That's the one thing I don't like.

For many people, fast food has negative connotations. This is partly because
of beliefs that food mostly should be eaten slowly and deliberately, as a
mark of gratitude and a time for relaxation. It is contrasted with home-
made food. At the boundary of the cusp of the restaurant and the takeaway,
it has for most people the least prestige of any place where a meal can be
taken on the premises, but its functional role is decried by a relatively small
minority. Thus, it would seem that the negative associations of fast food are
diminishing in parallel with its gradually increasing prevalence. It is far
from being unconditionally celebrated, but few condemn it.

## Vegetarians and vegetarianism

In the twenty-first century the eating of meat has become increasingly
controversial. The case for less or no meat is canvassed on environmental and health grounds (Röös et al., 2017), as well as for longer-standing
ethical and religious reasons (Regan, 1975; Singer, 1975). These topics
are regularly covered in mass and social media, partly the consequence
of social movement activity around food consumption. At the time of
writing, the promotion of veganism is particularly strong and vocal
(Twine, 2017). Less radical proposals for eating less meat in households
and workplace canteens revolve around observance of 'meat free days'
(Mylan, 2018). Also, an increasing number of people describe their diets
as 'flexitarian', a rather nebulous notion which implies eating more vegetarian meals and less meat or fish than previously. The catering trade is
adapting to these trends. Specialist vegetarian restaurants are probably
a little more common than before but most restaurants offer vegetarian

and, increasingly, vegan dishes on their menus. These, along with an almost universal acknowledgement that allergies of many kinds require care, consideration and special provision by the catering trade, impact upon dining out. One indication is that the pre-eminence of meat, potatoes and two veg, the most common format for a main meal in the third quarter of the twentieth century, has gradually dissipated.

In the light of media coverage it may seem surprising that the same proportion of respondents in both years (9%) claimed to follow a vegetarian diet. What did change was an increase in veganism. In 1995 it was very marginal, with only 3 people (0.3%) saying they followed a vegan diet, but the proportion had risen to 2 per cent by 2015. Vegans tend to be students or to hold degrees. They are in the vanguard of increasingly vocal social movements campaigning for the alteration of current food practices. Meanwhile vegetarianism, once seen as personally eccentric and politically radical, has become normalised. In 1995 vegetarians were likely to be female, youngish (but not very young), possessing a degree-level qualification, identifying as other than white British and without dependent children. Vegetarians were much less easy to characterise in 2015 when their only significant social characteristic was having a degree.[5] Normalisation is also indicated by a substantial reduction in the proportion of respondents who agree with the statement 'A vegetarian meal would never be my first choice' which dropped from 56 to 41 per cent, while the proportion strongly disagreeing rose from 17 to 27 per cent. Moreover, many more main dishes reported contained neither meat nor fish; the proportion rose from 4 per cent to 14 per cent. Examining the social characteristics of those consuming vegetable main dishes in 2015 indicates that being a vegetarian is the most powerful predictor but that being upwardly mobile and having a degree also matter. Meals without meat and fish tend to be of relatively short duration.

The interviews reveal some reasons for the wider consumption of vegetarian meals. Four interviewees claimed to be vegetarian (Tristan and Crispin, and their partners, and Robert and Magdalina). Their principal justifications were animal welfare and health. Neither environmental concern nor matters of taste were significant. Several others had in the past followed a vegetarian diet and Camilla had been vegan for a time following a serious illness. Lapsing is not considered very remarkable, for it is a fairly common occurrence. Mal, for example, had been brought up by his vegetarian mother but has since begun to eat meat. Others said

[5]   Variance explained by regression equations (pseudoR$^2$) fell from 0.14 in 1995 to 0.06 in 2015, implying that the determinants were increasingly personal conviction and situated circumstance rather than social position.

they were trying to reduce their meat consumption, as did 23 per cent of respondents to the survey (Mylan, 2018). In addition, for religious reasons, Laxmikant and Uma mostly ate vegetarian foods.

Other indications of changing reactions to meat include a decline in beef used as a main dish. It remains popular especially for special occasions among white British respondents. There were minor increases in the consumption of lamb, pork and ham, and more so of chicken. The proportion of fish and seafood dishes also rose (from about 8 to 12%). As the proportion of meals containing neither meat nor fish increases – if still mostly among sections of the educated middle class – vegetarianism seems less faddish, eccentric or noteworthy. In the context where special dietary regimes proliferate, it becomes an unremarkable minority practice, with a constant proportion of adherents over time, and subject to regular inflows and outflows of individuals.

## On innovation and diversity

The increasing popularity of curry, a more relaxed attitude to fast food and a growth in vegetarian meals are but three of many developments in the British landscape of eating out. Others include the incorporation of small dishes, as in tapas menus and the tasting menus of chefs with pretentions to celebrity; the celebration of street food; the redesign of interiors of restaurants to make cooking more visible; more means for securing advice and recommendation about venues on social media; and a greater dispersion of prices. These are all features of a landscape which fascinates journalists and enthusiasts, and which are highly relevant to actors in the catering industry because of their economic potential. However, it is not entirely clear how we should interpret these phenomena in a longer-term and academic perspective. Are they just minor turbulences in a climate where there is far more continuity than change? Are they the obsessions and intriguing adjustments of small minorities in the population with particular preoccupations with health or gastronomy? Clearly much variety can be obtained when eating out in Britain. Great diversity is reflected in the commercial and the communal modes of meal provision, in some part the consequence of innovation in the restaurant business. Nevertheless, behaviour and understandings of the practice of dining out remain socially patterned with consumption differentiated along lines of class, gender and ethnicity. The next two chapters (Part V) address the outstanding question of how much surface fluctuation in behaviour is underpinned by mechanisms for the expression of identity and distinction.

## Conclusion: aestheticisation and diversification

This chapter has both demonstrated a more sophisticated understanding of the effects of class on dining out and elaborated on the way in which other social divisions are expressed. All standard sociological measures of social position which generate inequalities – class, age, gender, ethnicity, place of residence, education, household structure, income – have appreciable effects upon some aspects of dining out. Those with the most consistent and strong effects in predicting access to variety are class, ethnicity, education and city. Gender affects orientation more than practice, age affects frequency rather than style preferences, as does the presence of dependent children in the household. The independent effect of city is regularly observed, partly arising because larger cities can offer a wider range of provision but multiplied because residents have social attributes which encourage eating out. London offers most options, Preston the fewest, and consequently the people living in the capital have the broadest experience. Ethnicity is the other variable which appears consistently to affect behaviour and orientation.

Ethnic minorities find some types of restaurant more conducive and congenial than others. They visit more often places selling Indian and 'other kinds' of cuisines and much less often traditional British or modern British food. They are much less likely to be major omnivores or to restrict themselves to eating only popular cuisines, and they are much more likely to eat only in restaurants serving foods unfamiliar from the standpoint of many white British respondents. Such uneven under-representation probably has several causes, ranging from fears of racial antagonism to indifference to the foods served in popular types of outlet. It is also a matter of selection of which types of restaurant to patronise. While CARs models reduce substantially the statistical effect of ethnic identity on access to more and broader cuisine styles, that does not apply to *types* of restaurant. The relative popularity of the fourteen types listed in the survey reveals a distinct structure of preferences among the ethnic groups. The liking for fine dining restaurants among minority ethnic groups is interesting and suggests that they appreciate formality, and perhaps even that pursuit of conspicuous consumption, eliminated from the practices of the ethnic majority by casualisation and informalisation, is still appealing. CARs models also show that ethnic identity can be compensated for by distribution of capital; those from ethnic minorities with higher incomes and greater social and cultural capital are major omnivores in the same way as white British.

The use of different measures of class offers a more complex and better-grounded understanding of the social processes which create class effects. Occupational class measures, when supplemented by information about income, offer solid models of differences in behaviour. The alternative assets model tends to give even more robust results, explaining more variance, picking up on the cultural aspects of class experience and increasing the capacity for sociological inference. However, using both the trajectory and the assets model together, by comparing inferences, allows discrimination between preconditioning influences and the current situation. It also brings the situational aspect of cultural practice to the fore, indicating that how opportunities are taken differentiates current experience both within and between social classes.

In addition, money matters rather a lot. To dine out regularly in relatively expensive venues is a significant burden upon household budgets. The hierarchy of styles is roughly correlated with the price of a meal, so those who are well versed in restaurants delivering many culinary traditions require significant extra funds. Nevertheless, it is not just money that matters. Models always show that other socio-demographic factors play a role. Taste, when expressed through activity, is always a matter of opportunity, and in this field, as in many others, cosmopolitan London offers more options. Yet social position remains a powerful determinant of both the breadth and content of experience. Variety is almost universally valued, offering a medium through which to express taste, but in practice it is more accessible to some sections of the population, exhibiting a pattern which parallels and echoes social inequalities more generally.

# Part V
# Continuity and change

# 12

## The practice of eating out

### Introduction: towards a practice-theoretical account of dining out

This chapter deploys theories of practice to frame an account of dining out in 2015. After a brief résumé of theories of practice to dispel misgivings about their capacity to describe and explain social change, a synoptic account of the practice of dining out is presented. We discuss the rationale of the practice and identify three core guiding principles widely shared across the population – variety, comfort and concern. The implementation of the principles is not uniform. Eating out events can be arranged in many different ways to satisfy these requirements. They must be tailored to particular occasions, companions and venues. We stress the central importance of conviviality. When people translate these principles into specific events, dining out is fundamentally a social and sociable event. Arrangements are, in addition, tinged by contrasting orientations towards 'Art' and 'Ease'. We emphasise the use of variety in the style and type of restaurant in marking distinction and social status. We illustrate the modal approach, exemplified by two interviewees, emphasising the central importance of conviviality. So, despite a shared dominant understanding and persistent basic orientations, performances vary a great deal, raising the question of whether there is a specifically British way of dining out. Finally, we examine how dining out fits with other practices, eating at home, cooking, shopping and other leisure and recreational activities. This discussion hints at how theories of practice differ from other approaches to explaining change and continuity.

Theories of practice operate on the basis that practices are the fundamental unit of social scientific analysis and emphasise habit and routine, know-how, practical understanding and performances. They appeal when studying consumption because they promise to make a double correction to previous work, first by providing an alternative framing to models of individual choice and by uncovering and exploring phenomena normally concealed in cultural analysis. This is best considered as a matter of the emphasis put on different aspects of conduct. Against the model of the sovereign consumer, practice theories emphasise routine over actions, flow and sequence over discrete acts, dispositions over decisions, and practical consciousness over deliberation. In reaction to the cultural turn, emphasis is placed upon doing over thinking, the material over the symbolic, and embodied practical competence over expressive virtuosity in the fashioned presentation of self.

There are many versions of theories of practice (Nicolini, 2012). The one applied here has been prominent in the sociology of consumption and has its philosophical origins in the synthesis of Schatzki (1996), subsequently adapted by Reckwitz (2002) and Warde (2005). Its primary analytic categories are understandings, procedures and engagement. Practice is viewed as a scientific object in itself and is located through its conditions of possibility and its wider institutional setting (Warde, 2016). It is reconstructed from evidence of typical doings and sayings, habitual and routine conduct, normative imperatives, and practical purposes, generating performances in the world which are observed and measured through various sociological devices. The protocol for describing practice requires the description of dominant shared features of performances and their socially differentiated variants.

Robust accounts of the internal operations of practices entail their perpetual modification. Schatzki (2013) addressed the issue explicitly, if in a preliminary way, when he distinguished between stability, evolution and dissolution of practices, which is to say that some practices change very little over time, some alter to a moderate degree but in a developmental manner, while others are transformed. Applying these concepts to dining out suggests that the basic features of the practice either remain stable or steadily evolve. There are no signs of the dissolution which 'happens when changes are large, disruptive, or cascading' (Schatzki, 2013: 40).

## The constitution of the practice

To demonstrate that a practice has an identity, and thus the potential for continuity through time, requires evidence of some sufficiently constant relationship between elements configured around practical understandings and practical procedures which are capable of initiating and orchestrating many discrete recognisable performances. In this section we show that dining out in England has such qualities. There is a shared sense of purpose or rationale, the operationalisation of which revolves around three guiding principles – variety, comfort and concern. The latter are configured in arrangements which meet the requirements of particular categories of social occasions. The principles are also interpreted in different ways depending on people's practical orientations towards the activity of eating. These structuring features reveal the anatomy of the practice of dining out.

## Mutual understandings of purposes

Eating out is primarily understood, as it was in 1995, as a substantial meal, paid for in a commercial establishment, eaten with other people, and usually primarily for enjoyment. Most meals out now are considered as ordinary, occurring in an impromptu or regularised manner which renders them a normal part of everyday life, although they are still exceptional in the sense that the home remains the primary site of eating. So, while the basic reasons for wanting to eat out are similar to 1995, fewer events are considered special occasions. Not only does almost everyone in the population dine out occasionally, most, especially the younger cohorts, are now very accustomed to eating in restaurants. Dining out is a familiar experience and a recreational activity expected to deliver pleasure.

Companionship and food quality are the primary concerns, although service, comfort and relief from domestic labour all matter. Almost everyone would agree strongly that good companions are the nub of the experience. For many the food is a secondary consideration. Opinion is also divided over the relative merits of being at home and eating out. Many prefer the comfort of home and the familiarity of the meals eaten there. Others, especially those whose labour is expended in providing domestic meals, see significant benefit in dining out at least sometimes.

Eating out events are differentiated along three principal dimensions: food content, the company, and relative valuations of public and domestic space. Eating out generates a tension between familiar and enjoyable foods and dishes not normally eaten at home. If dining out remains Britain's most popular out-of-home recreational activity, it occurs in different versions. Many people are keen to extend the range of dishes that they eat. There is greater excitement about food overall, and acknowledgement that eating out can be used to extend and expand culinary horizons. Aversions such as the fear of unfamiliar food or a dislike of vegetarian meals are diminishing. Although eating incurs much more media and popular attention than in the past, not everyone is attracted in the same way. Some interviewees who are very enthusiastic about eating out and about food more generally express great interest in dining at restaurants. Most people are less interested because they are primarily concerned with the sociability afforded or the convenience of an accessible meal requiring no preparation. Nevertheless, those who take a cautious approach still affirm that they try new and different things, adapting practically in the context of a food-conscious and food-suffused environment.

### Principles guiding engagement

Almost everyone subscribes to the three guiding principles governing arrangements for dining out – variety, comfort and concern. Pursuit of variety is the most frequently articulated priority. Major omnivores make breadth of experience an imperative; they are prolific in the accessing of cuisine styles, types of restaurant, and other channels, including takeaway outlets and specialist food shops. However, they are not exceptional in valuing diversity. Most other people do too, propelled by the injunction to be or become adventurous when deciding where to go and what to eat. A greater proportion of the population are now excited about going to new places, say that they eat things that they would not at home, and like to talk about food which they have eaten out. The appeal of this orientation towards food – a preference for diversity and novelty – is confirmed by the apologetic tone of those who perceive themselves as limited in the breadth of their tastes. For everyone there are limits, but the boundaries lie at a further remove for some. Foodies are characterised by cultivating super-diversity and maximum variety.

A second principle involves feeling comfortable and at ease when eating out. This is facilitated through normalisation and underpinned by the general societal tendency towards informalisation. Two-thirds of respondents say that they 'feel comfortable in any type of restaurant'. A similar proportion deny feeling 'on show' when eating out. The excessive formality of restaurants, which was a significant form of complaint in the 1970s (waiters kept ties to lend to men who had failed to put one on, for example) has dissolved to the point where fewer people, now only about half, say they dislike stuffy places. Also, fewer want their fellow diners to be smartly dressed. Few examples of embarrassment are reported. Diners are mostly relaxed, achieving adequate control of the social aspects of the occasion by being sufficiently attuned to the conventions of the venues they visit. Distinction is demonstrated by the capacity for feeling comfortable in a greater range of places where different implicit rules of behaviour and conventions apply. A general feature of middle-class cultural capital and competence in public is an apparent effortlessness in matching behaviour to different occasions and settings. To be able to traverse comfortably a wide variety of settings and experiences facilitates participation and is consistent with the third principle of cultivating a suitable level of informed appreciation of eating out.

The third principle is concern, implying that people should both pay attention to and develop adequate knowledge, awareness and appreciation of dining out. Not all people require the same amount or type of knowledge in order to be able to get by as customers in restaurants. Horizons of experience and the characteristics of companions affect what it is necessary to know or to be able to say. Interviewees differ markedly in their awareness of the panoply of restaurant experiences, their ability to describe their experiences, and their capacity to ground judgements about what they like or dislike. They share understandings of what it means to eat out and what, for instance, main meals might be. The least articulate and least engaged describe and pass judgement on food quality, atmosphere, menus and value for money. They rarely exhibit embarrassment or anxiety if asked for an opinion. Even when admitting to having less mastery than others over the range and intricacies of food culture, they are not ashamed. Some, like Gerald, are proud to stand up for their positive preference and convictions about traditional food. He wants to be seen as a defender of tradition, not in the foodie sense of authenticity but rather as custom. It is his wife who tries to defend him against the accusation that he is a died-in-the-wool conservative. Knowledge, genuine or pretended, exhibits competence and engenders a feeling of being in control. So, while connoisseurship is rare, a modicum of knowledge is commonplace.

As an aside, because these principles framing practical understanding are shared more or less universally, they have implications for the analysis of distinction. Those who might seek to derive cultural capital from their mode of participation are able to 'go with the flow' of the practice. Making most profitable use of the affordances of material privilege is predicated upon class pedigree, having high income and higher education. However, claims about the value of activities are neither contested nor rejected by other class fractions. To express or display distinction does not require action popularly deemed inappropriate or offensive. The difference in approach from persons without cultural pretension or concern with the symbolic status of their behaviour is marked only by more intensive engagement. Distinction in 2015 is expressed by obtaining greater varieties of food, attending more varied social occasions and having greater knowledge of the field. It probably also involves maintaining control over how eating (and dining out) impinges upon other social practices and recreational pursuits. Cultivation or exploitation of these possibilities may, *in extremis*, result in pretentiousness. However, when avoided, the boundaries between cultivation and vulgarity blur and differences of social position are more easily managed intersubjectively. Thus, food enthusiasts can, without appearing pretentious, talk to those who are less knowledgeable because the same principles are shared and accepted.

### Arrangements: situational adjustment

Organising an eating out event requires learning how to align the occasion, its purposes and its personnel, to the venue and its menu in order to create a congenial context for a pleasing meal. The many different types of venue vary in size, decor, atmosphere, layout, service culture, menu, style, quality and price. These features of a setting can generally be anticipated; a restaurant's offer does not change much from day to day. Selecting a setting, the site for an event, is a basic condition for ensuring that arrangements and procedures will be appropriate to the occasion, suitable to the main reason for eating out and the status and dispositions of companions. This requires some degree of judgement, as upon it depend the quality of the food and the success of the overall event. Greater familiarisation with the activity of dining out helps people develop skills of judgement and enables them to anticipate what certain types of place will deliver even if they have never been before. By the same token, many people go back to the same place because of its known qualities (Karpik, 2000). In 2015, 67 per cent of reported last visits involved returning to a place previously visited. There are also many subsidiary considerations in organising an event, such as the time of day, travel distance, other practices sequenced (including where your next meal is coming from), anticipated duration, price and accessibility, all of which give a steer towards a type and style of restaurant and menu. Nevertheless, these procedures affecting selection of the venue are mostly secondary to the generic imperative of finding a site suitable to the occasion and its participants.

The potential organiser of a meal out solves an equation, although they would rarely perceive it as such and they accomplish the task without much deliberation, seeking a good fit between companions, the purpose of the occasion and the food served:

Event = Location (venue) + Occasion (purpose + company) + Appetite (selection and incorporation of dishes)

It is possible to get such an equation badly wrong. However, people mostly solve it with little thought and great success. This is sometimes because they are routinised in their selection (to eat with the same people at the same place, with similar people at the same place, or the same people at a similar place are all safe bets often wagered). However, the principle of variety and the vagaries of social circumstance mean that this is not always the only desideratum. Eating alone usually means a simple calculation, with the occasion being a quick meal and the venue a place visited previously. Sometimes more thought is required, when, for example, the diners are not regular companions, or have incompatible dietary restrictions, or would not all be equally accepting of the price and quality of the food or the level of formality involved. Note that, regarding domestic hospitality, the location rarely offers any options and therefore simplifies the solution. The range of possible venues makes available more possibilities for greater success but may equally make such calculations more complicated. If Bauman (1988) is correct in suggesting that organisers can expect to be judged by others as if they had a free choice which expresses their taste and identity, decisions may be burdensome. Once a site has been selected, however, degrees of freedom are much reduced.

Suitable arrangements for any particular event also depend in part on the social position of companions and the dispositions they have acquired over time. Familiarisation means that people typically have attended many events, the resulting knowledge influencing expectations and the making of arrangements in the future. In addition, frequent discussion of eating out in the media and within social networks, which transmit ideas, standards and awareness of variety, enhances the capacity for nuances and making more specialised or specific arrangements when organising meals out.

The structure of the event is thus a 'cause' of what is eaten. It is easier to forecast what will be eaten if the other features of the event are known. While there is a great deal of heterogeneity in the performance of meals with the same principal purpose, certain features will occur more frequently. Conceptually it is helpful to think of the site of the meal as coordinating companions, occasions and food. Someone planning a restaurant meal has many degrees of freedom. Almost every restaurant will accept almost anybody as a customer (although it was not always thus). However, successfully moulding the social situation requires a congenial setting and a suitable alignment of elements which not every restaurant can provide.

### Differentiation of taste

The guiding principles are modulated and implemented in ways which reveal differences in cultural and culinary taste. Differences in taste appear in dispositions towards the practice. Almost everyone values conviviality, which is derived from connections to the companions. That is, however, often combined with, although sometimes occluded by, two contrasting dispositions towards eating out which might be deemed Art and Ease.

For some, eating in restaurants is approached as an aesthetic experience. Edward, the prototypical major omnivore, treats meals in restaurants as opportunities to engage in intricate evaluative judgements, as when he conducts comparative taste tests in restaurants. His disposition produces careful attention, deliberation, comparison, and the type of critical evaluation associated with judgements of art. Some, less dedicated, omnivores share aspects of that disposition; Camilla, Siobhan, Nadine and Penny all engage in judgements of the quality of preparation of dishes, but are less focused on culinary art. Penny, for example, pays close attention to the food, but holds companionship in higher regard. Asked 'What makes you enjoy food so much, do you think?', she replies:

> I get to talk about it with friends and colleagues [...] It's something to talk about and have fun with. It can signal a birth or looking after someone because they've had a bad time. You can treat people. So for me, (a) it's about the food itself and the flavours and the enjoyment you get from that but (b) like I said, it's the company and interaction. I've always associated food with a positive thing and always had positive experiences and I've liked being able to share my experiences with other people.

Others are even less concerned with the food and give primacy to the ways in which dining out makes for ease. Pete, a good example, eats in casual dining restaurants often but does not approach his meals with aesthetic criteria in mind. His priorities are company and the opportunity to 'get out of the house'. He seeks value for money, freshness, taste and prompt delivery. Much eating out alone is considered rather similarly as a matter of convenience, a way of avoiding the work of preparation, usually justified in terms of distance from home, shortage of time, tiredness or lack of a domestic alternative.

While everyone acknowledges the importance of conviviality and also considerations of health, dispositions towards Art and Ease differentiate the population. These dispositions exist on the basis of some similar institutional foundations; commodification, global culture, international trade, commercial competition, urban concentration, affluence and publicity underpin both dispositions. In addition, however, a taste for Art is fostered by aestheticisation, the search for distinction and cosmopolitan sympathy, while Ease reflects the informalisation of social conventions and pressures of everyday life prompting temporal reorganisation of schedules. Learned and cultivated through repeated experience these dispositions have become more pronounced in the period between 1995 and 2015.

### Orientations to the practice: procedural approaches and the effects of social position

Chapter 4 disclosed a pattern of orientations towards dining out. Respondents' answers to questions about purposes, opinions and behaviour associated with dining out tentatively capture the contours of the practice. The responses to a series of statements tapping aspects of understandings, procedures and engagement reveal prevalent and alternative orientations towards the activity. Identical data about the dispositions and orientations which guide people in context in both years, offer a means to determine both the shape of the practice and to detect change. Responses give information about regular behaviour, how the activity is approached, feelings about it, and general expectations and wants. While exercising due caution about interpreting such evidence it does give insight into the organisation of practices.[1] This is not, of course, evidence about what people actually do but is an indication of the range and content of dispositions and predispositions which constitute the practice and set the context of action.

Differences in orientation are one instrument for establishing social differentiation of taste. Recall that the first and most powerful orientation derived from the principal component analysis reported in Chapter 4 isolates a tendency for some people to use eating out as a channel for exploration of new experiences with food. Key indications include being excited about going to new places, learning from such excursions and talking to others about dining out (Table 4.2, pp. 63–64). Strengthening significantly after 1995, this orientation is prevalent among certain sections of the population. High social capital and a high

---

[1]   Many cogent criticisms can be levelled at the use of questions about attitudes and opinions. Reported attitudes are subject to understandings of the question and are flimsy guides to behaviour. Nevertheless, when the same question is asked at intervals its interpretation becomes more reliable. The aggregate changes in response also give some indications about changes in understanding and procedure.

rate of cultural participation are powerful influences. Moderate levels of household income are also significant, implying perhaps that the richest have already attained a level of exposure and knowledge which they take for granted and do not aspire to extend. Having a partner is a strong predictor too. A contingent effect of partners eating out together often is the opportunity to experiment by sampling a dish which one of them would not otherwise select. Importantly, women are significantly more adventurous in orientation than men, even though that disposition is not converted into greater breadth of practice. This is an aspect of gender disparity; women are more inquisitive and communicative about food consumption but are denied opportunities to capitalise on their interests. Overall, people professing an expansive and exploratory orientation are the same people who currently enjoy the widest experience of eating out and who exhibit omnivorous inclinations when eating out. The young, women, and those with above average but not the highest household incomes, have an exploratory orientation but lack the means to put it into practice.[2]

Other sections of the population approach matters differently. Caution when eating out is one distinct orientation (see Chapter 4). Some people profess to be suspicious of foods that they do not know, they prefer when eating out to choose things which they also eat at home, they feel themselves to be on show, and want quick service (suggesting that they want eating out events to be as brief as possible). This orientation is somewhat less prevalent in 2015 than in 1995, but nevertheless remains a strong orientation which was most prominent among those in the working class, without a degree, with low household income, living in Preston, with dependent children, who were not white British, and who did not eat out frequently. A CARs model also picked up weak effects for having lived in the city of residence for a long time, and being older.

These two orientations, each strongly evident in both years, have almost diametrically opposed social foundations. People in different social positions and with contrasting dispositions exhibit variations in taste which lead them into different situations and therefore different performances. Some feel out of place in many of the contexts afforded by the apparatus of contemporary dining out while others simply prefer the experience of eating familiar foods at home. So, although almost

[2]   This is revealed in models showing that the positional attributes associated with an exploratory orientation differ from those associated with breadth of experience of cuisine styles and restaurant types in so far as a different age group is engaged, and gender matters, but city does not.

everyone subscribes to the validity of the three guiding principles of the practice, they encounter different situations and opportunities for performance. Despite such variation, the agents involved in industrial provision and cultural intermediation can, in association with a swathe of enthusiastic consumers, manage to legitimate a particular hegemonic definition of the practice.

### A consolidated practice

Practice theories view purposes, principles, arrangements, tastes and orientations as a configuration of mutually constitutive elements. They are the basic analytic elements of the practice of dining out. The elements are not arrayed in a temporal, linear or casual sequence but are analytically necessary components of making eating out in a restaurant possible. They are fundamental components of the practice. Competence in the practice requires permutation of procedures which are consistent with purposes and principles, channelled by recognised orientations and dispositions, and applied effectively to specific situations. Satisfactory performances come mostly not from reflection and deliberation, but from a feeling for practical tasks which are routinised and tacitly understood. Elements change a little, and a few change a lot, but they nevertheless constitute a continuing identity. There are no apparent 'cascading' consequences. The principles have become more firmly entrenched, with prevalent orientations the same in 2015 as in 1995.

### Ordinary practice: how dining out is adjusted to eating at home

Much attention is paid to omnivores at the expense of those with less distinctive food behaviour. The largest bloc of tastes, the modal bloc, comprises people who experience both uncommon and popular cuisines (pp. 182–184). Modal respondents, 37 per cent of the survey sample, avoid exclusive places and eat in restaurants serving popular and uncommon cuisines. They draw predominantly on traditional British, Italian, Indian and 'other ethnic' cuisines. Their experiences are pivotal and are neither feted nor disparaged as might those of foodies be. How they approach dining out is key to capturing the central tendencies of current practice.

Statistical aggregation of the characteristics of members of the modal bloc depicts the mean modal individual as female, aged late thirties, living in Bristol, white British, with no children, no degree, and no present or parental experience of service class, with a household income between £30–40,000, and dining out monthly. Her social contacts are of middling status and cultural participation is moderate, and her mother (but not father) would have had highbrow interests. Not easily distinguishable by social characteristics, the hallmark of the modal condition is moderate, balanced and unremarkable practice. Members of the category are not exceptionally enthused by eating out, but nor are they conservative. They share more social and behavioural features with minor omnivores than with people in the restricted category (Table 10.2, p. 192). The ordinariness of the behaviours associated with such tastes, and the ways in which that becomes embedded in routine food practice, can be illustrated by the cases of two women, Angela and Miranda, whose tastes in dining out allocate them to the modal category.

One lesson to be learned in encountering these two women is to appreciate how dining out is integrated into their wider eating regimes. Dining out in the commercial sector is shaped and given meaning by comparison with eating under other social circumstances. Understanding the practice of dining out requires examination of how people integrate their restaurant meals with other aspects of their food behaviour. Chapter 8 summarised how this is achieved by examining the mutual influences of domestic provisioning, domestic hospitality and commercial provision. From that perspective the effusive attention paid by the media and cultural sociology to food enthusiasts and professional cultural intermediaries is potentially misleading. Now familiar but not overly engaged with the culture of restaurants, many people have a pragmatic and prosaic relationship with dining out.[3] It is these undistinguished and nondescript cases, the ordinary bearers of the practice, whose performances are primarily responsible for reproducing the practice. Their engagement is often a mere residual effect of their wider social and cultural commitments.

### Modal taste: Angela

No interviewee has the ideal typical characteristics of the modal figure, but Angela is a close approximation and in no way exceptional to the category. Aged in her early forties, she lives in Preston with her teenage son and husband with whom she shares a household income of £30–40,000 per year. She currently works in a lower professional occupation although she has no degree. She went to restaurants with five different cuisine styles in the previous year – traditional British, Italian, Chinese, Thai and 'other ethnic'.

---

[3]    Journalism and sociology alike tend to work with ideal typical, emblematic and symbolic figures with rather exceptional qualities. Distinct figures at the end of continua are described, rather than those who cluster in the middle of the spectrum.

Angela's first preference among venues is for a not-too-busy and not-too-noisy pub serving traditional British cuisine. She has firm favourites but tries new places if recommended by friends. Her last main meal out described during the course of the interview was a fish pie with vegetables eaten in a local gastropub, a regular haunt that she has known since she was a child, and where she and her husband eat at least six times a year. Indeed, 'we go back to what we know and what we like'. She values quality, characterised as the home-made over the pre-prepared or fast foods typically served by chain restaurants. Decisions about where to eat out are based on 'what we fancied for a start, where we are, who we are with, what we know'.

Angela's habits are shaped by social and caring responsibilities and work schedules. Once a fortnight Angela and her husband take her elderly and unwell father-in-law out for a meal, which is a 'break for him'. In addition, her mother hosts all of her children and their partners every Saturday morning by treating them to a mid-morning meal in a garden centre cafe.

Angela eats out with her husband and different sets of friends with some regularity, mostly in venues serving traditional British or 'socially near' cuisines such as Italian and Mediterranean foods. Indian and Chinese takeaway meals are bought occasionally but less often than fish and chips which are collected on the way home from the weekly supermarket shopping trip. They also eat once a year with a large group of friends as part of social club outing; the quality of the food on the last occasion was described as 'horrendous', but the food is not the purpose, rather 'it's about being together as a group'.

Sociability is more important than the food itself. Angela explicitly declares that she is not a foodie. In her opinion, a good restaurant will look nice and have a good reputation which she would glean from friends or from websites such as TripAdvisor. Angela has been inspired by meals eaten at a restaurant or pub, for example a 'cheese and onion pie' for which she 'googled' the recipe and proceeded to cook the dish at home. Describing herself as a 'good cook', Angela takes an active interest in 'basic good family food', and she cooks traditional British dishes with some contemporary influences; the 'Sunday roast dinner' is followed by a 'risotto' on Monday. New recipes are incorporated in an evolutionary, haphazard way, influenced by food fashions and travel. Asked whether travel has affected her cooking, she replies:

I guess it has really without thinking about it (...) this year we went to Turkey and they do cater for the English anyway but the restaurant that was our favourite was a traditional Turkish one and that was like the chickpeas and sauces and things like that, vegetables, yes. I've made things like that since we've come back. So yes, I guess it does influence.

Angela is unexceptional and lies near to an imaginary central point of contemporary tastes. She is relaxed and pragmatic, interested in food but not an enthusiast. She is sceptical about foodies, whom she views as 'pretentious', and among whom she includes people on specialised diets. She is unimpressed by the symbolic or communicative aspects of restaurants. Dining out serves family and social purposes, and excursions to restaurants fit in an integral manner into domestic routines.

### Modal taste: Miranda

Another example from the modal group, Miranda, aged late fifties at the time of interview, lives with her husband on a household income of approximately £70,000 a year. She is a skilled and enthusiastic domestic cook and eating at home is core to her eating habits. Nevertheless, she engages regularly in different types of eating out events. When asked what she understands by the term 'eating out', Miranda replies 'anything'. She recounts a repertoire of different kinds of dining out experience in a way that makes clear their correspondence with quotidian circumstantial demands as well as serving particular social purposes. She eats out around four or five times a month and, without prompting, she differentiates these occasions between 'one really nice meal' and several 'cheapie meals'. Elaborating, Miranda cites her husband's dismay at 'quick' home-made meals. On the occasions where there is a risk of 'something quick, even if it's home-cooked from the freezer' being served, as on days when Miranda has been caring for their grandchild, he is likely to suggest that they eat out, for 'nothing sensible is going to come out of the kitchen'. These occasions range from a casual meal where they 'share a pizza and have a beer each' to a 'splash out, and have a steak and share a pudding, and have, you know, wine and coffee' when she and her husband feel they can 'stretch a bit further' with their budget. Miranda also dines both in and out with a group of female friends with whom she has been meeting regularly since their respective children were infants. This group – the 'Thursday Girls' – meets approximately once a month, either over home-cooked food, or out at a restaurant, where they prioritise their own personal tastes rather than the preferences of their families. Summarising their preferences as 'ordinary class things', Miranda mentions vegetarian food, fish dishes and lighter dishes of flaky pastry.

Relaxed dining and an informal style is what Miranda claims to like most of all, which are principles she applies equally to home-cooking and dining out. British and Italian meals, with 'an Indian meal occasionally', provide enjoyment of a moderate variety of styles. Trips to the cinema are associated with a burger – 'cinema and a burger seem to sort of go together' – while Italian meals are greatly favoured for their propensity to deliver 'lovely, easy suppers'. Adding to the sense that eating out is an occasion for relaxation, Miranda says that she most likes not having to cook and wash-up herself. Indeed, she then 'enjoy[s] that glass of wine even more'. A highlight is a dessert which she would not make herself at home where she prepares hearty desserts designed to serve several people from one dish, such as cakes, crumbles and puddings. At a restaurant, Miranda likes to order 'something really extra special' like 'panna cotta' or 'crème brulée'. Testament to her unfussy attitude to dining out, she says that she will 'go anywhere if someone else is paying the bill' but also notes that she avoids places that are simply too 'grungy' – 'I'm of a certain age now, it's got to be nice'.

Miranda's wide and varied taste and knowledge about cuisine styles is partly the result of an interest in everyday cooking and entertaining. Her enjoyment of everyday and uncommon cuisines is matched with knowledge and opinions about the evolution of popular dishes which do influence her home-cooking. Recipes are adapted and improved over time though; she gives an elaborate description of how her shepherd's pie has come to involve browning the mince and deglazing the pan with red wine. She remarks on how new pizza toppings are evolving beyond purist Italian rules to include feta cheese, spices and salad leaves such as rocket. Reflecting on items presented as 'innovative' at food festivals and pop-up restaurants, Miranda concludes that she hasn't 'tried anything really new. You just try their variation on a theme'.

### Learning from the ordinary

Both Miranda and Angela use episodes of eating out to supplement and complement the other parts of their wider food arrangements. They appreciate such events, for their relief from domestic tasks, for the variety that restaurant meals offer, and for the relaxation afforded by being served. They are not food enthusiasts, although they are highly competent in preparing meals for their families and for guests. Dining out is a part of their culinary routine, and while regular and ordinary it remains relatively infrequent and still a treat. Miranda clearly has learned about food from mass media and incorporates that knowledge when organising domestic meal preparation. Neither woman would want to stop dining out, for it is a source of pleasure, but its role in their overall food regime is contained. They incorporate lessons from eating out, including cooking dishes which their parents would never have countenanced, but restaurants are not central to their practice. They nevertheless accede to the principles of variety, comfort and concern, distinguish effectively which venues are suitable for which occasions, and cleave to the poles of sociability and ease when dining out. They epitomise ordinary consumption in the field of dining out.

## Is there a 'British' way of dining out?

It is interesting to reflect on whether the modal approach to dining out, adopted by a large minority among the population, epitomises a meaningful and specifically English way of dining out. Food plays a role in the everyday creation of national identity (Ichijo and Ranta, 2016). Recent decades have seen 'cuisine' attributed to regions and countries, a process which DeSoucey (2010) conceptualises as 'gastronationalism'. The idea of national cuisine serves commercial interests, with opportunities for advertising restaurants, branding foodstuffs and promotion of tourism. However, some countries are hard-pressed to give a coherent and recognisable representation, as was argued by Sidney Mintz (2002 [1996]). He was able to describe common patterns of consumption in the US but could identify nothing with a sufficient aesthetic or historical foundation to justify the accolade 'cuisine'. The same may be true of contemporary Britain.

It is very hard to discern the components of a British cuisine when food content and cooking styles are so varied and subject to international influences. There is no orthodoxy. Diners feel no obligation to conform to a legitimated culinary order. Currently many people subscribe to particular named diets among a multiplicity; 41 per cent of respondents reported that, mostly for reasons of health but also of politics, they had followed a special diet in the last twelve months, including vegetarian, vegan, pescatarian, gluten-free and lactose-free. A search for communal or collective commitment to particular food content seems doomed to failure because of low attachment among the population to a shared and definable culinary tradition. Remnants of post-war practices perhaps still provide a notional idea of what is specifically British. In the 1950s French cuisine remained highly regarded, alongside domestic repertoires founded in the industrial nineteenth century, using imported ingredients especially from the British Commonwealth, when 'meat and two veg' dominated dinner plates. Some dishes surviving from that era are consumed on specific occasions and discussed as if they had some symbolic national significance for the dominant ethnic majority, such as roast meats, English breakfasts and fish and chips. In restaurants classified by respondents as 'traditional British' the most popular dishes proved to be roast dinners, steak, fish and chips, and burgers.[4] However, these comprise a small proportion of the dishes at meals eaten out. With food content enormously varied, it is no accident that the term 'eclectic' is commonly invoked to describe the dishes appearing on menus.[5] In restaurants and at dinner parties the range of items is heterogeneous as are the favourites. Making a virtue out of uncontrolled or unregulated diversity is a way to present favourably a rather ill-disciplined mix of traditional, international and experimental cooking in the professional trade. A mild echo of such a miscellany is discernible in domestic cook-ing, in for example Miranda's personal recipe book (Figure 5.1, p. 77), which features traditional British staples, Italian-influenced pasta and rice dishes, curries, and improvised dishes which mirror weakly the eclectic menus of restaurants in the UK.

Despite the heterogeneity of menus, travellers rarely get confused about which country they are in when they go out for dinner. Perhaps, therefore, it is less by means of food content and more by reference to orientations towards the arrangements, procedures and social norms of dining that British specificity is made recognisable. If British cuisine can-not be defined by content, perhaps it is shared orientations, oscillating between art and ease, that drive a national understanding and practice. British distinctiveness is a matter of the organisation of the field, which is governed by commercial competition and mandates variety on the one hand and weakly disciplined recreational social worlds which preclude formality on the other. Eclecticism coexists with plural social and culi-nary conventions.

Everyone wants food to be healthy (an injunction which mostly trans-lates into securing balance through sufficient variety). Otherwise they feel free to pursue particular and specialised diets, such as vegetarian, Mediterranean, gluten-free, or the gastronomic adventuring of foodies. All are acceptable and each has advocates. Tolerance for leisure activi-ties, appearance, matters of lifestyle (a term which in current usage implicitly defines choice between alternatives to be a personal matter) extends to eating out. Compared with other countries, Britain perhaps

---

[4]   The designation 'modern British' is much harder to delimit. At the high end of the commercial trade it was described in terms of fresh, seasonal and local produce in the 1970s, with echoes of nouvelle cuisine. However, this does not translate into particular dishes.

[5]   Note that eclecticism is not personal eccentricity but, like other diets, is a collective rather than an individual phenomenon.

emphasises health over gastronomy, and recreation and relief over connoisseurship and expression of national identity. When compared with other parts of Europe it supports informality of rules and conventions around event types and food content. By comparison with East Asia or North America, dining out remains exceptional because it is still a minor part of integrated eating arrangements. Ultimately the British way of dining out might be characterised by eclecticism, informality and its typical configuration with other eating practices whereby people pursue variety and comfort within the contours of plural dietary principles.

## Reflections on practice

Practices do not generate uniform performances. Settings, social positions and dispositions create diversity. Dining out is a socially differentiated practice. There are systematic variations in enjoyment (and rationale); engagement (frequency, type and style); procedures (manners, integration, planning, length of meals); and selection (potential for strategies of distinction, gender and divisions of labour, expression of commitment to ethnic minority culture). Nevertheless, despite the fact that the activity of eating out can be carried out in many alternative ways, it is one of the more regulated sub-species of the practice of eating. An orderly activity, its form is partly ensured by the way in which provision is organised and partly through shared understandings of appropriate conduct when dining in public. There is much flexibility but no compulsion or punishment incurred. There is limited embarrassment or disapprobation regarding how people eat, partly because people mostly eat with people from similar social circles and in similar circumstances to themselves. Deviation and non-compliance are a limited threat to reputation or self-esteem. Nevertheless, standards, preferred procedures and understandings are widely shared and few demur.

Even if there is no common manner in which the population of Britain eats out, the practice has a set of well-entrenched characteristics that sustain its eclectic menus and commensal conventions. Almost everyone dines out sometimes. The activity is legitimated in terms of acceptable purposes. All endorse the principles of variety, comfort and concern. People are mostly able to solve the equation which matches venue to occasion to menu. Settings are selected to sustain suitable forms of social interaction around the dinner table. Shared understandings include cognisance of the manners and conventions of behaviour on site which keep commercial venues orderly. They also include acknowledgement of the centrality of the sociability and conviviality of events. A recognisable hierarchy of cuisine styles is evident, differential engagement with which occurs in accordance with the predilections of different social groups. Both social position and disposition towards the practice inflect patterns of behaviour. A career of dining out will entail often wide experience organised sequentially in accordance with life-course changes and social and geographical mobility. Such experience, the product of many different individual performances, becomes sedimented into a set of dispositions and inclinations which reinforce the norms of the practice. Performances and practice are mutually constitutive, with identifiable features that are stable and reproduced over time.

# 13

## Explaining continuity and change

### Introduction

The previous chapter typified and synthesised approaches to dining out in 2015 as reported by interviewees and respondents to the survey. The impression is of diverse cuisine and informal organisation. This chapter considers the origins of contemporary practices. It is written with an awareness of the difficulty of explaining circumstances where a condition of the continuity of practice is both internal pressures and adjustment to movements in an external environment. Social scientists, social commentators and indeed many other inhabitants of modernity are primed to look for and mostly to welcome change. In presenting the results of our research to different audiences the first question asked is almost always 'what has changed?'. Of course, the purpose of the project is comparison over time in order to be able to examine similarities and differences between the evidence for 1995 and 2015. However, a primary focus on change is in danger of minimising an appreciation of continuity by overemphasising features of the activity, especially where the survey shows a statistically significant difference between 1995 and 2015. This chapter seeks to adopt a more subtle historical perspective which pays attention to the persistent identity of the practice of dining out in the context of wider social and cultural change.

### The difference that twenty years makes

#### Accounting for change

The mechanisms through which practices are shared become institutionalised and, when reproduced, work imperfectly. The vocabulary of practice theories includes concepts such as trajectory, career; recruitment, defection and generations; controversy, contestation and competition; differentiation; and obsolescence. These are all mechanisms impelling the evolution of practices. In addition, processes external to the focal practice create a wider institutional context for evolution including adjustment to changes in adjacent practices; adoption of innovations in technological systems and infrastructure; and new forms of regulation. Last and not least, individual and collective projects explicitly formulate strategies around which people mobilise in order that practices may be changed in ways more to the liking of the participants. In some instances these mechanisms cause only surface perturbation and trendless fluctuation, in other circumstances they define and propel a developing trajectory. Focusing on different component elements of the practice, to identify rates of change and compare different spans of time, provides elements of an explanatory account. Representing the balance between continuity and change is difficult. Even with, or perhaps because of, exactly comparable data obtained from a purposeful re-study, what remains the same is difficult to establish definitively.

### Tendencies and counter-tendencies: familiarisation and diversification

Two overarching trends in the practice of dining out, actually counter-tendencies each with several strands, can be detected: familiarisation and diversification.

Familiarisation occurs when a practice becomes ever more taken for granted as an unexceptional form of activity. In 1995 eating out was held to be special, a significant treat and something out of the ordinary. That is less true of 2015 when, for example, Crispin responds to the interviewer's question, 'What's the special thing about eating out?', by saying:

> I don't know. I think it's because we don't do it every day and the kids get to choose what they eat and it's sort of… it's seen as a bit of an occasion, so… and there might be nice food even. I don't think… it's not like it's an amazing treat … It's just something nice.

Familiarisation has several dimensions. Manifestations include fewer people expressing a wish to eat out more often and the evidence that it delivers declining pleasure. One dimension is regularity of practice. As people get experience of different types of establishment, fears and anxieties diminish. People feel more readily at ease in the semi-public space of the restaurant. They make recurring arrangements and expect to incorporate dining out events into their social diaries. Uniformity of provision in congenial settings aids regularisation. The proliferation of casual dining restaurants and frequent eating in pubs provide unchallenging contexts. Such popular types of restaurant sustain familiarisation. A second dimension might be called casualisation. More meals are described as 'quick/convenient' as more visits occur for functional purposes. Popular types of restaurant pride themselves on their informal atmosphere and ease of use, with less formal structure and less rigid manners. Children are more welcome and fewer people say they prefer child-free restaurants. Booking a table in advance is less common and the decision to eat out is less often premeditated. The interactions between staff and customers are also increasingly informal. A third dimension is simplification of both procedures and food content. With fewer special occasions, meals become quicker on average, have fewer courses and often less-elaborate dishes. This reinforces informality and lowers the social and economic stakes associated with an event.

These developments are consistent with a process of greater uniformity, of mass consumption associated with globalisation. Connoisseurs might feel that this is the thin end of a wedge, portending a loss of distinctiveness and difference. However, another set of trends appear to be working in the opposite direction. Witness a greater interest in food, more types of food, more cuisines, more publicity and discussion of food, aestheticisation and, overall, greater diversity.

In the early twenty-first century, popular enthusiasm for food and eating is rampant. Media coverage is very extensive and encourages concern and excitement. Ordinary people express considerable interest in food and cooking (in 2015, 69% declared themselves very or fairly interested in everyday cooking and 71% in special cooking). One facilitating factor is the considerable diversification within the commercial sector. More types of restaurant serve a wider range of cuisines and dishes. Temporal deregulation allows people to eat more types of meal out; the recent growth in the proportion of breakfasts purchased away from home is one example. These options are capitalised most by those with an omnivorous orientation, with some experiencing a very wide range of venues and foodstuffs. A greater variety of foods and dishes are available, drawing on global sources of styles of cuisine and their typical dishes. Such people undoubtedly get much enjoyment from their enthusiastic engagement with food and eating, and perhaps also garner valuable cultural (and social) capital. A minority of enthusiasts pursue variety purposefully and gain experience of ever more segments of the market. Enthusiasts, privileged financially and culturally, show obsessive tendencies towards voracious engagement in all kinds of eating experiences. Restaurant-going is a central concern, where they extend their already varied culinary experience and polish their knowledge.

Encouraged by cultural intermediaries, they are proud of their adventurousness and keen to display culinary prowess. Our data cannot say, but the levels of enthusiasm and publicity are probably greater than in 1995.

However, it is not only omnivores who experience a significant range of cuisine styles. Diversification reflects the two faces of globalisation. The first is a tendency for the same cultural items to occur uniformly in many places in the world as a function of international trade, global culture and global corporations. The second is local resistance to pressures for homogenisation as regional specificities are asserted and traditional institutional forms fill ecological niches.

### Institutional explanation

To explain the currently normal standards governing dining out requires consideration of the institutional forces that make the objectives of comfort, variety and concern seem practicable, sensible and natural. The forces underpinning the observed fluctuations and continuities broadly affect very many cultural activities in England. They take specific forms with respect to eating out.

As Burnett (2004) points out, informalisation of manners around meals has been happening for several decades as meals at home have become less structured and less uniform. They occur less often at a dining table, not taken with all other family members, without the setting of the table, and with less rigidly scheduled starting times.[1] Meals out have also become more informal in reaction to the view that restaurants were indeed stuffy and formal. Popular formats require *relaxed* manners.

The emergence and proliferation of restaurants seeking to provide a more relaxed experience has tilted the balance towards informality. The most popular types of restaurant among our respondents, indexed by where they ate the last meal on commercial premises, were casual dining restaurants (30% of occasions) and pubs (27%). Despite a perceptible variation in the regimes of different casual dining restaurants and pubs – for example, some gastropubs provide smart surroundings and forms of service similar to exclusive restaurants – it is easy to feel comfortable in most, and they provide little threat of embarrassment because of inadequately mannered performances. Market research reports observe that the casual dining restaurant is one of the major commercial creations of the 1990s. The name encapsulates the arrangements and processes within the restaurant, and confirms that many

---

[1]   Note, however, that the deregulation of domestic routines can easily be over-estimated (Yates and Warde, 2015 and 2018).

diners appreciate more casual forms of interaction, atmosphere and service. The spread of restaurants run by and staffed by migrant workers may also have had some effect; the conventions and procedures have fewer echoes of the norms of bourgeois patriarchy prevalent in post-War western Europe and the clientele may be less in awe of the staff. Both diners and staff behave more informally. The same trend to informality is apparent in domestic hospitality. Informalisation reflects a wider change in social atmosphere whose origins are attributed to cultural change in the 1960s and which escalates in multicultural contexts.

Not all occasions are informal. Some people welcome formality sometimes. Even informal settings present many potential embarrassments. Chopsticks may be just as daunting as serried ranks of knives and forks. Tipping is no less problematic. Informality is not without challenges, and the skills of confident informal interaction are a mark of social distinction. Ensuring fitting in harmoniously with other diners remains challenging and presupposes implicit rules prohibiting some kinds of behaviour. As Wouters (2007) might say, a constant rebalancing of formalisation and informalisation is a process without end. Dealing with people in the absence of formal or authoritative rules may make social interaction more rather than less delicate; exercising freedom requires the skills of selection of a suitable context on the part of the interactants. That the interaction is scripted by proprietors and staff who circumscribe behaviour *in situ* does, however, mitigate uncertainty.

Commercial processing of food has steadily reduced the amount of preparation required in the home prior to consumption. This reflects in part a need to adapt the changing household schedules in the post-Fordist service economy. The role of married women in the labour market in the last third of the twentieth century is often cited as a driver of change. The male breadwinner wage supporting a housewife and children gave way to dual-career households and much greater difficulty in coordinating the temporal and spatial itineraries of household members around fixed time points for meals. This should not be exaggerated, for routine and regularity persist (Yates and Warde, 2015, 2018). Nevertheless, Brannen et al. (2013) show, although with an admittedly small sample of people, that almost all households with more than one person in employment were having considerable difficulty in managing to eat together even once a day. Requirements of employment, fitting in time for recreation (often children's out-of-hours classes and pastimes), adapting to hours of employment that did not coincide for partners, and finding time for domestic labour and preparation of meals were the background to the imperatives, problems and potentials of flexible time–space paths. Some difficulties may be alleviated by smaller households, fewer dependent children, and the simplification of lunch. Work and family continue to be primary framing forces behind daily meal schedules and eating regimes as Grignon (1993) demonstrated for industrial societies. Couples with dependent children dine out less frequently, those with higher incomes and in professional and managerial jobs more frequently. Diversity of household structure and the irregular schedules of household members encourage new patterns of eating out. Household reorganisation provides an impetus to eat out occasionally both to reduce the burdens of domestic cooking and because flexibility obviates unforeseen disruptions. In conjunction with widely expressed concerns about gender inequality and a gradual redistribution of food-related domestic labour (Sullivan, 2000; Kan et al., 2011), differences between women and men in their levels of engagement in dining out has almost been eliminated.

Burnett's (2004) account emphasises the extent to which economic prosperity influenced patterns of eating out in England. Austerity during two world wars and their aftermath had very distinct impacts on eating out. Rationing and problems of supply imposed restriction on the commercial sector, although the inauguration of collective and communal systems of providing meals to the public compensated in part. The British restaurants set up during the Second World War are well known, but the extent to which factories, schools and military installations provided main meals to significant sections of the population until the 1970s was important in maintaining levels of eating out. Burnett (2004: 320) consequently concluded that

> it is probable that the total volume of eating out in England has not significantly increased over the whole period [1830–2000] … What has changed is the balance between eating out from necessity which has always been associated with work, and eating out from choice and for pleasure, that is, as a leisure activity.

The latter is true, although the balance may be readjusted as more people eat meals which they describe as quick and convenient. The functional meal is increasingly supplementing the leisurely social occasion which had proved one of the most popular of all British recreational activities of the later twentieth century. One other interpretation might be that some of the changes observed by 2015 might themselves be a result of policies of economic austerity pursued by Conservative governments after the global economic crash of 2008. Burnett argued that prosperity had helped found 'a revolution at table, 1970–2000'. That may have been reversed as incomes have stagnated, social support for the less privileged reduced, and wealth has become steadily more unequally distributed. A smaller proportion of food expenditure was devoted to eating out in 2015 than in the years immediately before the crash. Market research since 2010 suggests that people did not reduce the frequency of eating out but spent less on each occasion. Familiarisation is thus not hampered as people improvise to maintain their accustomed levels of engagement, even if that requires eating simpler meals in casual surroundings. Expense is not an insuperable obstacle to at least occasional meals out of the home.

A final institutional force is globalisation, long emerging, but with effects recognised now as increasing both uniformity and difference. Familiarisation with dining out is in part an effect of the ease of access to casual and fast-food restaurants, often global chains providing dishes and meal formats common in most cities throughout the Americas, Europe and Asia. International in scale, but barely distinguishable in aesthetic or symbolic terms, they are neither socially nor gastronomically challenging. On the other hand, globalisation has generated both conservation of local variation and an experimental approach to cuisine. The commercial sector has enhanced the aesthetic status of food by celebrating authenticity, novelty and quality. Aesthetic principles used to increase diversity include invoking the symbolic significance of local food, seen now as having a role in the spread of gastronationalism, the introduction of yet more obscure national cuisines, and the tendency to create variation in an experimental way by fusing the flavours of disparate culinary traditions (DeSoucey, 2010; Lane, 2018). This aspect of diversification, alighted upon by foodies, restaurateurs, journalists and cultural intermediaries, has accentuated material and symbolic variation in consumption conducive to both enthusiasm and distinction.

These key institutional processes have helped consolidate the contemporary approach to eating out. Their profound and uneven impact underpins familiarisation, informalisation and diversification. However, the practice of eating out intersects with others, most notably other ways of obtaining dinner, but also with other cultural and leisure activities, work and its scheduling, household and family management routines, the marking of rites of passage, and the maintenance of social connections and networks. To understand the dining out routines of specific individuals therefore requires an appreciation of the complexities of situation, position and their insertion within many different practices as well as overarching institutional forces.

### What interviewees say about change

Most people, for practical purposes, are oblivious to the institutional pressures within whose orbit they conduct their daily lives. Nevertheless, especially if pressed by an interviewer, they may be able to reflect informatively upon changes that they have experienced. So, while the interviews were directed at current and immediate past practice, the topic of change arose in discussion. References to change are couched more in terms of personal biography rather than wider cultural and commercial contexts, but the latter are considered.

Many interviewees recognised that the life-course stage affects how they behave. They acknowledged as turning points setting up home with a new partner, divorce, the birth of children and their leaving home. For example, Tristan had become a vegetarian after beginning to live with his new girlfriend. Siobhan comments on the difference between being childless, having young children and having older children. Robert also remarks 'we had little children and then big children … that was a different world really.' With children come changes in the frequency of eating out and preferred venues. The effect of changing health status is also often associated with ageing. Lara, for example, remarking that she is recovering from a stroke, says 'You don't get time, things change in your life. You go through different stages.'

Occupational and geographical mobility are also mentioned as factors influencing change. Felicity's recent move to Preston means that she has fewer friends, less money and new surroundings:

> I think the reason that I was in those places was because of jobs and things, so I probably would say that in Manchester and Bristol I ate out a lot more because I had a better-paid job and so did my husband, and we had more friends there. We don't really have many friends in Preston so I think that's influenced it as well. The bigger places that we've lived we've definitely been more times and we've gone into different places.

She underlines the importance of having other people to eat with, especially friends. Social capital is a key resource for benefiting from eating out. Friends are often credited with introducing new tastes and new restaurant experiences. Arlie, whom we met earlier, clearly feels indebted to her friend Pat for helping broaden her food horizons. Lara, Felicity, Miranda and Luke all attribute fresh tastes to friends.

Some autobiographical accounts attribute radical change to principled decisions about diet. Laxmikant and Uma explain their shifts in terms of religious commitment; Tristan credits his vegetarianism to his partner showing him films about animal welfare; Lara, Gerald and Camilla refer to serious health threats (stroke, diabetes, cancer); and Magdalina mentions her adoption of a strictly disciplined bodily maintenance regime to counter anxiety. Such transformational change is, however, the experience of a minority and happens only once or twice in a lifetime.

Older interviewees are better able to discuss change. Those born before 1960, who thus would have come of age before the major shifts in the commercial provision of meals in England, are much more likely to elaborate extensively.[2] They often make rather dramatic comparisons with their childhoods or their very early adult days. For example, they refer to the very highly routinised nature of domestic meals in the times of their grandparents especially (Miranda, Karina and Robert). They often have memories of change which relate to people other than themselves. Increased variety, particularly of ingredients, flavours and menus is a common theme. Robert remarks that the range of foods has 'got much greater'. Gerald says 'I think people are definitely much more diverse in their eating habits.' Karina says 'we've become more adventurous, whereas the older generation stick to what they know' and Arlie notes that 'we've all become a lot more foody in the last twenty to thirty years'. More spicy foods and new flavours were identified, usually with reference to specific dishes or holiday trips, as significant indicators of change.

Gerald, in his late sixties, identifies many changes; he observes more children in restaurants, greater diversity in provision, more takeaways, 'the menus have changed a lot', curries are popular, there are more venues, and eating out is no longer a luxury. He contends that 'as a country we're more cosmopolitan'. Like many others he is of the view that 'definitely people eat out more than they did twenty years ago.' Also, as do other older interviewees, he draws strong contrasts with his childhood:

> when I was a child, going back donkey's years, going out for a meal was a big, big treat. Yes, and it was always a cafe. It was something that you looked upon as you were so fortunate. And going out for your Christmas lunch.

Accounts sometimes become elaborate, when for example Miranda distinguishes between the traditional food that she prepares for her now adult children and 'the modern stuff' that they serve or buy her: 'from the children we get the younger style, the new style foods', among which she includes Japanese dishes, couscous and sashimi, while 'from us they get the classic shepherd's pie'. She has a clear sense of what is traditional,

---

[2]   Of sixteen interviewees who talked about change, the seven born before 1960 contributed twenty-five pages of transcript, while the nine born later filled only ten pages. The young major omnivores say little about change (three of them – Edward, Penny and Nadine – nothing at all) and then only about changes in their own habits rather than about context, manners or culinary trends.

including roast joints of meat, shepherd's pie, trifles and chocolatey puddings. She says, apropos of a dish of ham hock, 'there's a resurgence of the classic English, British dishes', and she accuses celebrity chefs of 'reinventing the wheel'.

Importantly, Miranda is an enthusiastic and skilled domestic cook, as were her mother and grandmother. Asked whether she would like to eat out more, she says 'no, because I enjoy my own cooking. And if I ate out more it would spoil it, eating out still has to be a treat'. Perhaps as a result of her interest in cooking – she entertains both family and friends in explicitly informal ways but with very varied foods – she is able to evaluate change and can offer a wide-ranging and nuanced account of developments. She is attuned to changes in the environment, locally and more broadly: 'pubs have become restaurants now', 'burgers have become posh' and 'we've got lots of exciting things to try'. She notes the current availability of vouchers promising two meals for the price of one, which she uses. She attributes her recently reduced consumption of Indian cuisine to the closure of a good nearby Indian restaurant, and some of her newer likes to the cooking of her children. She remembers when some ingredients such as avocados and capsicums became commonly available. However, she is in something of a quandary when estimating how her preferences have altered. She says, 'I don't think my tastes have changed. My tastes have always been very broad. I enjoy trying all sorts of things.' She also, however, says, offering many examples, 'I feel I have just moved with the times'. Posing herself a rhetorical question, she comments, 'Have my tastes changed? Well, I guess they have but I can't define it ...'. Perhaps a gradual evolution in tastes but without any significant change in disposition is the most common form of transition.

Finally, mark what interviewees do not say. No one disparages or condemns eating out. No one thinks that variety has diminished. No one is of the view that the quality of meals when dining out has, overall, declined. No one mentions social differences; despite awareness that other people eat in different ways to themselves, that is never attributed to social position.

## Appreciating stability and continuity

### Continuity

A thorough explanation requires the examination of cultural reproduction and an account of what has *not* changed. The essential structure of events persists, as evidenced by definitions of going out, having companions, travelling, spending time, ordering courses in sequence, and eating dishes from menus. When explicitly listed, these invariant parameters appear as trivial truisms. Yet it is possible to imagine, for example, that menus might disappear. The tasting menu, beloved of chefs with pretensions to inventiveness, is a form of table d'hôte which eliminates choice although not as yet the listing of dishes. A return to service *à la francaise*, where several dishes appear simultaneously at each course, might become the dominant rather than an alternative format. People might come to prefer to have meals delivered to the home and cease visiting restaurants. If, as now, home deliveries mostly involve basic dishes, they could be replaced by more elaborate services supplied by peripatetic chefs. One could imagine co-production, where consumers go to the restaurant kitchen and prepare the food themselves, or with others, before eating a meal. That is to say, radical transformations in the practice are imaginable. However, changes on this scale seem not on the horizon.

Inspection in detail of changes between 1995 and 2015 reveals much stability. Understandings of key defining features of eating out remain in place. The understandings of 'eating out' and 'main meal' were the same in both years. No new reasons for eating out have appeared over the twenty years. Identical questions on the survey met with similar levels of recognition. Dispositions identified in the battery of questions about attitudes and behaviours cluster in the same way in both years and the ways in which adherence to those clusters is distributed socially within the population are the same.

Of course, almost no features are identical. As Abbott (2001: 266) observed, it seems more realistic, in general, to expect that personal and social circumstances will change than that they should remain the same. Thus, he maintains that the challenge for sociology is to explain continuity. In that vein, factors militating towards reproduction are worthy of note. Retrospective estimates of the frequency of eating out in restaurants are the same in both years, although the mean frequency probably has increased a little. Eating out is still subordinate to eating at home, primarily seen as an occasional interlude rather than the foundation of dietary intake. Foodstuffs have changed incrementally as some new dishes and menu formats have become common, yet while specific dishes and cuisines rise and fall in popular estimation, concern for diversity remains. Social continuities are especially marked. Commensal occasions continue to be situationally defined; with whom, when, and in which category of venue an event occurs is calculated using the same formula as earlier. Also, social differentiation looks very similar, with the social underpinnings of symbolically distinguished behaviour, primarily in the form of cultural omnivorousness, still dominant.

The structure, pattern and frequency of domestic hospitality is, likewise, little altered. The same categories of person act as hosts and guests and a norm of reciprocity governs events which are very highly valued as a source of personal affinity and conviviality. The social construction of hospitable meals remains similar, involving small groups of family members and friends maintaining relationships through sharing food and exchanging labour. In 1995 such events were modelled in the light of the template of the dinner party, although most actual performances deviated in the direction of greater informality (Warde and Martens, 2000: 57–61). That tendency to informalisation has continued and if the classic dinner party is a little less common, its retreat is a *continuing* process. Domestic hospitality thus evolves more slowly than its commercial equivalent and, like other household arrangements, responds primarily to external institutional shifts.

In most respects, given the evidence from 2015, the main conclusions of the first study (Warde and Martens, 2000: 215–227) can be reiterated. Dining out is a socially differentiated activity, motivated by a search for conviviality and companionship, which delivers great pleasure and coexists comfortably with domestic family meal arrangements. Informalisation was already occuring, yet the activity remains disciplined and subject to widely shared conventions. Variety of experience, obtained from breadth of contact with foreign cuisine, is symbolically significant and a sign of socio-economic privilege and cultural refinement. So, while the study in 1995 had no systematic prior point of comparison, no radical tendencies have appeared subsequently.

Among the forces which retard rapid change is the continuing presence of conservative and cautious orientations among consumers. Commercial diversity serves the cautious and conservative as well as the adventurous for the former remain a valuable sector of the market whom producers are compelled to serve. To the extent that cohorts and categories of persons who have a disposition to maintain their conservative habits comprise an increasing proportion of the population – and Britain has more elderly and more ethnic minority groups than in 1995 – then bearers of stable preferences and practices are identifiable.

### Observed changes and the longue durée

While it would obviously be wrong to claim that the structure of eating out is invariant, there are no radical ruptures. Change is not dramatic. Familiarisation and diversification are important tendencies, but they partly cancel one another out, and do not erode the basic features of the experience of dining out. That they are not harbingers of radical transformation will be corroborated by viewing changes in dining out in a longer-term perspective. However, it might be objected, if continuity is so marked, why is there such a strong popular perception that eating out is subject to perpetual rapid mutation? One reason is publicity and the way that food and activities around eating out are addressed in mass (and social) media. News values concentrate attention on novelty, on 'the new'. Constant commercial innovation and advertising have effects on the climate of opinion; while innovations may be more sheen than substance, and many fail and therefore disappear rapidly, they are the subject of publicity. Publicity creates an aura of rapid change which is not confirmed by the research evidence. In addition, impressions deriving from personal careers, as behaviours change in parallel with geographical mobility, life-course stage and income levels, contribute to a sense of restless change. Given the props to an impression of permanent transformation, a look at the *longue durée* is informative as it gives a perspective on which are radical and which are surface changes.

Probably there is still a prejudice or preference for seeing change as good, an echo of modern ideologies of progress which have flourished for centuries, despite it often being directionless fluctuation, replacing typical behaviours with others functionally and morally equivalent. In no obvious sense can we measure progress towards perfection in the practice of eating out. There is no best way of dining out. The tendencies detected in this study – the mix of familiarisation, informalisation and diversification – are not straightforward evidence of improvement.

Perhaps assessment over a longer period justifies a positive impression. Viewed over a hundred years, dining out has spread to virtually the whole population. No longer an upper-middle-class preserve it has become a source of comfort and pleasure for all, implying that access and procedures have altered for the better. A much expanded and more differentiated catering industry provides meals which are prepared by a larger number of chefs and cooks with different international backgrounds. Chefs are given recognition and are probably better appreciated, while waiting staff in almost all establishments, especially in popular ones, interact less stiffly. Restaurants operate with greater informality with fewer white tablecloths and fewer glad rags. More ingredients are more widely and readily available and distributed, with seasonality of produce no longer an impediment to menu design. The clientele is socially much broader and is prepared to spend larger proportions of food budgets on commercial premises. Customers are better travelled, have a more detailed knowledge of international trends and dishes, and have developed tastes for more exotic foods derived from cuisines across the globe. Such tastes are inflected by a massive increase in popular food commentary as mass and social media make it a central topic for examination. Experience is also extended by the availability of restaurant dishes to be eaten at home, courtesy primarily of supermarket ready meals but also of domestic delivery. However, changes are slow and gradual.

Hence, the landscape is very different from a century ago when dining out decorously and elaborately was an activity for a small middle class. Many people ate out as a matter of necessity but rarely for recreational purposes. Economic fluctuations, and more so war, caused some significant discontinuities. By comparison, the period 1995–2015 is one of gradual evolution, with trends and counter-trends apparent at surface level but with strong continuities in the structural underpinnings of the activity. This is partly because the key tendencies of familiarisation, informalisation and diversification are themselves part of longer-term evolution rather than recent transformation. The persistence of institutional forces in the period since 1970 is the basis of coherence and continuity in the practice of dining out. Eating out as recreation, its spread to all sections of the population and the growing acceptability of different foreign cuisines were products of the 1960s and 1970s. By comparison, the emergence of tasting menus, sushi, tapas, and the still relatively arcane cuisines of Africa and South America are mere transitory detail.

### Innovation and the future

The practice of dining out was being consolidated in the twenty-year period under scrutiny rather than exhibiting features signifying transformation or dissolution. Nevertheless, some of the changes identified, were they to accelerate or intensify, might eventually result in the destructuring of the practice. It is worth briefly reviewing candidates for such a transformative role, for some changes may have the potential for cascading consequences which might thoroughly transform the practice. Candidates might include more eating in restaurants with family members, undermining the domestic setting as the nexus for food consumption; stronger separation of foods consumed in the commercial mode when compared with other modes of provision; rejection of the commercial mode as boredom sets in or value for money appears poor; re-privatisation and retreat from public life. Alternatively, one or more of the many social movements attempting to change eating behaviour in the light of health considerations, environmental sustainability or gastronomic persuasion might come to have transformative effects. Perhaps more likely, cumulative changes in adjacent practices which bear upon dining out might have significant effects. Patterns of employment and time-use, household structure and family formation, or the pull of other recreational activities might make dining out seem a less sensible way of obtaining food, meeting social obligations or having fun.

However, none of these possibilities seem imminent. Dining out is well established, resistant to change in other aspects of eating and not under much pressure from adjacent or distant practices. There is little indication of new moves in provision likely to undermine the structure of the activity. Certainly the last twenty years have seen some novel developments, including tapas bars and tasting menus, additional foreign cuisines, casual dining restaurants, the normalisation of foodie enthusiasm, dietary regimes, and new channels of communication about eating out. Significantly these are mostly commercial or culinary rather than social innovations. The social foundations of the practice are more stable. The understanding of commensality and conviviality, manners and purposes, are firmly established and entrenched. The normalisation of familiarity and diversity applies a social brake to commercial innovation.

## Conclusion

The principal features of the contemporary ideal of dining out began to form in the 1970s when the appeal of variety and greater flexibility in respect of new foods, procedures, timings and venues grew. Informalisation of manners occurred in parallel. The glimmerings of a new informed appreciation of food appeared in print and visual media and, enhanced by the educative effect of the supermarket, laid the foundation for enthusiastic interest in food. Heightened awareness and intensification of interest accelerated sharply from the 1990s. More publicity, more media and newspaper coverage (food columns were restricted to women's magazines until the 1980s), reviews and latterly online and blog commentaries on restaurants, the multiplying of celebrity chefs on television (thin on the ground until the 1990s), and habits of photographing dishes, have all increased the attention paid to food and eating out. Recreational and aesthetic engagement was supplemented from the 1990s by national campaigns about healthy eating, an interest in alternative diets and closer scrutiny of what people should eat. Familiarisation of dining out, informalisation of manners and the expectation of greater variety in practice sustained the trend for a gradual revision in orientation towards eating.

Similar modifications in understandings and behaviour associated with dining out occur in other contemporary cultural practices. Aestheticisation, an omnivorous orientation, the drawing of cultural boundaries, the complex interweaving of local and global influences on taste, commercial promotion, and market segmentation are common features of many cultural practices and not specific to dining out. These features of the general cultural landscape are underpinned by powerful processes of globalisation, commodification and cultural intermediation. Globalisation – the acceleration in the circulation of ideas, products, people and messages, associated with international trade, migration and information – expands the scale, scope and meanings of culinary options. Few can remain unaware of ingredients, dishes and cuisines that connote faraway places. Commodification increases the rate of circulation and accessibility of products. The expansion of a private and commercial catering industry, ceaseless in its promotional activities and aiming to sell more experiences to customers, adds novel foods and formats as part of a process of market differentiation. In respect of eating out, intermediation is crucial. Associated with commodification, it has come to play a significant part in the profusion of promotional materials which underscore tendencies to aestheticisation and introduce more elaborate vocabularies and frameworks for judgement. The prominence of food enthusiasm would not have been possible without the greater publicity given to eating and dining out. Simultaneously, professional intermediation makes aspects of the world of eating out accessible to a much wider audience, thus also playing a part in familiarisation.

Commercial innovation, driven by competition for profit, is a constant motor of change. Innovation is often trivial, usually minor tweaks to already existing formulae. The turnover rate of small businesses is rapid. New restaurants are opened, themes reformulated, menus rejuvenated, dishes modified, furniture repositioned, decor refreshed and staff reprogrammed. All enhance the impression of rapid change. Catering businesses encourage consumers to buy food in the high street rather than from the supermarket in order to colonise additional meal events. The industry hopes to draw more eating events into the commercial sector and to induce new habits among customers. To the extent that people engage with food differently depending on where it comes from, shifts between modes of provision do matter.

Notwithstanding the powerful impetus for change represented by the commercial sector, the practice of dining out displays strong social continuities. Key structural features and understandings are little changed since 1995. The same understandings of 'eating out' and 'main meal' pertain. There is little change in the frequency of main meals.

Judgements of quality and topics of complaint have similar foundations. Social differences in approach and behaviour are also similar; the same factors of age, class, education, income and ethnicity differentiate the population. Changes in the direction of informalisation and diversification were already well underway by 1995, with Burnett and Panayi detecting their origins in the 1970s. Apart from a couple of decades after the end of the rationing imposed during the Second World War which were characterised by relative uniformity and homogeneity, variety and informality have been the watchwords of the entire half century after 1970. These are continuities associated with normal evolution. Panayi's so-called revolution has not stalled and nor have the tendencies been reversed that Burnett emphasised as originating after 1970. These tendencies did not, however, accelerate significantly in the years to 2015. The basic structural framework of the activity remains much as it was in 1995. This is not to suggest that the observed changes are all trivial or merely surface fluctuations, but twenty years is a short period for examining culture change, and eating habits resist rapid and radical change.

Finally, let us return to one initial question about the advantages and disadvantages of dining away from home. On balance, from the vantage point of early twenty-first-century England, current arrangements for dining out appear largely positive. It delivers a good deal of satisfaction and pleasure. The range of options has grown significantly, including not only more varied foods but allowing people to fit social occasions to different contexts in which they might comfortably enjoy convivial meals with friends and family. Restaurants have improved, starting without doubt from a low point in the years after the Second World War (Driver, 1983; Burnett, 2004; Warde, 2009). They have served as a vector for aestheticisation without causing any great harm to most of their clientele. Developments are not unaffected by the resistance of habits and routines which serve to guide people's preferences and practices. In the last analysis, cultural change is slow and what has been observed is the gradual and unobjectionable evolution of practice and taste which continues to grant relief from labour, exposure to new foods, and sociable gatherings which enhance relationships and a sense of well-being. Whether other less benign processes are working behind the backs of diners is a slightly different question, but experiences seem mostly to be enhanced by processes of familiarisation, informalisation and diversification.

# Methodological appendix

This appendix describes in more detail the survey samples, interview procedure and the socio-demographic characteristics of interviewees. It also contains supplementary tables referred to in the main body of the text.

## The survey samples

Table A2.1 shows some key characteristics of the survey samples in 1995 and 2015.

Table A2.2 compares the characteristics of the samples with the population of England as reported in the Censuses of 1991 and 2011. The characteristics selected as a basis of comparison are different because of changes in the nature of reporting in the Censuses. When comparing the sample with the population of England it is important to bear in mind that the sample is drawn from cities which have younger populations than average. Comparison of the samples with the populations of the three cities indicates that the sample is much more closely representative.

Both survey and household interviews were conducted in English. No significant difficulties arose. It is not possible to estimate whether respondents with English as a second language differed systematically in their understanding of questions or issues as there were comparatively few cases.

## The interviews

### Social and demographic characteristics of the interviewees

Table A2.3 records key features of the thirty-one interviewees. Pseudonyms are used and age is rounded to the nearest five years.

**Table A2.1** Survey sample characteristics, 1995 and 2015 (percentage by column)

|  | 1995 | 2015 |
|---|---|---|
| **Sex** | | |
| Male | 50 | 49 |
| Female | 50 | 51 |
| **Age group** | | |
| 16–25 | 24 | 18 |
| 26–35 | 28 | 25 |
| 36–45 | 20 | 16 |
| 46–54 | 16 | 19 |
| 56–65 | 12 | 12 |
| 66+ | 0 | 12 |
| **Marital status** | | |
| Cohabiting | 60 | 53 |
| Other | 40 | 47 |
| **Economic activity** | | |
| Full-time employment | 44 | 49 |
| Part-time employment | 18 | 11 |
| Other | 38 | 40 |
| **Ethnic identity** | | |
| White | 89 | 78 |
| Asian/Asian British | 5 | 10 |
| Black/Black British | 4 | 5 |
| Other | 3 | 6 |
| **Education** | | |
| Degree level qualification | 24 | 41 |
| Other | 76 | 59 |

## Topics

The checklist of questions for qualitative interviews in 2015 was as follows:

### MODULE 1 Another last meal out

- What do you understand by the term 'main meal'?
- Indeed, what do you understand by the term 'eating out'?
- Tell us about your last main meal eaten away from home...(public eating place/restaurant)
  - Why did you eat out on that occasion?
  - How unusual is the event, or the reason for the event?
  - Did you like it? Do you have a favourite restaurant or restaurant meal?

**Table A2.2** Survey sample characteristics, 1995 and 2015, compared to Census for England in 1991 and 2011 (percentage)

|  | 1995 sample | Census 1991 | 2015 sample | Census 2011 |
|---|---|---|---|---|
| **Sex** | | | | |
| Male | 50 | 50 | 49 | 48 |
| Female | 50 | 50 | 51 | 52 |
| **Age group** | | | | |
| 16–24 | 21 | 20 | 16 | 14 |
| 25–34 | 28 | 24 | 23 | 17 |
| 35–46 | 20 | 22 | 27 | 17 |
| 50+ | 31 | 34 | 34 | 52 |
| **Ethnic identity** | | | | |
| White | 89 | 94 | 78 | 85 |
| Asian/Asian British | 5 | 4 | 10 | 8 |
| Black/Black British | 4 | 2 | 5 | 3 |
| Other | 3 | 1 | 6 | 3 |
| **Child(ren) under 16** | | | | |
| Adult-only household | 62 | 68 | 68 | 72 |
| Child under 16 | 38 | 32 | 32 | 28 |

- What affects your choice of restaurant?
- What are the characteristics of a good meal out?
- What considerations do you give to where to eat and what to eat (health, novelty, convenience, ethics etc.)
- Are there things you dislike about eating out?
- Is there any kind of regular pattern to when you tend to eat out? Or is it more random?
- What affects your decision to eat out?
  - How do you decide where to go?
  - Are there places you avoid?
- Who do you eat out with?
  - How often do you eat out with them?
  - Do you regularly eat out with the same people?
  - How often is it your partner/family?
- Do you adjust what you eat at home if you know you are going out to eat? How?
- Have you ever cooked what you ate last time? [We know whether they cook]
- Would you be pleased if you had to eat out more often? What sort of food/place would that be?

**Table A2.3** Interviewee characteristics, 2015

| Name | Gender | Age[1] | City | Ethnicity | Household structure | Equivalised Household Income (tertiles)[2] | Class mobility |
|---|---|---|---|---|---|---|---|
| Edward | M | 35 | London | White British | Couple only | Highest | Sideways intermediate – working class |
| Lara | F | 65 | London | White British | Couple only | Middle | Upwardly mobile into service class |
| Arlie | F | 70 | London | White British | Living alone | Middle | Upwardly mobile into service class |
| Penny | F | 35 | London | White British | Non-related adults | Highest | Stable service class |
| Siobhan | F | 35 | London | White non-European | Couple with children | Unknown | Upwardly mobile into service class |
| Douglas | M | 35 | London | White British | Non-related adults | Highest | Upwardly mobile into service class |
| Eleni | F | 35 | London | White European | Couple only | Highest | Upwardly mobile into service class |
| Isaac | M | 45 | London | White British | Living alone | Lowest | Stable service class |
| Pete | M | 55 | London | White British | Living alone | Highest | Upwardly mobile into service class |
| Noah | M | 35 | London | White non-European | Couple only | Highest | Stable service class |
| Gerald | M | 70 | Preston | White British | Couple only | Highest | Downwardly mobile from service class |
| Simon | M | 40 | Preston | White British | Couple with children | Highest | Unknown |
| Angela | F | 40 | Preston | White British | Couple with children | Middle | Stable service class |
| Tyler | M | 20 | Preston | White British | Couple only | Middle | Downwardly mobile from service class |
| Felicity | F | 30 | Preston | White British | Couple only | Middle | Upwardly mobile into service class |
| Karina | F | 40 | Preston | Indian | Single parent | Lowest | Downwardly mobile from service class |
| Enid | F | 60 | Preston | White British | Couple with children | Middle | Upwardly mobile into service class |
| Stephen | M | 60 | Preston | White British | Living alone | Highest | Stable service class |
| Tristan | M | 30 | Preston | White British | Couple only | Highest | Upwardly mobile into service class |
| Jeff | M | 65 | Preston | White British | Couple only | Middle | Upwardly mobile into service class |
| Camilla | F | 40 | Bristol | White European | Single parent | Middle | Upwardly mobile into service class |
| Nicola | F | 50 | Bristol | White British | Couple with children | Middle | Downwardly mobile from service class |
| Laxmikant | M | 60 | Bristol | Indian | Couple only | Highest | Downwardly mobile from service class |

**Table A2.3** Continued

| Name | Gender | Age[1] | City | Ethnicity | Household structure | Equivalised Household Income (tertiles)[2] | Class mobility |
|---|---|---|---|---|---|---|---|
| **Magdalina** | F | 30 | Bristol | White European | Non-related adults | Unknown | Downwardly mobile from service class |
| **Luke** | M | 25 | Bristol | White British | Couple only | Middle | Sideways intermediate – working class |
| **Nadine** | F | 30 | Bristol | White British | Couple only | Highest | Upwardly mobile into service class |
| **Robert** | M | 60 | Bristol | White British | Couple only | Unknown | Stable service class |
| **Miranda** | F | 50 | Bristol | White British | Couple with children | Highest | Sideways intermediate – working class |
| **Mal** | M | 30 | Bristol | White British | Living alone | Lowest | Sideways intermediate – working class |
| **Cheryl** | F | 65 | Bristol | White British | Couple only | Middle | Stable working class |
| **Crispin** | M | 50 | Bristol | White British | Couple with children | Middle | Upwardly mobile into service class |

[1]Rounded to the nearest 0 or 5
[2]Reported annual household income adjusted for number of persons in the household. Lowest (£300–£13,000); Middle (£13,001–27,500); Highest (£27,501–£130,000); Unknown 3 Partners were present at four interviews: Nicola, Enid, Samir and Gerald. In two instances they participated extensively, and we sometimes quote Rasmi, wife of Samir, and Jane, wife of Gerald.

## MODULE 2 What sorts of restaurants do you (ever) go to, and do you like them?

- What are your favourite types of restaurant?
- Do you go to lots of different types (which would be a follow-up from the survey responses – take those responses as a starting point)?
- Has your range got greater over time?
- How interested in food and cooking are you?
- Are you interested in TV cookery shows?
- Do you read about food?
- Do you use online sources for recipes, choosing restaurants, etc.?
- Has travel affected your tastes, or your practices, and does what you have eaten on holidays matter? Do you like 'foreign' foods?
- Do you know the term 'foodie'?
- Would you consider yourself a foodie? If not, why not?
- Have you ever been a vegetarian? Do you have any specialised diet now or have you in the past?

## MODULE 3 How do you put together/plan/achieve a mix of eating at home and eating away from home on a regular basis?

- Do you have a particular routine of eating during a week?
- Are weekends different?
- Tell me about this week, for example...
- Would you prefer to cook more, or less often? Why?

## MODULE 4 Domestic entertaining

In the survey, you said that you have people over for a main meal in your home. Can you tell me about...

- Who you tend to have over? For what reason?
- What do you serve? Is it different depending on who you have over?
- Who does the work? Do your guests contribute in some way?
- Do you like entertaining others with food in your home?
- What are your favourite ways of doing/things to cook when having people over to eat in your home?

And what about the last time you ate at someone else's home?

- Who entertained you?
- Who else was there?
- What did you eat? What did you think of the food?

- What sort of occasion was it?
- How does this compare to the other times you've eaten at other people's homes? (Who, what, when, occasion etc.)

### Coding procedures for qualitative interviews

Thematic codes were derived both deductively – nodes were created for responses to key questions such as 'what do you consider a main meal to be' – and inductively, for example, seeing that respondents identified different 'types of occasion' we interpreted and named these as 'regular', 'just social', and 'special' occasions. Such thematic inductive and deductive codes were indexed into 'parent and child' nodes, which were used to retrieve narratives by category when further analysing the data both in conversation with the survey, and in writing case vignettes. In this way, as noted by Mason (2002) we distinguish between making our data manageable and creative analysis. For the latter, we treated each transcript as a narrative, or collection of stories pertaining to eating practices (Reissman, 1993). We did not adhere to conventions of narrative analysis as set out by Labov (1997), such as sequence of storytelling (Coffey and Atkinson, 1996). Instead we attended to the ways in which stories and utterances contributed to a portrait of eating and feeding both in and outside the home.

### Additional tables

See over.

**Appendix Table A4.1** Principal component analysis, eight orientations: regression of factor score loadings, 1995, 2015 and combined

| | Eigenvalue | Rotated loadings | Significant coefficients: All | Significant coefficients: 1995 | Significant coefficients: 2015 |
|---|---|---|---|---|---|
| **1 Exploration** | 3.601 | | 2015*** <br> (–) Male*** <br> Degree* <br> High £*** <br> Middle £*** <br> Freq EO*** | (–) Male*** <br> High £*** <br> Middle £* <br> Freq EO*** | (–) Male* <br> Degree* <br> High £** <br> Middle £** <br> Freq EO*** |
| I have learned about foods through eating out | | 0.522 | | | |
| I eat things now that I learned about on holidays abroad | | 0.466 | | | |
| I often talk with others about eating out | | 0.462 | | | |
| I get excited about going to eat in a new place | | 0.423 | | | |
| **2 Relief** | 2.343 | | (–) 2015*** <br> (–) Male*** <br> White Brit*** <br> (–) Unknown £** | (–) Male*** <br> Age* <br> (–) Age2** <br> (–) Degree* <br> (–) Stable service* <br> (–) Other class* <br> (–) Unknown class* <br> (–) Unknown £* | (–) Male* <br> White Brit*** <br> (–) Unknown £** |
| I like eating out because it means I do not have to prepare the meal myself | | 0.575 | | | |
| I like eating out because it gets me out of the house | | 0.538 | | | |
| I would like to eat out more often than I do now | | 0.403 | | | |
| **3 Home-centredness** | 1.538 | | (–) Male* <br> (–) White Brit*** <br> Children* <br> (–) High £*** <br> (–) Middle £*** <br> (–) Unknown £*** <br> (–) Freq EO*** | (–) Upward mob** <br> High £* <br> (–) Middle £** <br> (–) Unknown £*** <br> (–) Freq EO*** | (–) Male* <br> (–) White Brit*** <br> Children* <br> Unknown mob* <br> (–) High £* <br> (–) Middle £* <br> (–) Freq EO*** |
| Eating out is poor value for money | | 0.551 | | | |
| Meals prepared at home are superior in quality | | 0.467 | | | |
| I prefer the comfort of my own home to eating in public place | | 0.432 | | | |
| I only eat out on special occasions | | 0.407 | | | |

**Appendix Table A4.1** Continued

| | Eigenvalue | Rotated loadings | Significant coefficients | | |
|---|---|---|---|---|---|
| | | | All | 1995 | 2015 |
| **4 Caution** | 1.395 | | | | |
| I am suspicious of foods that I do not know | | 0.584 | (–) 2015* | Children** | (–) White Brit** |
| When I eat out, I like to choose things which I don't eat at home | | –0.430 | (–) White Brit** | (–) Degree*** | (–) Degree** |
| Quick service is important to me | | 0.307 | Children** | (–) Stable service*** | (–) Stable service*** |
| When I eat out I feel I am on show a little bit | | 0.306 | (–) Degree*** | (–) Upward mob*** | (–) Upward mob** |
| | | | (–) Stable service*** | (–) Downward mob*** | (–) Downward mob*** |
| | | | (–) Upward mob*** | (–) Other mob* | (–) Other mob* |
| | | | (–) Downward mob*** | (–) Unknown mob*** | (–) Unknown mob** |
| | | | (–) Other mob*** | (–) London*** | (–) Unknown £* |
| | | | (–) Unknown mob*** | (–) Bristol** | (–) London* |
| | | | (–) London*** | (–) Freq EO*** | (–) Bristol** |
| | | | (–) Bristol*** | | (–) Freq EO*** |
| | | | (–) Freq EO*** | | |
| **5 Indulgence** | 1.211 | | | | |
| I am not as concerned about the healthiness of the food served | | 0.673 | (–) 2015* | Male** | Male*** |
| A vegetarian meal would never be my first choice | | 0.508 | Male*** | White Brit*** | (–) Age* |
| When I eat out, I like to eat more than I do at home | | 0.317 | White Brit*** | (–) Degree*** | White Brit*** |
| I prefer there to be no children around when I eat out | | 0.312 | (–) Degree*** | (–) Stable service* | (–) London* |
| | | | (–) Stable service* | (–) Upward mob* | (–) Bristol*** |
| | | | (–) London*** | (–) Other mob** | |
| | | | | (–) Unknown mob*** | |
| | | | | (–) London*** | |
| | | | | Freq EO* | |

(Continued)

**Appendix Table A4.1** Continued

| | Eigenvalue | Rotated loadings | Significant coefficients | | |
|---|---|---|---|---|---|
| | | | All | 1995 | 2015 |
| **6 Decorum** | 1.143 | | | | |
| I dislike eating out at places that are formal and stuffy | | −0.600 | (−) Degree* / High £* / (−) Bristol* | Stable service* / Upward mob* / High £* | (−) Bristol*** / Freq EO*** |
| I like to go to places where the other diners are smartly dressed | | 0.581 | Freq EO*** | Freq EO*** | |
| I feel comfortable in any type of restaurant | | 0.471 | | | |
| **7 Efficiency** | 1.085 | | | | |
| If I was served an unsatisfactory meal I would complain | | 0.646 | (−) 2015*** / Male** / Age** | Male** / Age** / (−) Age2* | (−) Children* / (−) Degree* / High £*** |
| Quick service is important to me | | 0.439 | (−) Degree** / High £** / Freq EO*** | White Brit** / (−) Degree* / Freq EO*** | Middle £* / Freq EO*** |
| I prefer there to be no children around when I eat out | | 0.343 | | | |
| **8 Sociability** | 1.061 | | | | |
| I like to eat out because I don't like the meals I have to eat at home | | −0.613 | (−) 2015*** / (−) Male* / Children*** | (−) Male* / Children*** / (−) Downward mob* | (−) White Brit* / Children*** / High £** |
| When I eat out I dislike eating alone | | 0.587 | High £** / Middle £** / (−) London*** / Bristol*** / (−) Freq EO** | Other mob* / (−) London*** / Bristol* / (−) Freq EO* | Middle £* / Bristol** / (−) Freq EO* |
| I prefer there to be no children around when I eat out | | −0.366 | | | |

# References

Abbott, A. (2001) *Time Matters: On Theory and Method*. Chicago, IL: Chicago University Press.

Ahn, Y. Y., Ahnert, S., Bagrow, J. and Barabasi, A. L. (2011) Flavor network and the principles of food pairing, Scientific Reports, December. www.npr.org/blogs/thesalt/2011/12/20/144021294/what-a-global-flavor-map-can-tell-us-about-how-we-pair-foods.

Albala, K., Belasco, W., Bentley, A., Heldke, L. and McIntosh, A. (2017) *FCS* editors' roundtable: Reflections on the twentieth anniversary of the journal. *Food, Culture and Society*, 20 (1), pp. 1–14.

Alkon, A. H. and Agyeman, J. (2011) *Cultivating Food Justice: Race, Class and Sustainability*. Cambridge, MA: MIT Press, pp. 263–281.

Allegra (2009) *Eating Out in the UK, 2009: A Comprehensive Analysis of the Informal Eating Out Market*. London: Allegra.

Appadurai, A. (1990) Disjuncture and difference in the global cultural economy. *Theory, Culture & Society*, 7 (2–3), pp. 295–310.

Appadurai, A. (1996) *Modernity at Large*. Minneapolis, MN: University of Minnesota Press.

Arsel, Z. and Bean, J. (2012) Taste regimes and market-mediated practice. *Journal of Consumer Research*, 39 (5), pp. 899–917.

Ascher, F. (2005) *Le mangeur hypermoderne*. Paris: Odile Jacob.

Ashley, B., Hollows, J., Jones, S. and Taylor, B. (2004) *Food and Cultural Studies*. London: Routledge.

Barthes, R. (1975 [2000]) *Mythologies*. London: Vintage.

Baudrillard, J. (1998 [1970]) *The Consumer Society: Myths and Structures*. London: Sage.

Bauman, Z. (1988) *Freedom*. Milton Keynes: Open University Press.

Beardsworth, A. and Keil, T. (2002) *Sociology on the Menu: An Invitation to the Study of Food and Society*. London: Routledge.

Beck, U. (1992) *Risk Society: Towards a New Modernity*. London: Sage

Beck, U. and Beck-Gernsheim, E. (2001) *Individualisation*. London: Sage.

Bennett, T., Savage, M., Silva, E., Warde, A., Gayo-Cal, M. and Wright, D. (2009) *Culture, Class, Distinction*. London: Routledge.

Berris, D. and Sutton, D. (2007) *The Restaurants Book: Ethnographies of Where We Eat.* Oxford: Berg.

Bianchi, S. M., Milkie, M. A., Sayer, L. C. and Robinson, J. P. (2000) Is anyone doing the housework? Trends in the gender division of household labor. *Social Forces,* 79 (1), pp. 191–228.

Bianchi, S. M., Robinson, J. P. and Milkie, M. A. (2006) *Changing Rhythms of American Family Life.* New York, NY: Russell Sage Foundation.

Bianchi, S. M., Sayer, L. C., Milkie, M. A. and Robinson, J. P. (2012) Housework: Who did, does or will do it, and how much does it matter? *Social Forces,* 91 (1), pp. 55–63.

Bourdieu, P. (1984[1979]) *Distinction: A Social Critique of the Judgement of Taste.* London: Routledge & Kegan Paul.

Brannen, J., O'Connell, R. and Mooney, A. (2013) Families, meals and synchronicity: Eating together in British dual earner families. *Community, Work & Family,* 16 (4), pp. 417–434.

Buettner, E. (2008) Going for an Indian: South Asian restaurants and the limits of multiculturalism in Britain. *The Journal of Modern History,* 80, pp. 865–901.

Bugge, A. B. and Almås, R. (2006) Domestic dinner representations and practices of a proper meal among young suburban mothers. *Journal of Consumer Culture,* 6 (2), pp. 203–228.

Burawoy, M. (2003) Revisits: An outline of a theory of reflexive ethnography. *American Sociological Review,* 68, pp. 645–679.

Burnett, J. (2004) *England Eats Out: 1830–Present.* Harlow: Pearson.

Cabiedes-Miragaya, L. (2017) Analysis of the economic structure of the eating-out sector: The case of Spain. *Appetite,* 119, pp. 64–76.

Campbell, C. (1987) *The Romantic Ethic and the Spirit of Modern Consumerism.* Oxford: Blackwell.

Caplan, P. (1997) *Food, Health and Identity.* London: Routledge.

Cappeliez, S. and Johnston, J. (2013) From meat and potatoes to 'real-deal' rotis: Exploring everyday culinary cosmopolitanism. *Poetics,* 41(5), pp. 433–455.

Cappellini, B., Parsons, E. and Harman, V. (2016) Right taste, wrong place: Local food cultures, (dis)identification and the formation of classed identity. *Sociology,* 50 (6), pp. 1089–1105.

Charles, N. and Kerr, M. (1988) *Women, Food and Families.* Manchester: Manchester University Press.

Cheng, S.-L., Olsen, W., Southerton, D. and Warde, A. (2007) The changing practice of eating: Evidence from UK time diaries, 1975 and 2000. *British Journal of Sociology,* 58 (1), pp. 39–61.

Coffey, A. and Atkinson, P. (1996) *Making Sense of Qualitative Data: Complementary Research Strategies.* London: Sage.

Cohen, P. N. (1998) Replacing housework in the service economy: Gender, class, and race-ethnicity in service spending. *Gender and Society,* 12, pp. 219–231.

Crang, P. (1994) It's showtime: On the workplace geographies of display in a restaurant in southeast England. *Environment and Planning D: Society and Space,* 12 (6), pp. 1767–1768.

Crompton, R. (2008) *Class and Stratification.* Cambridge: Polity.

Darmon, I. and Warde, A. (2016) Senses and sensibilities: Stabilising and changing tastes in cross-national couples. *Food, Culture & Society*, 19 (4), pp. 705–722.

Darmon, I. and Warde, A. (2018) Habits and orders of everyday life: Commensal adjustment in Anglo-French couples. *British Journal of Sociology*, 70 (3), pp. 1025–1042.

Deloitte/BDRC Continental (2011) The taste of the nation: the future trends for the going out market.

Department for Environment, Food and Rural Affairs (DEFRA) (2017) Family Food 2015.

DeSoucey, M. (2010) Gastronationalism: Food traditions and authenticity politics in the European Union. *American Sociological Review*, 75 (3), pp. 432–455.

DeVault, M. (1991) *Feeding the Family: The Social Organisation of Caring as Gendered Work*. Chicago, IL: University of Chicago Press.

Díaz-Méndez, C. and García-Espejo, I. (2014) Eating practice models in Spain and the United Kingdom: A comparative time use analysis. *International Journal of Comparative Sociology*, 55 (1), pp. 24–44.

Díaz-Méndez, C. and García-Espejo, I. (2017) Eating out in Spain: Motivations, sociability and consumer contexts. *Appetite*, 119, pp. 14–22.

Diaz-Mendez, C. and Van den Broek, H.-P. (2017) Eating out in modern societies: An overview of a heterogeneous habit. *Appetite*, 119, pp. 1–76.

Douglas, M. (1975) 'Deciphering a meal', in M. Douglas (ed.) *Implicit Meanings: Selected Essays in Anthropology*. London: Routledge and Kegan Paul, pp. 249–275.

Douglas, M. (ed.) (1984) *Food in the Social Order*. New York: Russell Sage Foundation.

Driver, C. (1983) *The British at Table 1940–1980*. London: Vintage.

Edwards, J. S. A. (2013) The food service industry: Eating out is more than just a meal. *Food Quality and Preference*, 27, pp. 223–229.

Ehgartner, U. (2019) 'Environmentally and socially responsible consumption? A study on food sustainability discourses' (PhD thesis, University of Manchester).

Erikson, R. and Goldthorpe, J. H. (1992) *The Constant Flux: A Study of Class Mobility in Industrial Societies*. Oxford: Oxford University Press.

Family Spending (various years), Office of National Statistics.

Featherstone, M. (1991) *Consumer Culture and Postmodernism*. London: Sage.

Ferguson, P. (2004) *Accounting for Taste: The Triumph of French Cuisine*. Chicago, IL: The University of Chicago Press.

Ferry, L. (1990) *Homo aestheticus: l'invention du gout a l'age démocratique*. Paris: Grasset.

Fine, G. A. (1996) *Kitchens: The Culture of Restaurant Work*. Berkeley, CA: University of California Press.

Finkelstein, J. (1989) *Dining Out: A Sociology of Modern Manners*. Cambridge: Polity Press.

Finkelstein, J. (2013) *Fashioning Appetite: Restaurants and the Making of Modern Identity* (Vol. 26). London: IB Tauris.

Firat, A., Fuat, A. and Ventakesh, A. (1995) Liberatory postmodernism and the re-enchantment of consumption. *Journal of Consumer Research*, 22 (3), pp. 239–267.

Fischler, C. (2011) Commensality, society and culture. *Social Science Information*, 50 (3–4), pp. 528–548.

Food Standards Agency (2014) The 2014 food and you survey: UK Bulletin, FSA Social Science Research Unit.

Gabriel, Y. (1988) *Working Lives in Catering*. London: Routledge Kegan Paul.

Garthwaite, K. (2016) *Hunger Pains: Life Inside Foodbank Britain*. Bristol: Policy Press.

Giddens, A. (1991) *Modernity and Self-Identity: Self and Society in the Late Modern Age*. Cambridge: Polity.

Goffman, E. (1959) *The Presentation of Self in Everyday Life*. New York, Ancho.

Goldthorpe, J. H. (2000) *On Sociology: Numbers, Narratives, and the Integration of Research and Theory*. Oxford: Oxford University Press.

Goldthorpe, J. H. and Lockwood, D. (1969) *The Affluent Worker in the Class Structure*. Cambridge: Cambridge University Press.

Goldthorpe, J. H., Llewellyn, C. and Payne, C. (1980) *Social Mobility and Class Structure in Modern Britain*. Oxford: Oxford University Press.

Grignon, C. (1993) 'La règle, la mode et le travail: la genèse social du modèle des repas français contemporain', in M. Aymard, C. Grignon C and F. Sabban (eds) *Le Temps de Manger: alimentation, emploi du temps et rythmes sociaux*. Paris: Maison de Sciences de l'Homme, pp. 275–324.

Grignon, C. and Grignon, C. (1999) Long-term trends in food consumption: A French portrait. *Food and Foodways*, 8, pp. 151–174.

Gronow, J. and Holm, L. (eds) (2019) *Everyday Eating in Denmark, Finland, Norway and Sweden: a comparative study of meal patterns 1997–2012*. London: Bloomsbury.

Gronow, J. and Warde, A. (2001) *Ordinary Consumption*. London: Routledge.

Guthman, J. (2011) '"If they only knew": The unbearable whiteness of alternative food', in A. H. Alkon and J. Agyeman (eds) *Cultivating Food Justice: Race, Class and Sustainability*. Cambridge, MA: MIT Press, pp. 263–281.

Hardyment, C. (1995) *Slice of Life: The British Way of Eating since 1945*. London: BBC Books.

Haug, W. F. (1986) *Critique of Commodity Aesthetics*. Cambridge: Polity.

Heldke, L. M. (2003) *Exotic Appetites: Ruminations of a Food Adventurer*. Oxon: Routledge.

Herpin, N. (1988) Le repas comme institution, compte rendu d'uneenquete exploratoire. *Revue Francaise de Sociologie*, 19, pp. 503–521.

Hirschman, A. (1982) *Shifting Involvements: Private Interest and Public Action*. Princeton, NJ: Princeton University Press.

Hochschild, A. (2012) *The Outsourced Self: What Happens When We Pay Others to Live our Lives for Us*. New York, NY: Picador.

Hochschild, A. and Machung, A. (2012) *The Commercialization of Intimate Life: Working Life and the Revolution at Home*. London: Penguin.

Hollows, J. (2016) 'The feminist and the cook: Julia Child, Betty Friedan and domestic femininity', in L. Martens and E. Casey (eds) *Gender and Consumption: Domestic Cultures and the Commercialization of Everyday Life*. Oxon: Routledge, pp. 33–48.

Holm, L. (2001) 'The social context of eating', in U. Kjaernes (ed.) *Eating Patterns: A Day in the Lives of Nordic Peoples*. Oslo: National Institute for Consumer Research, pp. 159–198.

Holm, L., Ekström, M. P., Gronow, J., Kjærnes, U., Lund, T. B., Mäkelä, J. and Niva, M. (2012) The modernisation of Nordic eating: Studying changes and stabilities in eating patterns. *Anthropology of Food*, (S7), pp. 2–14.

Holm, L., Lauridsen, D., Bøker Lund, T., Gronow, J., Niva, M. and Mäkelä. J. (2016) Changes in the social context and conduct of eating in four Nordic countries between 1997 and 2012. *Appetite*, 103, pp. 358–368.

Hook, J. L. (2006) Care in context: Men's unpaid work in 20 countries, 1965–2003. *American Sociological Review*, 71 (4), pp. 639–660.

hooks, b. (2012 [1992]) 'Eating the other: Desire and resistance', in M. G. Durham and D. M. Kellner (eds) *Media and Cultural Studies: Keyworks*. Second edition. Malden, MA: Wiley-Blackwell, pp. 308–318.

House, J. (2019) Modes of eating and phased routinisation: Insect-based food practices in the Netherlands. *Sociology*, 53 (3), pp. 451–467.

Household Family Expenditure Survey (various years), Office of National Statistics.

Huggan, G. (2001) *The Post-Colonial Exotic: Marketing the Margins*. New York, NY: Routledge.

Huxley, R., Land, J. and Lobley, M. (2011) *A Review of the UK Food Market*. Exeter: Cornwall Food & Drink and University of Exeter Centre for Rural Research.

Ichijo, A. and Ranta, R. (2016) *Food, National Identity and Nationalism: From Everyday to Global Politics*. Basingstoke and New York, NY: Palgrave Macmillan.

Jackson, P. (2009) *Changing Families, Changing Food*. Basingstoke: Palgrave Macmillan.

Jackson, P., Brembeck, H., Everts, J., Fuentes, M., Halkier, B., Hertz, F. D., Meah, A., Viehoff, V. and Wenzl, C. (2018) *Reframing Convenience Food*. Basingstoke: Palgrave Macmillan.

Jacobs, M. and Scholliers, P. (2003) *Eating Out in Europe: Picnics, Gourmet Dining and Snacks since the 18th Century*. Oxford: Berg.

Johnston, J. and Baumann, S. (2010) *Foodies: Democracy and Distinction in the Gourmet Foodscape*. London: Routledge.

Julier, A. P. (2013a) *Eating Together: Food, Friendship, and Inequality*. Chicago, IL: University of Illinois Press.

Julier, A. P. (2013b) 'Meals: "Eating in" and "eating out"', in A. Murcott, W. Belasco and P. Jackson (eds) *Handbook of Food Research*. London: Bloomsbury Academic, pp. 338–351.

Kan, M. Y., Sullivan, O. and Gershuny, J. (2011) Gender convergence in domestic work: Discerning the effects of interactional and institutional barriers from large-scale data. *Sociology*, 45 (2), pp. 234–251.

Karpik, L. (2000) Le guide rouge Michelin. *Sociologie du Travail*, 42 (3), pp. 369–389.

Karsten, L., Kamphuis, A. and Remeijnse, C. (2015) 'Time-out' with the family: The shaping of family leisure in the new urban consumption spaces of cafes, bars and restaurants. *Leisure Studies*, 34 (2), pp. 166–181.

Kaufman, R. L. (2010) *Race, Gender, and the Labor Market: Inequalities at Work*. Boulder, CO: Lynne Rienner.

Kjaernes, U. (ed.) (2001) Eating patterns: a day in the lives of Nordic peoples, Oslo, SIFO Report No.7 – 2001.

Klein, N. (2000) *No Logo*. London: Flamingo.

Labov, W. (1997) Some further steps in narrative analysis. *Journal of Narrative & Life History*, 7 (1–4), pp. 395–415.

Lambie-Mumford, H. (2017) *Hungry Britain: The Rise of Food Charity*. Bristol: Policy Press.

Lamont, M. (1992) *Money, Morals and Manners: The Culture of the French and American Upper-Middle Classes*. Chicago, IL: University of Chicago Press.

Lamont, M. (2000) *The Dignity of Working Men: Morality and the Boundaries of Race, Class and Immigration*. Cambridge, MA: Harvard University Press.

Lane, C. (2011) Culinary culture and globalization: an analysis of British and German Michelin-starred restaurants. *British Journal of Sociology*, 62 (4), pp. 696–717.

Lane, C. (2014) *The Cultivation of Taste: Chefs and the Organization of Fine Dining*. Oxford: Oxford University Press.

Lane, C. (2018) *From Taverns to Gastropubs: Food, Drink, and Sociality in England*. Oxford: Oxford University Press.

Lane, C. (2019) Reverse cultural globalization: the case of haute cuisine in one global city, *Poetics*, 75.

Lash, S. and Urry, J. (1994) *Economies of Signs and Spaces*. London: Sage.

Leach, R., Phillipson, C., Biggs, S. and Money, A. (2013) Baby boomers, consumption and social change: The bridging generation? *International Review of Sociology*, 23 (1), pp. 104–122.

Leidner, R. (1993) *Fast Food, Fast Talk: Service Work and the Rationalisation of Everyday Life*. Berkeley, CA: University of California Press.

Leschziner, V. (2015) *At the Chef's Table: Culinary Creativity in Elite Restaurants*. Stanford, CA: Stanford University Press.

Levenstein, H. (1993) *The Paradox of Plenty: A Social History of Eating in Modern America*. Oxford: Oxford University Press.

Lhuissier, A. (2014) Anything to declare? Questionnaires and what they tell us. *Anthropology of Food*. Online S10aof.revues.org/7625.

Li, Y., Savage, M. and Warde, A. (2008) Social mobility and social capital in contemporary Britain. *British Journal of Sociology*, 59 (3), pp. 391–411.

Li, Y., Savage, M. and Warde, A. (2015) 'Social mobility, social capital and cultural practice in the UK', in Y. Li (ed.) *The Handbook of Research Methods and Applications on Social Capital*. Cheltenham: Edward Elgar Publishing, pp. 21–39.

Lin, N. (2001) *Social Capital*. Cambridge: Cambridge University Press.

Longhurst, B. (2007) *Cultural Change and Ordinary Life*. Milton Keynes: Open University Press.

Lopata, H. Z. (1971) *Occupation: Housewife*. Oxford: Oxford University Press.

Lupton, D. (2000) Where's me dinner?: Food preparation arrangements in rural Australian families. *Journal of Sociology*, 36 (2), pp. 172–186.

Lury, C. (1996) *Consumer Culture*. Second edition. Cambridge: Polity.

Mallard, A. (1998) Compare, standardize, and settle: On some usual metrological problems. *Social Studies of Science*, 28 (4), pp. 571–601.

Marshall, D. and Anderson, A. (2002) Proper meals in transition: Young married couples on the nature of eating together. *Appetite*, 39 (3), pp. 193–206.

Martens, L. (1997) Gender and the eating out experience. *British Food Journal*, 99 (1), pp. 20–26.

Mason, J. (2002) 'Linking qualitative and quantitative data analysis', in A. Bryman and B. Burgess (eds) *Analyzing Qualitative Data*. London: Routledge, pp. 89–110.

Mason, J. (2017) *Qualitative Researching*. London: Sage.

McCracken, G. (1990) *Culture and Consumption: New Approaches to the Symbolic Character of Consumer Goods and Activities*. Bloomington, IN: Indiana University Press.

Meah, A. and Jackson, P. (2013) Crowded kitchens: The 'democratisation' of domesticity? *Gender, Place and Culture*, 20 (5), pp. 578–596.

Meah, A. and Watson, M. (2011) Saints and slackers: Challenging discourses about the decline of domestic cooking. *Sociological Research Online*, 16 (2), pp. 10–13.

Mellor, J., Blake, M. and Crane, L. (2010) When I'm doing a dinner party I don't go for the Tesco cheeses. *Food, Culture & Society*, 13 (1), pp. 115–134.

Mennell, S. (1985) *All Manners of Food: Eating and Taste in England and France from the Middle Ages to the Present*. Oxford: Blackwell.

Mennell, S., Murcott, A. and van Otterloo, A. (1992) *The Sociology of Food: Eating, Diet and Culture*. London: Sage.

Mintel (2014) Eating Out Review: UK, June 2014. Mintel Group.

Mintel (2015) Eating Out Review: UK, June 2015. Mintel Group.

Mintel (2017) Eating Out Review: UK, September 2017. Mintel Group.

Mintz, S. (1997) *Tasting Food, Tasting Freedom: Excursions into eating, culture, and the past*. Boston, MA: Beacon Press.

Mintz, S. (2002) 'Eating American', in C. Counihan (ed.) *Eating in the USA*. New York, NY: Routledge, pp. 23–34.

Murcott, A. (1982) On the social significance of the 'cooked dinner' in South Wales. *Social Science Information*, 21, pp. 677–695.

Murcott, A. (1983) *The Sociology of Food and Eating: Essays on the Sociological Significance of Food*. Aldershot: Gower.

Murcott, A. (1997) The nation's diet: An overview of early results. *British Food Journal*, 99 (3), pp. 89–96.

Murcott, A. (2018) *Introducing the Sociology of Food and Eating*. London: Bloomsbury.

Mylan, J. (2018) Sustainable consumption in everyday life: A qualitative study of UK consumer experiences of meat reduction. *Sustainability*, 10 (7).

Naccarato, P. and Lebesco, K. (2012) *Culinary Capital*. London: Berg.

Neuman, N., Gottzén, L. and Fjellström, C. (2017) Masculinity and the sociality of cooking in men's everyday lives. *Sociological Review*, 65 (4), pp. 816–831.

Nicolini, D. (2012) *Practice Theory, Work and Organization*. Oxford: Oxford University Press.

Oakley, A. (1972, 2016) *Sex, Gender and Society*. London: Routledge.

Oakley, A. (1974) *The Sociology of Housework*. Oxford: Martin Robertson.

Oleschuk, M. (2017) Foodies of color: Authenticity and exoticism in omnivorous food culture. *Cultural Sociology*, 11 (2), pp. 217–233.

Ollivier, M. (2008) Revisiting distinction: Bourdieu without class? *Journal of Cultural Economy*, 1 (3), pp. 263–280.

Ollivier, M., Van Eijck, K. and Warde, A. (eds) (2008) Models of omnivorous cultural consumption: New directions in research. Special edition. *Poetics*, 36 (2–3), pp. 115–119.

ONS (2017) Business Demography: Business Survival 2011–2016. Office of National Statistics.

Paddock, J. (2016) Positioning food cultures: Alternative food as distinctive consumer practice. *Sociology*, 50 (6), pp. 1039–1055.

Paddock, J., Warde, A. and Whillans, J. (2017) The changing meaning of eating out in three English cities 1995–2015. *Appetite*, 119, pp. 5–13.

Panayi, P. (2008) *Spicing up Britain: The Multicultural History of British Food*. London: Reaktion Books.

Parasecoli, F. (2008) *Bite Me: Food in Popular Culture*. Oxford: Berg.

Park, K. (1997) *The Korean American Dream: Immigrants and Small Business in New York City*. Ithaca, NY: Cornell University Press.

Pearlman, A. (2013) *Smart Casual: The Transformation of Gourmet Restaurant Style in America*. Chicago, IL: University of Chicago Press.

Peterson, R. A. (1997) The rise and fall of highbrow snobbery as a status marker. *Poetics*, 25, pp. 75–92.

Peterson, R. A. and Kern, R. (1996) Changing highbrow taste: From snob to omnivore. *American Sociological Review*, 61, pp. 900–907.

Phull, S., Wills, W. and Dickinson, A. (2015) Is it a pleasure to eat together? Theoretical reflections on conviviality and the Mediterranean diet. *Sociology Compass*, 9 (11), pp. 977–986.

Poulain, J.-P. (2017) *The Sociology of Food: Eating and the Place of Food in Society*. London: Bloomsbury.

Poulain, J.-P. (2002a) *Sociologies de l'Alimentation: les mangeurs et l'espace social alimentaire*, Paris: PUF.

Poulain, J.-P. (2002b) The contemporary diet in France: 'De-structuration' or from commensalism to 'vagabond feeding', *Appetite*, 39, pp. 43–55.

Prieur, A. and Savage, M. (2011) Updating cultural capital theory: A discussion based on studies in Denmark and in Britain. *Poetics*, 39 (6), pp. 566–580.

Prieur, A., Rosenlund, L. and Skjott-Larsen, J. (2008) Cultural capital today. A case study from Denmark. *Poetics*, 36, pp. 45–71.

Rao, H., Monin, P. and Durand, R. (2003) Institutional change in Toque Ville: Nouvelle cuisine as an identity movement in French gastronomy. *American Journal of Sociology*, 108 (4), pp. 795–843.

Ray, K. (2011) Dreams of Pakistani grill and Vada Pao in Manhattan: Re-inscribing the immigrant body in metropolitan discussions of taste. *Food, Culture & Society*, 14 (2), pp. 243–273.

Ray, K. (2016) *The Ethnic Restaurateur*. London: Bloomsbury.

Reckwitz, A. (2002) Toward a theory of social practices: A development in culturalist theorizing. *European Journal of Social Theory*, 5 (2), pp. 243–263.

Regan, T. (1975) The moral basis of vegetarianism. *Canadian Journal of Philosophy*, 5 (2), pp. 181–214.

Reissman, C. K. (1993) *Narrative Analysis*. Newbury Park, CA: Sage.

Reissman, C. K. (2002) 'Narrative analysis', in A. M. Huberman and M. B. Miles (eds) *The Qualitative Researcher's Companion*. London: Sage.

Ribbat, C. (2017) *In the Restaurant: Society in Four Courses*. London: Pushkin Press.

Röös, E., Bajželj, B., Smith, P., Patel, M., Little, D. and Garnett, T. (2017) Greedy or needy? Land use and climate impacts of food in 2050 under different livestock futures. *Global Environmental Change*, 47, pp. 1–12.

Rose, D. and Pevalin, D. (eds) (2003) *A Researcher's Guide to the National Socio-Economic Classification*. London: Sage.

Rotenberg, R. (1981) The impact of industrialization on meal patterns in Vienna, Austria. *Ecology of Food and Nutrition*, 11, pp. 25–35.

Rousseau, S. (2012) *Food Media: Celebrity Chefs and the Politics of Everyday Indifference*. London: Berg.

Said, E. (1978) *Orientalism*. New York, NY: Vintage.

Sassatelli, R. (2007) *Consumer Culture: History, Theory and Politics*. Oxford: Berg.

Savage, M., Warde, A. and Devine, F. (2005) Capitals, assets and resources: Some analytical points. *British Journal of Sociology*, 56 (1), pp. 31–47.

Schatzki, T. (1996) *Social Practices: A Wittgensteinian Approach to Human Activity and the Social*. Cambridge: Cambridge University Press.

Schatzki, T. (2001) 'Introduction: Practice theory', in T. Schatzki, K. Knorr Cetina and E. von Savigny (eds) *The Practice Turn in Contemporary Theory*. London: Routledge, pp. 1–14.

Schatzki, T. (2013) 'The edge of change: On the emergence, persistence and dissolution of practices', in E. Shove and N. Spurling (eds) *Sustainable Practices*. London: Routledge, pp. 31–47.

Schlosser, E. (2012) *Fast Food Nation: What the All-American Meal is Doing to the World*. London: Penguin.

Scholliers, P. (2001) *Food, Drink and Identity. Cooking, Eating and Drinking in Europe since the Middle Ages*. Oxford: Berg.

Shove, E. and Southerton, D. (2000) Defrosting the freezer: From novelty to convenience; a narrative of normalization. *Journal of Material Culture*, 5 (3), pp. 301–319.

Shove, E., Trentmann, F. and Wilk, R. (eds) (2009) *Time, Consumption and Everyday Life: Practice, Materiality and Culture*. Oxford: Berg.

Singer, P. (1975) *Animal Liberation: A New Ethics for our Treatment of Animals*. New York, NY: New York Review.

Slater, D. (1997) *Consumer Culture and Modernity*. Cambridge: Polity.

Slocum, R. (2007) Whiteness, space and alternative food practice. *Geoforum*, 38 (3), pp. 520–533.

Sobal, J. (2000) 'Sociability and meals: facilitation, commensality, and interaction', in H. Meiselman (ed.) *Dimensions of the Meal: The Science, Culture, Business, and Art of Eating*. Gaitherburg, MD: Aspen, pp. 119–133.

Southerton, D. (2006) Analysing the temporal organization of daily life: social constraints, practices and their allocation. *Sociology*, 40 (3), pp. 435–454.

Southerton, D. (2013) Habits, routines and temporalities of consumption: From individual behaviours to the reproduction of everyday practices. *Time & Society*, 22 (3), pp. 335–355.

Stebbins, R. A. (1992) *Amateurs, Professionals, and Serious Leisure*. Montreal: McGill-Queen's Press-MQUP.

Stewart, A., Prandy, K. and Blackburn, R. (1980) *Social Stratification and Occupations*. London: Macmillan.

Sullivan, O. (1997) Time waits for no (wo)man: An investigation of the gendered experience of domestic time. *Sociology*, 31 (2), pp. 221–239.

Sullivan, O. (2000) The division of domestic labour: 20 years of change? *Sociology*, 34 (3), pp. 437–456.

Sullivan, O. (2006) *Changing Gender Relations, Changing Families: Tracing the Pace of Change over Time*. Oxford: Rowman & Littlefield.

Sullivan, O. and Gershuny, J. (2013) Domestic employment and multitasking: How much do they really contribute. *Social Science Research*, 42, pp. 1311–1324.

Sullivan, O. and Gershuny, J. (2018) Speed-up society? Evidence from the UK 2000 and 2015 time use diary surveys. *Sociology*, 52 (1), pp. 20–38.

Thompson, L. (1991) Family work: Women's sense of fairness. *Journal of Family Issues*, 12 (2), pp. 181–196.

Twine, R. (2017) Materially constituting a sustainable food transition: The case of vegan eating practice. *Sociology*, 52 (1), pp. 166–181.

Valentine, G. (1999) Eating in: Home, consumption and identity. *The Sociological Review*, 47 (3), pp. 491–524.

Warde, A. (1997) *Consumption, Food and Taste: Culinary Antinomies and Commodity Culture*. London: Sage.

Warde, A. (2000) 'Eating globally: Cultural flows and the spread of ethnic restaurants', in D. Kalb, M. van der Land, R. Staring, B. van Steenbergen and

N. Wilterdink (eds) *The Ends of Globalization: Bringing Society Back In.* Boulder, CO: Rowman & Littlefield, pp. 299–316.

Warde, A. (2004) La normalita del mangiare fuori (The normality of eating out). *Rassegna Italiana di Sociologia,* (special issue on 'Sociology of Food', editor R Sassatelli), 45 (4), pp. 493–518.

Warde, A. (2005) Consumption and theories of practice. *Journal of Consumer Culture,* 5 (2), pp. 131–153.

Warde, A. (2008) Dimensions of a social theory of taste. *Journal of Cultural Economy,* 1 (3), pp. 321–336.

Warde, A. (2009) Imagining British cuisine: Representations of culinary identity in the Good Food Guide. *Food, Culture and Society,* 12 (2), pp. 149–171.

Warde, A. (2012) 'Eating', in F. Trentmann (ed.) *Oxford Handbook of the History of Consumption.* Oxford: Oxford University Press.

Warde, A. (2016) *The Practice of Eating.* Cambridge: Polity.

Warde, A. (2018) 'Accounting for taste', in Z. Arsel and J. Bean (eds) *Taste, Consumption, and Markets: An Interdisciplinary Volume.* New York, NY: Routledge, pp. 215–234.

Warde, A. and Martens, L. (2000) *Eating Out: Social Differentiation, Consumption and Pleasure.* Cambridge: Cambridge University Press.

Warde, A., Martens, L. and Olsen, W. (1999) Consumption and the problem of variety: Cultural omnivorousness, social distinction and dining out. *Sociology,* 33 (1), pp. 105–127.

Warde, A, Cheng, S.-L., Olsen, W. and Southerton, D. (2007) Changes in the practice of eating: A comparative analysis, *Acta Sociologica,* 50 (4), pp. 365–385.

Warde, A., Wright, D. and Gayo-Cal, M. (2008) The omnivorousness orientation in the UK. *Poetics,* 36 (2–3), pp. 148–165.

Warde, A., Whillans, J. and Paddock, J. (2019) The allure of variety: Eating out in three English cities, 2015. *Poetics,* 72, pp. 17–31.

Warren, G. (1958) *The Foods We Eat.* London: Cassell.

Watson, J. L. (ed.) (1997) *Golden Arches East: McDonald's in East Asia.* Stanford, CA: Stanford University Press.

Weeden, K. and Grusky, D. B. (2005) The case for a new class map. *American Journal of Sociology,* 111 (1), pp. 141–212.

Whyte, W. F. (1949) The social structures of the restaurant. *American Journal of Sociology,* 54 (4), pp. 302–310.

Wilk, R. (2006) *Home Cooking in the Global Village: Caribbean Food from Buccaneers to Ecotourists.* Oxford: Berg.

Wills, W. and O'Connell, R. (2018) Children's and young people's food practices in contexts of poverty and inequality. *Children and Society,* 32 (3), pp. 169–173.

Wood, R. C. (1995) *The Sociology of the Meal.* Edinburgh: Edinburgh University Press.

Wouters, G. (2007) *Informalization: Manners and Emotions since 1890.* London: Sage.

Yates, L. and Warde, A. (2015) The evolving content of meals in Great Britain: Results of a survey in 2012 in comparison with the 1950s. *Appetite*, 84 (1), pp. 299–308.

Yates, L. and Warde, A. (2018) Eating together and eating alone: Meal arrangements in British households. *The British Journal of Sociology*, 68 (1), pp. 97–118.

Yin, R. (2006) Mixed methods research: Are the methods genuinely integrated or merely parallel. *Research in the Schools*, 13 (1), pp. 41–47.

Zelinsky, W. (1985) The roving palate: North America's ethnic restaurant cuisines. *Geoforum*, 16 (1), pp. 51–72.

Zerubavel, E. (1981) *Hidden Rhythms: Schedules and Calendars in Social Life*. Berkeley, CA: University of California Press.

# Index

EU authorised representative for GPSR:
Easy Access System Europe, Mustamäe tee 50,
10621 Tallinn, Estonia
gpsr.requests@easproject.com

www.ingramcontent.com/pod-product-compliance
Lightning Source LLC
Chambersburg PA
CBHW050631280326
41932CB00015B/2601